Chasing the Rising Sun

The Journey of an American Song

Ted Anthony

Simon & Schuster
New York · London · Toronto · Sydney

SIMON & SCHUSTER
Rockefeller Center
1230 Avenue of the Americas
New York, NY 10020

For information about special discounts for bulk purchases,
please contact Simon & Schuster Special Sales at
1-800-456-6798 or business@simonandschuster.com.

Designed by Paul Dippolito

Manufactured in the United States of America

1   3   5   7   9   10   8   6   4   2

Library of Congress Cataloging-in-Publication Data is available.

ISBN-13: 978-0-7432-7899-7

ILLUSTRATION CREDITS

Courtesy of Ted Anthony: 3, 5, 6, 8, 9, 10, 12, 13, 16, 19, 20, 21
Courtesy of the AP: 2, 22, 23, 24, 25, 26, 27, 28, 29
Photo courtesy of Homer Callahan: 7
Photo courtesy of The Moaners: 14
Courtesy of Eva Ashley Moore: 4, 11
Photo courtesy of Melissa Rayworth-Anthony: 15
Courtesy of Georgia Turner's children: 1, 17, 18

For my father, Edward Mason Anthony Jr.,
who first sang me the old songs.

For my son, Edward Mason Anthony V,
who is just starting to learn them.

And for Georgia Turner Connolly,
who deserved better.

Contents

There is a house in New Orleans
they call the Rising Sun.
It's been the ruin of many a poor girl
and me, O God, for one.

If I had listened what Mamma said,
I'd a been at home today.
Being so young and foolish, poor boy,
let a rambler lead me astray.

Go tell my baby sister
never do like I have done,
to shun that house in New Orleans
they call the Rising Sun.

My mother, she's a tailor;
she sold those new blue jeans.
My sweetheart, he's a drunkard, Lord, Lord,
drinks down in New Orleans.

The only thing a drunkard needs
is a suitcase and a trunk.
The only time he's satisfied
is when he's on a drunk.

Fills his glasses to the brim,
passes them around
only pleasure he gets out of life
is hoboin' from town to town.

One foot is on the platform
and the other one on the train.
I'm going back to New Orleans
to wear that ball and chain.

Going back to New Orleans,
my race is almost run.
Going back to spend the rest of my days
beneath that Rising Sun.

—"THE RISING SUN BLUES," AS ASSEMBLED BY ALAN LOMAX
FROM FIELD RECORDINGS MADE IN EASTERN KENTUCKY IN
SEPTEMBER AND OCTOBER 1937.

Introduction

. . . you never can tell what goes on down below.
This pool might be bigger than you or I know!
This MIGHT be a pool, like I've read of in books,
connected to one of those underground brooks!
An underground river that starts here and flows
right under the pasture!
And then . . . well, who knows?

—DR. SEUSS, *MCELLIGOT'S POOL*

Tell me, man,
which way to the rising sun.

—OLD BLUES, SUNG BY HENRY SIMS

I do not belong to my own generation.

When I was born in the turbulent, musical spring of 1968, my father was forty-five years old and my mother forty-three. My sisters, born in 1947 and 1951, were grown. Though I grew up Gen-X in suburban Pittsburgh, my friends' parents were my sisters' ages. Generationally, I was a Baby Boomer. I look back more easily to American yesterdays because, I think, so much of it seems real to me.

And it has shown in my music.

The songs that played within my house were different from those that came from outside. When my mother's ubiquitous transistor radio, tuned to KDKA-AM, would pipe in Billy Joel, Fleetwood Mac and the Bee Gees, I absorbed them all. But the sounds coming from the family room, from my father's floor-model Magnavox phono-graph, were so different as to be barely recognizable. Glenn Miller. Benny Goodman. Tex Benecke. And from my father's own fingers, on the Grinnell Bros. upright piano, the music reached back even fur-ther—deeper into a distant history I didn't recognize as such just yet. Scott Joplin rags. "St. Louis Woman." "Oh, Susanna" and "Old Folks at Home" and "There Was an Old Woman Who Swallowed a Fly." Occasionally my mother would chime in with "I've Been Workin' on the Railroad."

Best of all was bedtime, when he would sit on the edge of my bed and sing. He could never say where he learned most of the songs, which I realize now is a standard characteristic of folklore. Some, he's sure, he got from his father or his grandmothers. Some he probably just heard. But he remembered them for me.

> *My grandfather's clock*
> *was too large for the shelf,*
> *so it stood ninety years on the floor.*
>
> *One dark night, when we were all in bed,*
> *Old Mother Leary put a lantern in the shed.*
> *And when the cow kicked it over,*
> *she turned around and said,*
> *"There'll be a hot time*
> *in the old town tonight."*
>
> *Oh, Mister Johnny Verbeck,*
> *how could you be so mean?*
> *I told you you'd be sorry*
> *for inventin' that machine.*
> *Now all the neighbors' cats and dogs*
> *will nevermore be seen.*
> *They'll all be ground to sausages*
> *in Johnny Verbeck's machine.*
>
> *Go tell Aunt Rhody*
> *that the old gray goose is dead.*

For me, those songs simply *were*. They entered my ears and joined the earliest of my memories, becoming as second nature as language.

As I grew, I wondered where they had come from. I think I realized, even then, that they hadn't materialized out of thin air; something between the lines told me they came from a place alien to me, recognizable to my father and even more familiar to the people who came before him.

In second-grade music class at Falk Elementary School in Pittsburgh, the teacher, Don Mushalko, taught us to sing about someplace called the Erie Canal:

> *We were forty miles from Albany*
> *forget it I never shall.*
> *What a terrible storm we had one night*
> *on the Er-i-e Canal.*

Only years later did I learn that my ancestors moved from upstate New York to Cleveland on the steamship *Daniel Webster,* which traversed the canal to Lake Erie. I thought of the song instantly: It was something real, a document of an experience that was about my country, my family, me.

As I prepared for college, my father insisted I couldn't leave the house unless I learned one of the two skills he felt were life's most important: typing and playing the piano. As much as I loved listening to him play, I had no interest in doing it myself. I took a typing class in my junior year of high school and became a writer.

To type and to make music. Both are the same act, really. In each, it is not the action that matters but the echo it produces. I never learned the piano; finally, today, I am teaching myself. And I have come to realize that the music was always within me. My father got it from long ago, and he gave it to me. I just needed to awaken it.

After writing this book, which documents my determined search for the history of the song "House of the Rising Sun" and the paths it has taken through the world, I understand now: The secrets of the American tapestry can be unlocked with its music, if you're using the right batch of keys. And Key Number One is realizing how much of us can be contained in just one song.

Several years ago, when I wrote an article about the latest inductions at the Rock and Roll Hall of Fame, I referred to rock as "mongrel music." Within hours, a reader dashed off an indignant email. "I don't appreciate your terminology," he snapped.

I thought about what "mongrel" means. We consider it a negative term: At best, it means diluted and ineffectual; at worst, it smacks of old hatreds and an ugliness that our nation is still purging. But I see it differently. Mongrel means a stew of ingredients—a blended batch of all the things that came before, hopefully with the good outnumbering the bad. In this country, "mongrel" means that we contain multitudes. It means that we—each of us, each in a different way—contain America.

We are mongrels. And like our canine counterparts, the mix of heritages and experiences and outlooks and travails makes us stronger and healthier—both in our culture and in the music and song that we use to describe it. We come from what we believe is a single world, but it is so many, all existing at once.

We are America's mongrels. All of us.

What could possibly be more exciting?

Prologue: The Moment

I met a girl who sang the blues.

—DON MCLEAN, "AMERICAN PIE"

She is blond, pretty, barely sixteen, too young to be singing the blues. But she does, all the time. After all, Middlesboro is a rough town these days, and every day is a struggle. Sometimes, when the songs are sad, she even cries along with them.

One song is her signature—a sad tune, weighed down with the ballast of misery, moist with the tears of bad choices, loved ones, and home left behind, a life inching balefully toward its end. *If I had listened to what Mama said, I'd have been at home today.*

The girl has a strong, beautiful voice, and she sings the song wherever she goes—around the neighborhood, hanging the wash outside her family's wooden shack, and especially when folks gather to play some harmonica, pick some banjo and forget about the day spent underground in the coal mines. Their voices echo across the hillside east of town. Sometimes the music from the poor cabins and stoops reaches the railroad tracks just a few yards away—the ones that shepherd the steam-belching trains that carry coal, people, and a tantalizing invitation: There are other places to claim, other choices to be made, other destinies to be fulfilled. Rounders and ramblers and gamblers and hoboes and wayfaring strangers and unfortunate rakes hurtling toward siren-song cities that shine atop distant plateaus at the end of the line. Nashville. Birmingham. Meridian. Atlanta. New Orleans. The road to possibility, rendered in steel and steam and thunder. Even if you can't hop aboard, you can dream. *One foot on the plat-form, the other one on the train.*

Everyone in the neighborhood knows her song is old, though no one seems sure where it comes from. They just know that Georgie Turner sings it, and they like it when she does. Music offers a sliver of respite from the blackness of the mines and the meanness of the Depression, which still seems to be gobbling up Middlesboro even as it begins to ebb in other places.

One day, a stranger shows up from back East. He is a young man in an old car weighed down by an enormous, unfamiliar machine. Even when he rolls up his sleeves and dirties his hands in the machinery, you can tell he's different—smooth and energetic and glib, cigarette occasionally dangling from the corner of his mouth, a dashing twenty-two-year-old who'll never be stuck, who goes from town to town sampling the world with the confidence of someone certain he'll be able to move on to the next challenge. He is trolling Kentucky's mountains with his bulky contraption to record people singing their songs. He is finding himself to be a popularizer, a fan of the folk, a blend of the academy and the frontier, a Southerner and a Northerner in one package. He's the kind of man who drives over bumpy dirt roads talking like Harvard and Yale: "Here the mountains have formed culture eddies where one can find the music of the American pioneer, in all degrees of purity—in some isolated spots, little affected by nearly a hundred years of change in the 'outland'; in others acquiring new vitality in the mouths of the miners."

The man will tell you that this place is part of heaven. Like his daddy, he loves the South. Ever since the first Turners crossed the Cumberland Gap in Daniel Boone's era and settled in the lush hills around Pine Mountain, this has been, to songcatchers from the outland, one of *those* places—where the Scotch-Irish ballad tradition survives unfettered, and people still sing on their front porches, isolated from the encroaching world of cities and recorded sound and national mass culture. But the man, Alan Lomax, is smart: He works for the Library of Congress and is conducting this quest like his father before him. He knows the gold of song collecting comes from two treasure chests: the untouched English balladry of centuries ago and the newer, earthier songs of American experience. His ears are open to both, and he hears fascinating things as he winds through Harlan, Bell, and Clay counties: songs from the 1700s, 1800s, and 1900s, all blending into something new. Song fragments carried like viruses by modern vectors—trains and cars and itinerant miners who infect new people with a verse here, a verse there, pressed into service to make a point, evoke a memory, remember a moment.

Middlesboro is fertile proving ground for this; old songs are coming down from the hills and, in the hands of visitors and miners, mutating and becoming something new. Even phonograph records are appearing, purchased by the fortunates who have electricity and some spending money. You might get a flash of recognition if you mentioned the name Roy Acuff: He's from the Smokies just over Cumberland Mountain in eastern Tennessee, and he's about to make a name for himself at the Grand Ole Opry. The outside world is changing a way of isolated living that is generations old, and Lomax is determined to capture the moment before the rising monoculture shoves it all out of the way.

He has written ahead to announce his appearance; after all, in these parts of the world, a smooth city man who uses big words—even one born in Texas—needs a sponsor or two, just to keep things from getting ugly. Through his contacts in Washington and New York City, he has arranged to stop in—on Wednesday, September 15, 1937—at the house of a man named Tillman Cadle, who lives by the railroad tracks in a desperately poor part of Middlesboro called Noetown. Few houses here have electricity; most are rickety wooden shacks. Cadle has invited some neighbors to sing for the the man and his machine. Among them is Mary Mast Turner—Mary Gill, they call her—a strict Baptist, a middle-aged housewife who lives nearby in an old log cabin with no front porch and a kitchen stove to heat the entire family. With her, she brings her teenage daughter Georgia.

Lomax unloads his Presto "reproducer," which runs on a big, heavy battery. He sets it up in Cadle's house alongside a stack of blank acetate discs upon which the machine will etch the grooves that capture the voices he craves. He wants to get things right on the first take because he's stingy about the discs; he keeps running out of them and has to send back to Washington for money to buy more.

The girl and her mother arrive. They are joined by Cadle's nephew, Edward Hunter, who, though barely a teenager, knows his way around a harmonica. When the girl's turn comes, she leans in (you have to lean in close with these Presto machines, or they won't pick up your voice) and opens her mouth. Then, on a blues scale, in a vigorous, nasal voice that resonates beyond her years, she sings. Georgia Bell Turner sings for her mother, for Tillman Cadle and Ed Hunter, for Alan Lomax, and for forever.

1 *The Way-Back Machine*

*I'm the man that signed the contract
to raise the rising sun.
And that was the biggest thing
that man has ever done.*

—WOODY GUTHRIE

*Sometimes I live in the country; sometimes
I live in town.*

—LEAD BELLY, "IRENE"

Somewhere in the hills where North Carolina, Tennessee, Kentucky, and Virginia meet sits The Village.

It's not a real town—at least, not the kind of reality we're accustomed to. Yet The Village defies logic and exists nonetheless. It lives outside of time and space. It's a place where possibilities—unsettling possibilities—dwell.

The Village is located in an American Oz of the late nineteenth and early twentieth centuries, a land of the imagination that is deeply *of* us and yet almost biblical in its longing and death and sacrifice and guilt and innocence and the sheer size of its myths. It is populated by ramblers and drunkards and rounders and vanquished Confederates and doomed train engineers, by two dead presidents named Garfield and McKinley and their assassins, by young women condemned to die at the hands of their lovers by knife or by smoking revolver or by flowing waters over and over again, each time a different voice sings the songs of their sad ends.

9

If The Village had a telephone directory (and it would be an early, wooden telephone for sure), it would list people immortalized in songs sung long ago, men and women named Willie and Polly and Tom and Omie and Little Sadie and Laura Foster, Sheriff Thomas Dell and Charles Guiteau and Darling Corey and John Henry and John Hardy and Stagolee. Some of its citizens have real-world counterparts, mirror-universe doppelgangers that resemble them but are different in fundamental ways. Some, like Barbara Allen, are kernels of English memories accentuated by centuries of American folk-song buildup. Dying cowboys and blind children and steel-drivin' men and roving gamblers and desperate men locked in the walls of prison listening to the locomotive whistle blowing or simply looking down that lonesome road. In and around The Village, the places of song wink in and out of our reality: Birmingham Jail and Jericho and Penny's Farm and Carroll County and Hazard County and the Banks of the Ohio and the depot where you catch the Wabash Cannonball, all teeming with poor boys and girls who leave their little mountain communities, bound for the city and its pleasures and ruinations, doomed to spend the rest of their wicked lives beneath places like the Rising Sun.

In The Village, many things—wonderful things, ugly things, things of magic—are always about to happen. Religion, folk belief, and a uniquely American, uniquely Christian paganism have created this enchanted land. *In the pines, in the pines, where the sun never shines.* Just as Dorothy wasn't sure exactly where Kansas ended and Oz began, so it is with The Village. Reality provides the raw material for legend, and legend repays it by bleeding back into reality. The Village has no physical boundaries, only songs and the stories they contain.

The roads that lead out of The Village—and the railroads, always the railroads—sweep south through the Appalachian Mountains, the Blue Ridges, the Smokies, the Cumberlands, winding all the way down past Nashville to the Mississippi Delta, where Robert Johnson did or didn't sell his soul to the devil at the crossroads of Highways 49 and 61 in exchange for the ability to play some superhuman guitar. They cut west into the Ozarks and south into Georgia, winding through settlements that are long forgotten or were never really noticed at all. All roads end down in New Orleans, where the train and the riverboat carried the runoff of human rambling and tragedy and it pooled in one glorious city of gluttony and racial mixing and fighting and drinking and sex.

Across this land, magic and music blend—British balladry, old-time Baptist hymnody, early Tin Pan Alley songwriting, and West African field hollers that, carried on the backs of slaves and their freed descendants, convulsed forward into the blues with the erratic abruptness of a teenager learning to drive a stick shift. The exuberance of song is palpable, yet always tempered by the melancholy of the worried man. *I am a man of constant sorrow; I've seen trouble all my days.*

These notions of an "other place" had careened through my head since long before the Rising Sun entered my life. But I could never articulate the images that danced at the corners of my vision until I read Greil Marcus's *Invisible Republic: Bob Dylan's Basement Tapes.* Marcus is a music critic, among other things, but using that label is a bit like describing Abraham Lincoln as a federal employee. In tracing the genesis of Bob Dylan's famed 1967 sessions with the Band—and of Dylan himself—Marcus not only sees this other America but also becomes its master cartographer. He charts its landscape like an existentialist urban-studies guru exploring an alternate universe that many of us Casey Kasem–weaned, Orange Julius–gulping, Styx-listening, Original Recipe–scarfing Americans never begin to encounter.

The music of The Village and the Invisible Republic around it—for I was certain, upon reading Marcus's book, that his republic was home to my Village—was heard by few until the early 1920s. Then, suddenly, "hillbilly" and "race" recordings began to capture it, amplify it, broadcast it across the land for the first time. Subcultures that had gone ignored or stereotyped for generations by outworlders like me could suddenly hitch their traditions to modernism's speeding wagon and tell their stories in their own voices. And people were *listening.* It was a revolution of the ear, but a revolution nonetheless. Marcus writes:

> For the first time, people from isolated, scorned, forgotten, disdained communities and cultures had the chance to speak to each other and to the nation at large. A great uproar of voices that were at once old and new was heard, as happens only occasionally in democratic cultures—but always, when it happens, with a sense of explosion, of energies contained for generations bursting out all at once.

Marcus, in turn, credits Harry Smith as the original mapmaker, the wizard of this Oz. Smith was the iconoclast who, in 1952, cobbled together dozens of old 78s from the 1920s and 1930s—tunes that came straight from The Village and the Invisible Republic—and issued them in an astonishing (and legally dubious) multirecord set called *The Anthology of American Folk Music*. It became one of the foundations of the American folk revival. It's great fun to read Smith's quirky liner notes, which feature headlines for songs, as if The Village published its own newspaper. The creatively spelled "Charles Giteau," about the president killer, is summed up this way: "Assassin of President Garfield Recalls Exploit in Scaffold Peroration." And the synopsis of "Stackalee" reads like a police blotter: "Theft of Stetson Hat Causes Deadly Dispute, Victim Identifies Self as Family Man."

Listening to Smith's *Anthology* from the distant vantage point of the early twenty-first century, it's easy to underestimate it or dismiss it as cliché. So much of the material feels familiar. But that's only because musicians like the Grateful Dead, the Rolling Stones, and Dylan made it their own, and it has wended in and out of rock and pop ever since—as has this notion of a somehow different world. Dylan himself reflected on the place in his 2004 autobiography: "I had already landed in a parallel universe . . . with more archaic principles and values; one where actions and virtues were old style and judgmental things came falling out on their heads," he wrote. "It was all there and it was clear—ideal and God-fearing—but you had to go find it."

In 1952, many of the old-time artists who made the recordings were still alive and had gone back to their jobs in mills and lumberyards and coal mines. The *Anthology* was a thunderclap from another era that had been forgotten. A good portion of the *Anthology*'s artists, Marcus writes, "were only twenty or twenty-five years out of their time; cut off by the cataclysms of the Great Depression and the Second World War, and by a national narrative that had never included their kind, they appeared now like visitors from another world, like passengers on a ship that had drifted into the sea of the unwritten."

Smith's accomplishment was so starkly bizarre because the old, weird America—as *Invisible Republic* was renamed in subsequent printings—had been steamrolled by modernism. This was lamented as early as 1919, when Sherwood Anderson published *Winesburg, Ohio*, his melancholy chronicle of an Ohio town grappling with the encroachment of the modern world.

The coming of industrialism, attended by all the roar and rattle of affairs, the shrill cries of millions of new voices that have come among us from over seas, the going and coming of trains, the growth of cities, the building of the interurban car lines that weave in and out of towns and past farmhouses, and now in these later days the coming of the automobiles has worked a tremendous change in the lives and in the habits of thought of our people of Mid-America. . . . Much of the old brutal ignorance that had in it also a kind of beautiful childlike innocence is gone forever.

Brutal ignorance and childlike innocence—the murder ballad and the love song, two sides of the same Morgan silver dollar—defined that other America. Now that country—the one beyond the Wal-Marts, the interstate exits, and the chain motels—exists only in pockets, a few geographic but most of them psychological. Somewhere in there, beyond the limited-access highways and the clusters of backlit plastic that represent our tacit agreement of national commerce, a story was lurking. It was the story of a single song and the many routes it had traveled. I was aiming to find it.

We like to believe there is a single, comprehensible world that we all share. Go to work, run to the store, pay the bills, order a Double Whopper with cheese at the drive-thru, drink a PBR at the roadside bar, stop at a freeway exit and fill the tank. It's a default point of view: We each eat, drink, sing, dance, make love, make children, and die on the same planet, so we must be sharing the world, right? This is the notion that keeps us sane from day to day and also pits us against each other: red state/blue state, black/white, urban/rural, American/foreign. We're all jostling for physical and cultural space because there's only one world, and we have to share.

I once believed that. I was wrong.

There are moments in our lives when doors slide open silently, when glimpses of other worlds are served up unexpectedly. Sometimes we choose to pass through the doors and explore. More often we don't; the doors beckon us and we move on, blissfully unaware, because the cataract has already obscured the lens.

The door that changes my life, that shows me one of these alternate worlds, slides open on a sunny afternoon in July 1998 in Keene, New Hampshire, in the semidarkness of a restaurant called the Thai Garden.

On this day, I am sitting in the restaurant with a lovely blonde named Melissa, who has recently become—to my somewhat stunned surprise—my girlfriend. This is one of our first trips together. The blonde does not know of my tendency for weird obsessions. She does not know that, during the summer of 1989, I ate beef MexiMelts at Taco Bell for three months straight. Or that, in college, I played the Grateful Dead song "A Touch of Grey" so many times in the stereo of the Delta Chi house at Penn State that my fraternity brothers absconded with the cassette and melted it. The blonde does not know that when I developed a nursery school crush, I sat on the floor of my room with my mother's Olympia manual typewriter and typed the little girl's name over and over. Sharon Simmons. Sharon Simmons. Sharon Simmons.

The blonde knows none of this. She is not yet my wife, not yet the mother of a boy who carries my name, not yet the partner of a man who will spend more than $10,000 chasing a song around the world. She does not know that she will offer to spend her honeymoon driving through Southern backroads stopping at dimly lit roadhouses and listening to country music. She is blissfully unaware that in two years, I will drag her through the sweaty streets of Bangkok after midnight, looking for an air-conditioned karaoke bar that will give me the opportunity to sing a song, just one song. *That* song.

She knows only that she wants to order, and that there is a small disturbance at the next table.

The couple next to us is speaking loudly and barking at the staff. Why, the man demands, isn't sweet-and-sour pork on the menu? I want to grab him by his lapels and tell him that sweet-and-sour pork is *Chinese*, for chrissake, and barely that to boot. But Melissa and I tune them out. The only distraction is the background music, and we begin to listen.

Background music is a subtle but ever-present part of our lives as consumers. It is calibrated to set a mood, grease the wheels, get the wallet out and—in many cases—to not be noticed. Usually, the mood and flavor of the music matches the surroundings.

Not here.

The tune is mellow, designed to insinuate itself unobtrusively. It sounds vaguely familiar, as if a memory of a memory: a minor key, lots of sweeping notes. We realize we should know this song. But its journey has been a winding one. By the time it arrives at this place, at this moment, watered down and stripped of its pain, it has become almost unrecognizable.

"I've heard it a million times. I just can't think of the name," Melissa says.

Somehow, a kernel of distinctiveness bursts through. It is a piece of music that the world came to know in the 1960s, in a version full of electric instrumentals topped off by a British bluesman's voice. It embedded itself in that subconscious, collective musical memory that we Americans accumulate through years of absorbing cultural background noises, lifetimes of listening to drive-time DJs and weekly Top 40s.

The song is "House of the Rising Sun."

Even in mellow background music, the words are implied: *There is a house in New Orleans . . . been the ruin of many a poor boy . . . mother was a tailor . . . gambling man . . . suitcase and a trunk . . . mothers tell your children . . . not to do what I have done . . . wear that ball and chain.* In my mind, I hear what I will come to know as the definitive version—the switchblade of a voice that came from Eric Burdon, front man for the Animals, the British band that made the song an unorthodox chart-topper in 1964.

On a balmy evening in 1998, a composition that began life somewhere in the South more than a century ago—that has been globalized and cannibalized, repackaged and rerecorded—is being presented to us as window dressing as we order our tom yum soup.

I don't believe in epiphanies; they're usually simplistic answers to complicated questions. But for some reason, a revelation hits: The story of this song, how it got from someone's front porch to a Southeast Asian restaurant in upper New England, is more than an interesting anecdote. It is about technology, globalization, packaging, marketing, and the rise of recorded sound. It is the story of American culture in the twentieth century.

We are taught that drama must be Very Dramatic, that those who shout the loudest have the most important stories to tell. Occasionally, men like Charles Kuralt or Alistair Cooke pass our way and show us that regular Americans are fascinating, too, but we seem to endorse the fifty-foot-billboard rule of human importance. Yet many stories of our age are more subtle and may not involve Schwarzenegger-style theatrics. Instead, they unfold in small towns, along lonely highways, in Midwestern apartment complexes and in rickety Southern shacks. In suburbs and office parks and rowhouses and tenements. Or in Yankeeland Thai restaurants with Buddhas kneeling at the door, even.

Rarely is human obsession obvious at the outset. It is born as a seed of curiosity and only later does it grow into an out-of-control beanstalk. But I should have seen this one coming.

I have always been fascinated with history and with charting connections between the worlds of yesterday and the lives of today—particularly when it comes to America. This comes from something very basic: My full name is Edward Mason Anthony IV, which means that there are Edward Mason Anthonys going back to 1826 in my family. The Anthony side of my family followed the epic sweep of early American history—immigration to New England in colonial times, enlistment in the Revolutionary War, migration west to upstate New York, then to Ohio and, finally, for some Anthonys, further west. I have been able to see how the events I learned about in high school history class played out in my own family and I have seen two gravestones with my own name on them. When I was growing up, my obsession was visiting old courthouses, scouring dusty archives, tromping through lichen-coated graveyards looking for distant ancestors. I was seeking proof, I think, that the people who came before me had actually lived real lives, that they were more than paper and microfilm and memories. Such experiences made the past more personal, more vivid, rather than something that belonged only to another world.

Now I had another obsession, and it would become a global one that expanded far beyond anything I ever expected. Before it was over, I would buy nearly five hundred CDs and more than two hundred books. I would stay in dozens of cheap motels as I traversed the American landscape and put close to ten thousand miles on various vehicles. I would eat far too much fast food and fill the floors of rental-car backseats with empty Diet Coke bottles and piles of greasy plastic packaging—from Slim Jim wrappers to pork rind bags. I would chase the song into Southeast Asian karaoke bars, through music stores in the frigid plateaus near the China-Russia border, and across the Blue Ridge and Smoky mountains. I would ask people about it while eating raw oysters in New Orleans, smoking cheap cheroots in Nashville, and gulping down pints of obscure bitter ales in an English seashore town. The search would consume me for years. And when I asked myself why, I would always come back to one answer: It was something small that connected to something much larger—to everything, really. It contained infinite chances for new knowledge, new experiences, and a fresh understanding of the world.

In my favorite Dr. Seuss book, *McElligot's Pool,* a boy goes fishing in a tiny pond and is scorned by a farmer. "You'll never catch fish in McElligot's Pool," the man scoffs. Then the lens pulls back. The pool in the distant meadow is connected—to an underground brook, to a river through the city, to the vast ocean and beyond. The tiniest of places is always touching the biggest, and things flow back and forth. I always loved that book as a child but never knew quite why. Now I do.

Connections mean stories. One person, alone in one place, is a small story. When people connect, when their connections produce new ideas and more connections, things get interesting. Stories multiply. That was what had happened with "House of the Rising Sun," I was sure: all these human interactions, quietly hidden in the overproduced notes of background music in the unlikeliest of places.

It could have been anything—a recipe, a folktale, an advertising logo drawn from tradition, a quaint saying that reaches back to Elizabethan England and beyond. But it wasn't. For me, it was this song. The connections were dancing right in front of me. Where had this song come from? Where had it gone? Who carried it there?

Quietly, the door had opened. My life had changed, and I was fortunate to recognize it. I was embarking on a quest to find something pure. There were new worlds to explore.

The saying on the back of the dollar bill, America's motto, is *e pluribus unum:* of many, one. This American story is just the opposite: of one, many.

In the decades after the Civil War, a generations-old way of life was ending in the Southern Highlands. Railroads were coming through. Towns were cropping up all over. In *Southern Crossing: A History of the American South, 1877–1906,* Edward L. Ayers notes that, by 1890, nine of ten Southerners lived in a county with a railroad. As they were linked by commerce and transportation, small communities began to realize how different they were from one another. "Any given year would find some places in a buoyant mood as a railroad approached or a new mill opened, while others, bypassed by the machinery of the new order, fell into decay," Ayers writes. "The arrival of a railroad could trigger many consequences: rapid population growth or population decline, a more diversified economy or greater specialization, the growth of a city or the death of small towns."

When it came to people, the railroad did two things: It brought 'em in and it carried 'em out. The Southern Railroad advertised in cities for passengers, saying it would help them get away from an increasingly complicated, confusing way of life. "Are you weary of the city's din and discord? Come to these grand old mountains and find peace and quiet. . . . To this wonderful country the Southern Railway takes you cheaply, swiftly, commodiously." Among those who came in were folks who roused rabble; the railroad became a way for the itinerant ne'er-do-well to try his best in one town, then hit the depot and get out of Dodge. Some were musicians, spreading songs here and there—hardly an honorable pursuit in that time and place.

It's difficult to fathom today, in an age when business travelers are called "road warriors" with no hint of the sardonic, that the very act of rambling—going from town to town—was once a questionable pursuit. Yes, the notion of changing your place to change your life is the most American of stories, but aside from actual migrations, most "civilized" people spent their days staying put. They didn't have business in other locales. Those who drifted were desperate for employment or had something to hide or to leave behind. And leaving community and family just because you wanted to? That was deemed unaccepable by fellow citizens, churches, and families.

At the same time, the railroad carried off the sons—and sometimes the daughters—of families that had been stationary for generations. These young people rambled, too, looking for opportunity. For the first time, it was not impossible for a young person to live out dreams and seek fortunes elsewhere. In the Southern Highlands—the hills of North Carolina, southwestern Virginia, eastern Tennessee, and eastern Kentucky—places like Atlanta, Nashville, Birmingham, Meridian, and New Orleans, railroad-line endpoints, crackled with possibility.

How could the prospect of a life of hillside farming or working underground in the mines, of hearth and home, compete with a chance to see the world, make easy money, play cards, and meet women and see actual stores where you could buy, in one place, the very things that the Sears catalog rhapsodized about? "Girls with a wild streak . . . often lost their hearts to the man in dapper clothes with a big gold watch-chain across his vest and with plenty of money," the poet Carl Sandburg, who was also a musicologist, wrote in his folk-song collection *The American Songbag*. "That the man was a stranger in town, that he was a gambler, that he introduced himself saying, 'Come with me, girlie,' were points in favor of his audacity."

New Orleans was a particular object of attraction and suspicion, and the railroad's arrival in Appalachia only accentuated that. It almost defied belief that the tracks that came through your very own little mountain town could be connected with that place *down there*. New Orleans had lurked in Appalachia's consciousness since Andrew Jackson's Tennessee volunteers and some Kentucky riflemen had helped fight the Battle of New Orleans during the War of 1812. They returned with knowledge of a place where the races mixed and women who were black, white, Asian, Hispanic, and every step in between were available for purchase.

Upper Appalachia is a religious place, well inside the Bible Belt; today, at every turn on the winding roads, signs point the way to churches or challenge passersby to repent before Judgment Day. Imagine what these good hill-bred Christians—who tried so diligently to struggle through difficult lives, with the only motivation the promise of a reward in the next world—must have made of stories about Nouvelle Orleans and its seductive Creole mystique. And now the hills were becoming less remote with the railroad and, after it, the automobile. Young men and women could hop aboard and simply ride into the darkness. Small wonder, then, that cautionary songs and laments were so popular in this setting.

The warning song has a rich history, and many traditional Elizabethan ballads brought over by Scotch-Irish pioneers start with an exhortation—"Come all you fair and merry men . . ."—before recounting a tale of woe to be avoided at all costs. And in an uneasy South after the Civil War, freshly crafted warnings and admonishments popped up everywhere in folk songs.

"O daughter, O dear daughter, how could you treat me so, to leave your dear old mother and with a gambler go?" the mother sings in "The Roving Gambler." "If I had my life to live over, I would not go there anymore," goes one floating lyric fragment, which appears in several songs of otherwise unrelated subject matter. Sometimes the railroad itself was the focus of the anger, as in this song from the Kentucky mountains: "I don't like no railroad man / railroad man he'll kill you if he can."

It's impossible to catalog the oral tradition of the nineteenth century definitively, because it was just that—oral. With its carriers long dead, the fog of history has prevailed. But one thing is clear: From this changing land, another ballad emerged. In its earliest incarnations, it shows evidence of that cobbled-together flavor so common among Southern songs that quickened from lyrics that were floating around—an idea here, a specific there, a folk saying or a figure of speech or a couple of borrowed verses for additional seasoning, maybe a local reference thrown in—all marinated until some critical mass made it a song or even a story. Greil Marcus says many songs that emerged from the Invisible Republic during this period were

> . . . made up of verbal fragments that had no direct or logical relationship to each other, but were drawn from a floating pool of thousands of disconnected verses, couplets, one-liners, pieces of eight. Harry Smith guessed the folk-lyric form came together some time between 1850 and 1875. Whenever it happened, it wasn't until enough fragments were abroad in the land to reach a kind of critical mass—until there were enough fragments, passing back and forth between blacks and whites as common coin, to generate more fragments, to sustain within the matrix of a single musical language an almost infinite repertory of performances, to sustain the sense that out of the anonymity of the tradition a singer was presenting a distinct and separate account of a unique life.

Viewing "House of the Rising Sun" through this prism, the possibilities abound. Somewhere in the region, as different traditions began to blend into a distinctively Southern aesthetic, a songster who wanted to build a warning song assembled a passel of familiar lyrics into a lament. Maybe the singer was trying to warn a particular young person about the wages of sin; maybe he or she had a memory of someplace called the Rising

Sun and simply added New Orleans. Perhaps there indeed was an actual House of the Rising Sun in New Orleans, and someone from the mountains had come back spinning true (or tall) tales about the bordello. Maybe someone's daughter met her ruin there and returned home to tell about it. Or maybe one particular singer on one particular day, with the notion of a rising sun kicking around in his head, thought New Orleans would be the perfect flashpoint for a warning.

In the early stages of my quest, preparing to travel to New Orleans for an exploratory trip that would ultimately prove I was in the wrong place to trace the song, I spent two months going from record store to record store in Manhattan, buying up any version that I could. I collected from all genres—blues, country, reggae, rock, jazz, even *Golden Trumpet Favorites*. The clerk at Tower Records began greeting me by a nickname—"Rising Sun Boy." Another record shop employee offered me a declaration I would hear over and over in the coming years: " 'House of the Rising Sun'? Oh, that was written by Eric Burdon and the Animals."

The song and its potential origins have generated an enormous amount of discussion on the internet and produced a rich vein of legend, much of it just plain wrong. I tracked these trails to their dead ends, methodically eliminating each. It's amazing what people will say, flatly, without any proof.

For example, the house itself as it appears in the song. Is it a brothel? A prison? A gambling hall? Almost every iteration of the song never says, and therein lies its universal appeal: Anyone hobbled by, or even tempted by, a pernicious vice can peer into its mirror and see themselves reflected. And yet, though most people believe it to be a whorehouse, I was shocked at how many simply state—quite vehemently, sometimes—that their particular theory is right.

So, before we embark upon our journey, let's tackle a few of these internet urban legends, courtesy of various newsgroup posts and websites.

• *"The song is based on a 16th-century British ballad ('The Unfortunate Rake')."* Possible, but the hard evidence is wanting. "Rising Sun" bears some thematic resemblance to "Rake" and the songs it begat, including "St. James Infirmary," "Gambler's Blues," and "The Dying Cowboy" (known more commonly today as "The Streets of Laredo"). All three are related and are laments from the end of a life lived in sin; "St. James" is often played by New Orleans jazz musicians. But is "Rising Sun" directly related? There's no evidence to suggest that, and dozens of versions of those songs, while similar in subject (death, wages of sin, et cetera), have little in common otherwise with our song.

- *"I understand that the song was written by Alan Price in 1910."* Impossible. That was more than three decades before the birth of Price, a member of the original Animals whose name is on their famous 1964 arrangement.

- *" 'House of the Rising Sun' is an old blues tune. Bessie Smith sang it way back in the days of the minstrel shows."* This was an interesting possibility, though the guy who posted it could offer me no evidence to back it up. I scoured Bessie Smith's entire discography and found nothing to point me in that direction.

- *"Prior to Eric Burdon, it was about a woman."* Survey says . . . Nope! The earliest known recording, by Clarence "Tom" Ashley in 1933, is about a rounder, a male character.

- *"I read a serious-looking text stating that the original is an English folk song from the eighteenth century called 'Rising Sun.'"* Ah, yes. The always reliable Serious-Looking Text. This one isn't out of the realm of possibility, though some of the nation's foremost music scholars, including longtime Library of Congress folklorist Joe Hickerson, don't know of it.

Finally, here's my personal favorite:

- *"The 'House of the Rising Sun' is about a parrish* [sic] *prison in La (the state, not the city). They all had 'House' names. Every freekin' body thinks it is about a slut house. Get real and get the facts."* Merits aside, obviously someone needs a tranquilizer dart. The folk musician Dave Van Ronk, who played a key role in the spread of "Rising Sun" in the early 1960s, died believing that the song was about a women's prison.

The most ubiquitous "fact," repeated so many times that it is now presented as reality, is the notion that the earliest version of "House of the Rising Sun" was recorded by "black bluesman Texas Alexander" in 1928. This assertion has made it into several Serious-Looking Texts. Trouble is, it's completely wrong. Yes, Alger "Texas" Alexander did indeed record a song called "The Risin' Sun" in 1928, but it bears absolutely no resemblance, musically or lyrically, to the song we're chasing. It's a traditional blues with no narrative, no hint of New Orleans or a house or a ruined young woman or man or a warning to a younger sibling. It's dreamy and torpid and not at all unpleasant, and it doesn't seem to be about anything in particular:

> *My woman got somethin'*
> *Just like the Risin' Sun . . .*
> *You can never tell when that work is done.*

It also offers this cryptic line: "She got somethin' round and it looks just like a bear / sometime I wonder what in the hell is there." Some people have suggested those lyrics refer to a prostitute or, obliquely, the female genitalia ("got somethin' just like the Risin' Sun"; "you can never tell when that work is done"). I've heard a rumor that "rising sun" has been used as an African American slang term for vagina, but I've never been able to track it down.

In fact, all of the early "black blues" songs with Rising Sun–related titles are unrelated to our search. I find this out, naturally, after tracking each down on obscure reissues, purchasing them at premium prices and holding my breath, waiting for some early, unnoticed blues version of the song to unfold, only to hear something entirely unfamiliar. Ivy Smith and Charles "Cow Cow" Davenport's "Rising Sun Blues" (recorded in Chicago in 1927) features a muted trumpet and Smith complaining how someone "wooed her man away": "I raised my window, looked at the rising sun. / No one can love me just like my sweet man does." No ruination or warning there. "I get up with the rising sun," Peetie Wheatstraw sings in "The Rising Sun Blues" (Chicago, 1935). And "Rising Sun Blues" from King David's Jug Band (Atlanta, 1930) is an amiable lament about a lost, perhaps dead love. "Woke up this morning, looked up at the rising sun. I thought about my good gal who done gone along."

Another "Rising Sun Blues," recorded in 1930 by Darby and Tarlton, a white duo from Georgia and South Carolina who sang gentle folk and sentimental songs from the late nineteenth century in the white country blues tradition, is entirely unconnected to "House of the Rising Sun." It does, however, exhibit echoes of early black blues. "Lord, the sun's a-risin', and the moon is sinking low," Tom Darby and Jimmie

Tarlton sing. "I been with you all night long, pretty mama, now your daddy's got to go."

The late music writer and advocate Robert Shelton, one of Bob Dylan's earliest supporters and eventual biographer, contributed to the racial confusion in the liner notes of *The Folk Box*, a compilation issued by Elektra in 1964. Alongside an ethereal version by a Texas folksinger called Hally Wood, Shelton asserts that "House of the Rising Sun" emerged expressly from the black tradition and is essentially urban blues.

> When the country blues moved to New Orleans and other cities, there was a great change in its form and sophistication. Instead of being a purely personal vehicle, it became a performer-audience medium. This song falls into the early city blues category. Its meaningful moral is torn out of the pages of New Orleans' large brothel area around the time of World War I. "House of the Rising Sun" is a classic example of the passage through tradition of a folk song. It has roots in an English ballad of the sixteenth century called "The Unfortunate Rake." This earlier version traveled to America and several centuries later was transformed into a cowboy song, "The Cowboy's Lament." After the Civil War, Negro Cowboys brought the song back with them into the South where it has attained, in part, this form.

Shelton cites no sources for any of this. Most important, the song definitely predates World War I. Alan Lomax, who collected the version that would become definitive in Appalachia in 1937, said, "We have heard it sung only by Southern whites."

You could argue that "House of the Rising Sun" is a piece of distinctly American blues by theme and subject matter alone. You could argue that, thematically, the song points right back to the night in 1903 when W. C. Handy found a lonesome black musician at a rural Mississippi train station playing guitar in the darkness and singing the earliest of blues about the lonesome whistle blowing. And of course many white mountain singers in the post–Civil War Southern mountains absorbed some of their styles—of both music and lyrics—from traveling black musicians. But that certainly doesn't mean that "Rising Sun" came from African American tradition.

So let's explore. That means traveling back to The Village and looking at the key moments when the song first bubbled up—and where it came from.

Despite its deeply American influences, "Rising Sun" seems directly connected in meter and subject to the British ballad tradition. Its melody, Alan Lomax wrote, resembled one arrangement of "Lord Barnard and Little Musgrave," also known as "Matty Groves," a well-known English ballad dating to the 1600s that chronicles a sad tale of infidelity and death. And if "Rising Sun" is indeed unrelated to "The Unfortunate Rake," it certainly seems as if it has distant ancestors in that old don't-do-what-I-have-done neighborhood.

In Britain, the term "Rising Sun" is a common name for pubs, though few say it's used for houses of prostitution. There exists one tantalizing clue, brought forth by our friend Alan Lomax.

In 1953, in Norfolk in eastern England, Lomax was recording a raft of fascinating old English ballads sung by a sixty-eight-year-old farm laborer and balladeer with an extensive repertoire named Harry Cox (1885–1971). Cox, who lived in a cottage with no electricity, had been singing in local pubs since he was eleven and learned hundreds of songs from listening to the singing of his father and other singers who performed in the taverns in the late 1800s and early 1900s. "There weren't no wireless," Cox recalled of those days. "None of it. You had to go—you used to go to a pub and made your own music—and sung these old songs and everybody join in it."

One day, Lomax made a request.

"Now what about this 'Rising Sun' song?" he asked Cox.

"What—that old bad song?" Cox shot back. "That t'aint worth doing, is it?"

"For me, I want it, 'cause I have it from the United States, you see," Lomax said.

Harry Cox (whose name, especially considering the material he's singing, sounds suspiciously like a 1970s porn pseudonym) proceeds to uncork a dirty ditty called "She Was a Rum One" about a john bedding a prostitute. It features verses like:

> *At last I found m'cock*
> *m'cock was in my hand*
> *and if you gave me all the world*
> *I couldn't get him to stand*

He finishes, and Lomax prods him. "There's another way to begin that song, isn't there, Harry?"

"Yeah."

"How's that go?"

"Like I said 'afore," Cox says, then offers this alternative intro:

> *If you go to Lowestoft,*
> *and ask for the Rising Sun,*
> *there you'll find two old whores,*
> *and my old woman's one.*

Here was the Rising Sun as a whorehouse, in England, entirely separated from its American context, sung by a singer whose ballad knowledge stretched back far beyond the song's first appearances in America. It's doubtful Cox picked up the "Rising Sun" notion from mass culture; he wasn't that kind of guy. He hated "all that squit you hear on the radio" with a passion. "I'd go anywhere, by and by, to go and sing an old song," he said during those 1953 sessions. But "I wouldn't listen to a song what they make today. I'd never pick up one to learn 'cause there ain't one worth it."

That fragment of Cox's song suggests that "Rising Sun" probably pre-dates its New Orleans setting—which suggests, in turn, that there may not have been an actual House of the Rising Sun in the Crescent City. Lomax, in his 1960 book *The Folk Songs of North America,* says that, in addition to our song, "the 'Rising Sun' occurs as the name of a bawdy house in two other traditional songs, both British in origin." Presumably one of those is the one Cox sang to him seven years earlier; he never elaborated on the other, and his archived papers reveal no clues to its identity.

I went to Lowestoft, a port town on England's eastern seaboard founded by the Danes many centuries ago. After a weekend of poking around, I came away with only two nuggets: First, there once was a pub there called the Rising Sun; second, Lowestoft itself, by virtue of it being so far east on the island, was occasionally called the "Town of the Rising Sun." No one had heard of Harry Cox or a similarly named bordello.

In America, the earliest hard evidence of a proto–"Rising Sun" is a song about the wages of sin, not a dirty ditty. It comes from one of the performers who was introduced to folk revival aficionados through Smith's *Anthology*—Clarence "Tom" Ashley, a white songster and balladeer whose grandparents came from Ashe County, smack in the middle of the Golden Triangle where Kentucky, Tennessee, Virginia, and North Carolina meet. Smack in the middle of The Village.

Ashley was born in 1895 in Bristol, a railroad town that straddles the border between Tennessee and Virginia. He was a rambling man. He was born Clarence Earl McCurry, but a thorny family situation produced a dispute between his grandparents and his father, whom he did not meet until decades later. Clarence was raised by his mother and his grandparents, Enoch and Martha ("Mat") Ashley, who were highly musical and sang an assortment of old ballads. According to Clarence Ashley, he learned "Rising Sun Blues" from his mother's parents when he was a boy, and he implied that it was already old then. That puts it squarely in the Golden Triangle in the years after the Civil War.

Ashley's family gave him a nickname when he was growing up: "Tommy Tiddy Waddy." He dropped the sillier part as he grew, but "Tom" stuck. When he began traveling around in a medicine show at age sixteen, and on some of his recordings after that, he alternated between the names Tom Ashley and Clarence Ashley.

Ashley's decision in 1911 to join a traveling medicine show as a performer was probably pivotal in the spreading of "Rising Sun" around the Golden Triangle. He spent the better part of three decades with this particular show, which was run, during most of Ashley's tenure there, by two "physicians," one a German named Doc Hauer and the other a purported American Indian named Doc White Cloud. They toured the mountain towns and mining camps of the Triangle selling patent medicine. Ashley's daughter, Eva, who sometimes accompanied him on the circuit, told me she remembered helping Doc White Cloud mix his elixirs from orchard fruits. "We used to gather wild cherries," she said. "We had a cherry tree out by the barnyard. I went out there all the time to get 'em."

Medicine shows, which flooded rural America in the 1800s and endured until the television era, were important vectors of early mass culture. Doctors and "doctors" selling cures and elixirs would employ minstrel shows and hillbilly musicians to perform and draw crowds from railroad communities, farm-to-market towns and mountain mining camps (think of Professor Marvel in *The Wizard of Oz*). Samuel Charters, in *The Country Blues*, describes what it was like:

> The entertainers sang loud, mugged ferociously, and relied on slapstick to get them through the show. When they were finished, the "doctor" would begin his sales pitch, trying to charm hard-earned money out of overall pockets and into his cashbox. The musicians hung around, helping him with the sales and passing out bottles. They were a hard-living, independent bunch. They slept wherever they happened to be, with anybody handy; drinking, gambling, getting run out of the county for chasing the wrong married woman, or getting a royal treatment for singing a song that went over big.

Though the medicine show is forgotten today, its musical ripples—black and white music blending and creating something entirely new—endure. Some of country music's most famous performers—including Roy Acuff, who makes a cameo appearance in the "Rising Sun" saga—got their start in such shows. "Until movies and radio were available to the majority of rural Americans, the medicine show was synonymous with entertainment," Ann Anderson writes in *Snake Oil, Hustlers and Hambones: The American Medicine Show*. That meant that sometimes isolated communities would, with the arrival of a medicine show and its motley band of performers, experience a sudden infusion of popular culture that they could never have sampled otherwise. In other words, a single man singing a single song could plant it like Johnny Appleseed in towns across the show's route—which in Ashley's case was the exact region where eruptions of "Rising Sun" began at about the same time.

In the mid-1920s, Ashley began appearing with various groups that performed in the Golden Triangle—Byrd Moore and His Hot Shots, the Carolina Tar Heels, the Blue Ridge Mountain Entertainers. He cut several sides for Vocalion, including his signature song, "Coo Coo Bird," recorded solo, in which he accompanied himself on the banjo in one of the most haunting performances of traditional music recorded in the 1920s. Brought back from the grave on Smith's *Anthology*, it sounds like a minor-key ghost from the past, a refugee from The Village. *Oh the coo-coo is a pretty bird, she warbles as she flies, / She never hollers coo-coo 'til the fourth day of July.*

Like his music, Ashley was at turns taciturn and exuberant. While he put his stamp upon such Appalachian standards as the remorseless murder ballad "Little Sadie" and the desolate "Dark Holler," Ashley's sense of humor was clear in his recording, with the Tar Heels, of a throwaway song called "You Are a Little Too Small." It must have been a sight to gather around the medicine show tent and see this little man—barely five feet tall—switch abruptly from chronicling Appalachia's blackest desolation to singing lyrics like

> *I asked her if I might be her escort*
> *some eve at her home I might call?*
> *She said she'd ask Ma, "But I really believe*
> *she'll say you're a little too small."*

Decades later, after he was "rediscovered," Ashley included "Rising Sun Blues" in his set. "I got it off some of my grandpeople," he told the crowd during one concert shortly before his death in 1967. "Now, I don't know who wrote this. It's too old for me to talk about." I can't help but wish that he had. But though he had known "Rising Sun" since he was a child, Ashley didn't record it. At least not at first.

Just as Ashley was about to make his first commercial recordings, Robert Winslow Gordon, who ran the Library of Congress's Archive American of Folk Song in the 1920s, was writing a newspaper column about folk music and printing submissions from correspondents around the country. One, William F. Burroughs, sent him what appears to be the earliest instance of "Rising Sun" committed to paper. Burroughs, who told Gordon, "I work for the railroad," sent it in late February or early March of 1925. He told Gordon that he heard the song, which he called "The Rising Sun Dance Hall," from

> . . . a southerner. He was of the type that generally call themselves:
> "One o'th' boys." He was not a crook, and not exactly a bum. His

working activities were confined to "Pearl diving" and other restaurant jobs. This and an occasional strike at the dice kept him away from the Associated Charities. However, he called on them at times. When he lacked the funds for railroad fare he simply stayed where he was until something "turned up." He "took his fun as he found it," and as a consequence had spent a total of something like five years in penal servitude on various misdemeanor charges.

Then Burroughs wrote down the lyrics for Gordon as he remembered them—"I believe complete, and I can say exactly as I heard it":

The Rising Sun.
There is a house in New Orleans,
It's called the Rising Sun,
It's been the ruin of a many poor girl,
Great God and I for one.

If I had of listened to what my mother said,
I'd be at home today,
But I was young and foolish poor girl
Let a rounder lead me astray.

Oh mother, mother, tell me why
You treat that rounder cold,
I'd rather be that rounder's wife
Than to wear your crown of gold.

Now tell my sister in Baltimore,
Not to do as I have done
To shun that house in New Orleans
It's called the Rising Sun.

Gordon was thrilled. " 'The Rising Sun' is bully, and I'm glad to have it," he responded. But he never did anything with it; it vanished into the Library's files.

Burroughs's version is interesting for two reasons. First, it means the earliest known text of "Rising Sun" in print is told from a girl's point of view, even though the person who sent it to Gordon was male. Second is its addition of a specific line that appears nowhere else: "Tell my sister in *Baltimore*." It shows, early on, how malleable our song can be. Maybe the guy who sang this for Burroughs was from Baltimore. It could have been Birmingham, Meridian, Atlanta—or Outer Mongolia. It's one of those things that folk songs and folksingers do to maintain their relevance among their audiences. And it's something that gets a lot harder when you have a national culture listening to nationally distributed recordings as we do today.

In August 1929, folklorist Mellinger Edward Henry collected a set of lyrics called simply "Song Ballet" from a man named Ray Bohanan in Sevierville, Tennessee—then a Smoky Mountains backwater, now a bustling tourist center full of miniature golf courses and themed attractions that is just up the road from Dollywood, the amusement park started by Dolly Parton. The song offered by Bohanan, who wasn't identified further, was pegged by Henry as a variation of something called "The Rambling Cowboy." Its first verses contained many images familiar to cowboy songs: "My papa always taught me well, and give me good advice / My mind it was on rambling, and we could not agree." But it was the ninth verse that caught my eye:

> There's a girl in Baxter Springs,
> They call her the rising sun;
> She has broken the heart of nine.
> Love, boys, and this poor heart is one.

Baxter Springs, it turns out, is hundreds of miles west in Kansas, just over the border from Missouri. It's a lonesome-prairie cowtown, and today it feels more Larry McMurtry than the Appalachia-like Ozark Mountains that it abuts. It's along old Route 66, and it's full of 1950s commercial signage, folks wearing cowboy hats, old stone buildings and roads that just taper off in gravel and grass. Nearby is "the Hanging Tree," or the site where it used to be. Today a plaque remembers it as "the site of vigilante justice. As many as seven horse thieves were hanged from the tree at one time."

On the day I drive through, the auto body lots are full of '50s-era Chevy pickups and the sign on the Bethel Church warns passersby to "live your life so the preacher won't have to lie at your funeral." There's a residue of Old West menace, though it dissipates when you reach the Wal-Mart at the edge of town. Something about discounted Milky Way Midnight multipacks tends to take the edge off.

That Baxter Springs might have appeared in a song about the wages of sin is understandable. "It was known, far and wide, as 'a tough place,' made up of a number of classes of people who would scarcely be taken into the aggregate of polite society," Nathaniel Thompson Allison wrote in a 1904 local history. Even earlier, in 1883, historian William G. Cutler's *History of the State of Kansas* made Baxter Springs sound even worse:

> Society was in a state of chaos. Here was a rendezvous for the notorious Texas cow boy, the gambler, prostitute, saloon keeper, and the multitude of villains and ruffians which infest these cattle towns. Saloons and bawdy and dance houses of the most virulent character were numerous, and the town, especially during the season when the cattle were being driven in, was in one continuous state of uproar, night and day.

The setting and characters of "Rising Sun" were present and accounted for.

The Kansas connection in Bohanan's song will remain a mystery. But what's instructive about the little lyric in an otherwise unrelated song is the absence of one key character: New Orleans. It shows that the "Rising Sun" is elastic enough to be superimposed on any rough-and-rowdy situation, and that—in the years when recorded music was just beginning to sell—the image was compelling enough to be pressed into service for the storytelling of a man in a rural Tennessee town 650 miles east.

Four years passed. Clarence Ashley made more recordings and traveled with the medicine show. By 1932, the Depression had ensured that people didn't have much money to spend on "hillbilly records." Record companies cut back their catalogs. But before one of them, Vocalion, retreated entirely, it brought Ashley in for another session in New York City. On September 6, 1933, he recorded Vocalion 02576-B—"The Rising Sun Blues." Years later, he would remember committing it to acetate. "This was a popular old song in my early days," he said during that concert in the 1960s. "I don't know how long it stayed on the market. I don't remember; didn't keep up with it. But it stayed on the market a period of time—reasonable, I guess. Then it died out."

This recording was what I had been waiting for—a postcard sent from The Village. Here was the moment when "Rising Sun" took its first baby step from the folk tradition into popular culture. One generous old-time aficionado emailed me an MP3 version, but it was promptly eaten by my computer. I had to immerse myself in that early Ashley piece, to hold the acetate record in my hand and see it spin as I heard his high, nasal voice sing about New Orleans. So where on Earth could I find an obscure old 78 that had never made it to any album? The Library of Congress didn't even have it.

But Joe Bussard did.

FREDERICK, MARYLAND

He sits in his cellar each day, awaiting his next customer. The ride he offers is free. Anyone is welcome aboard. The preconditions are these: a willingness to listen; an endorsement of his fundamental principles—that yesterday is far better than today, that music conquers all, that modern Americans have forgotten the wisdom of previous generations; and an appetite for his tales, his memories, which are legion.

If you think you qualify, then knock on Joe Bussard's door. Follow him to the kitchen and turn left, down the stairs. Proceed into the Room, which still smells of the cigars he finally quit smoking. He'll run toward the big machine with all the buttons. "Gotta fire up old Bessie here," he'll say. Then he'll dart to the wall and pluck a shellac disc from the library of twenty-five thousand that line the room.

Now the moment is at hand. Gangly and abrupt and delightfully manic—Buster Keaton via Don Knotts—he flips a switch. His machine begins to revolve until it reaches cruising speed: 78 rpm. The room crackles with the static of another age. Music begins to play—raw music, untethered music, created not by technology but by human beings. Bussard grins. And at that moment, anyone caught inside the warp bubble that is his basement will travel back in time.

Joe Bussard Jr. collects records. And not just any records. He collects records that shatter when you drop 'em. Records that spin so fast on the turntable, they'll make you feel dizzy if you try to read the labels while they're playing. Records that blare yesterday's tales through refrigerator-sized speakers. Like their owner, each disc opens doors from other eras into our own. Multiplied over four decades of accumulation, that means Joe Bussard is on a one-man crusade to let anybody within shouting distance know that American music ain't what it used to be. "When I play records down here at night," he says, "I get so high I'm up on the ceiling and it takes me hours to come down."

Bussard was in his early seventies when I visited him, a widower with a shock of white hair. He worked at regular jobs, but records are his career. He moves about like a ten-year-old playing kickball—a mass of arms and legs and proclamations going in every direction. If he likes you, he'll call you "Doc." If he's annoyed with you, he'll call you "Doc" really loudly.

He yanks out record after record by artists you've never heard of unless you're deeply into such things. John Dilleshaw, better known as Seven-Foot Dilly (and his Dill Pickles). The Skillet Lickers. Vernon Dalhart, who in 1924 made the first popular recording of the classic train song "Wreck of the Old '97." The Ozarkers, whose "Second-Class Hotel" documented the travails of a low-end boardinghouse ("If the butter gets a chance, it will do the Charleston dance"). The Beale Street Sheiks, whose 1927 "It's a Good Thing" is, Bussard asserts, the earliest rap record. "They don't call it rap, but it is," he enthuses, springing from his stool toward me. "Whaddaya think of that, kid? There's nothing new."

For Joe Bussard, nothing new is worth much. The Day the Music Died? He'll say it was the end of Prohibition (for jazz) or the early Eisenhower administration (for old-time country and most genuine blues). "Nashville?" he'll spit. "More like Trashville." Rock? "The cancer of the music world." He switches to a nyah-nyah voice and his eyes bulge. "There's no difference anymore—no difference between Itchy and the Leopards, Hank and the Hernias, Johnny Flush and the Commodes."

Then he'll grin, whisper sweet nothings to his cat and spin another record—probably something from a long-ago label like Gennett or Paramount or the absurdly rare Black Patti or the delightfully named Okeh, which specialized in "race recordings" and "hillbilly music." He'll listen, then start moving and jerking. Air guitar? He plays air sax, air banjo, air fiddle, even air cornet.

This personality did not develop recently. In the 1950s, the sixteen-year-old teenager who became Bussard used to troll his neighborhood with a gadget called an oscillator that disturbed the signals of early television sets. He and a friend would drive from house to house while a popular show was airing, turn on the oscillator, then peer in through the front window to watch their victims frantically adjusting the antenna.

During the week, Bussard records old-time music programs for Appalachian radio stations. On weekends, he welcomes all comers—from amateur musicians to jazz critics, folkies to researchers. Mail him your wish list, and he'll dub a cassette of anything he owns for fifty cents a track. "Our greatest works of American music are on these 78s," he says. Suddenly he's taking things personally. "And they're ignored by just about everybody!"

Like so many of the characters his favorite music immortalizes, Bussard is a rambler. That's how he got what he's got. "It took me forty-seven years," he growls. "I been all over the place. I've found out about so many people—sunup to sundown, fruit pie and a bottle of gutwash at the old country stores."

I am not sure I have any idea what he means.

Bussard started listening to country string bands on the radio in the 1940s, which led him to records by Jimmie Rodgers, the Carter Family, and Gene Autry. He began hunting around Frederick, his hometown, and a woman gave him a box of records with "some good stuff."

"I started listening," he says, "and one thing led to another."

When he got his driver's license, he began to range around the county, stopping at old houses and scoping out records. Then excursions to Virginia, West Virginia, the Carolinas. More door knocking. More folks who'd unload big boxes of discs for next to nothing. "Take 'em," they'd say. "Just give me a couple dollars." Bussard was glad to oblige; he was honing his instincts. "I usually could look at a house and tell you if it had records in it," he brags.

He began at a perfect time—the 1950s, when 78s were neither new enough to be trendy nor old enough to be antique. By 1960, he'd accumulated four thousand and realized that, instead of "a whole mess of records," he had a collection. Today, behind each record he pulls from the shelf is a story of how it arrived. Sometimes he'd play music for people, serenading them as he pried loose their records. In 1968, near Tazewell, Virginia, came his crowning achievement. En route to a flea market, he gave a guy a ride to the guy's house up in the hills. "He goes into this bedroom and he pulls this box out from under the bed. There was three foot of bed dust in it. I started going down through it. Some decent stuff—some Uncle Dave Macons, Carter Familys, some Jimmie Rodgerses. Then I hit the first Black Patti. All of a sudden I was looking at fifteen of them. Mint. *Mint!*"

The guy had played them once, long ago. Seems he didn't much like blues. One became the jewel of Bussard's collection—"Original Stack O' Lee Blues" by the Down Home Boys (Long Cleve Reed and Little Harvey Hull), an eerie version of the old Stagolee murder ballad that, with its harmonies and ghostly guitar, sounds as if it's piped in directly from The Village. *Standing on the hilltop, a dog begin to bark; well, it was nothin' but Stack O' Lee come creepin' in the dark.* It's the only known copy in existence. People have offered up to $30,000 for it; Bussard grins and sends them away. He'll copy it onto tape for you, though, for those two quarters. It's worth it. "It's beautiful. They were great artists. The world today doesn't know a thing about music. They listen to this horrible banging and rattling and squealing and bumping. All people want today is some kind of a thump."

Many who visit the Bussard cave want to borrow, but he sends them away with an admonishing look; he never lends. Would you? But if you're producing a compilation CD and you're nice to him, he might come to you and bring along the records you want to remaster. His scope in that respect is jaw dropping. If you buy a compilation CD of professionally recorded old-time music from the 1920s and 1930s, the odds are that some of the songs you hear will have been recorded from the Bussard stash.

He accommodates whomever he can because they're doing what he's doing—spreading the word. Maybe, he figures, people will eventually wake up.

There are folks like Bussard sprinkled across the land, men who stalk the aisles of self-assembled sound collections and hope people will come to listen. A decade earlier, I spent time with Paul Mawhinney, who runs a sprawling beast in suburban Pittsburgh called Record-Rama, which is part store, part sound archive. Mawhinney is as fascinating as

Bussard but nowhere near as vehement. Both are preservers, but while Bussard is an unabashed tastemaker, Mawhinney sees himself as a supplier. When I visited him in 1991, he had 250,000 vinyl LPs, 50,000 compact discs, and a record-holding 1.5 million 45 rpm singles—more than the Library of Congress. Unlike Bussard's purist sturm und drang, Mawhinney revels in modern culture's dreck und kitsch—including, God help us, every K-Tel album ever sold on television and the entire discography of a certain actor who played a certain pointy-eared Vulcan in a certain science-fiction show and liked to dabble in the musical arts. "I have all the Nimoys," Mawhinney told me. "I even have 'Sebastian Cabot Sings Dylan.'" Thinking about the implications of that statement makes me reassess my affection for the blending of genres.

I cold-called Bussard after hearing he had the Ashley version of "Rising Sun Blues" from the 1930s that had proven elusive. Even a wonderful 2001 compilation of Ashley recordings on CD, *Greenback Dollar*, didn't include it, though Bussard had contributed some of his records for remastering for the project. When I got him on the line, I made the mistake of asking to speak with Joe Buss-ARD rather than Joe BUSS-ard. That elicited something that emerged from the telephone on my end as a cross between the snort of an irritated boar and the low, rumbling thunder that accompanies heat lightning.

"I'm not *French*," he snapped.

Soon, though, he became his usual gregarious self and allowed that his collection did, indeed, contain "The Rising Sun Blues" by Ashley and Foster.

"Come on down," he boomed. "I got a speaker system that'll blow you out of the house."

This was before I became comfortable with my obsession, so driving from New York to Maryland still seemed like something odd to do just to hear a song. Nevertheless, on a gloomy February Saturday, I make my way to Frederick and arrive at Bussard's house, where he ushers me into a very normal-looking garage, through a very normal-looking kitchen and down some very normal-looking basement steps. What greets me at the bottom is decidedly not normal. In this mid-sized suburban house sits an entire countryful of music. Six-foot-high shelves groan with shellac 78s in protective sleeves, bordered by rows of cassettes and reel-to-reel tapes.

Already sitting there, clearly in heaven, is Ron Curry, a musician and old-time aficionado from Richmond, Virginia. "Do you know what you've gotten yourself into?" I remember Curry saying to me. This was before the full force of the Bussard blast furnace had revealed itself. Bussard immediately stalks to his turntable and queues up some really old jazz. I'm not a jazz fan, but this stuff grabs me and *squeezes*. It sounds like sex—like late-night city sex, the kind of urgent, indulgent sex you have in a mid-rise hotel after an extended evening of drinking in some narrow club where blue smoke lingers just above your eyes, an available woman is everywhere you turn and the knowledge of things like consequences and stupidity and headaches at dawn drains from your mind and your nether regions get behind the wheel and start driving the whole machine. And suddenly, just as things are getting really explicit, a snowy-haired, bulging-eyed guy, grinning like a devil's head, is three inches from your nose shouting, "That's *hot*. Is that not *hot*? That's *jazz*, baby!" And the dream dissipates into Joe Bussard's face.

That's what this music was like. That's how my extraordinary Saturday afternoon at the Bussard abode began. Most of Bussard's Saturdays, however, are like this—a parade of obsessives cheerfully insisting that he be their personal DJ. They always prevail. "I never turn anybody down," he says.

I wait an hour, allowing Bussard to introduce me to records I never imagined, before I remind him of the reason why I came. "Right, right, 'Rising Sun,' " he says. Without looking it up, he walks over to a spot in the middle of his racks at about chest level, extends a paw and withdraws a record. I can't help but imagine how horrible it would be if this place ever caught fire; it's probably for the best that Bussard gave up cigars.

He holds it up so I can photograph it. It's far more beautiful than today's CDs or the 33 rpm albums I grew up with. The black grooves gleam like the freshly washed straight hair of a 1970s Breck Girl. The label is etched in gold leaf. "Vocalion" is written in one of those Olde English fonts that seems too grandiose for the folk music that the record contains. "Work of art, that Vocalion label," Bussard says.

Below the logo is written, "U.S. Pat. 1,637,544, Rising Sun Blues, Ashley and Foster, Vocal with Guitar and Harmonica Acc. Not Licensed for Radio Broadcast." This is the earliest known recorded version of the song. Bussard is hoisting the record into the air and going on about

Ashley. "He was about this high," he says, holding his hand about five feet in the air. "Just a great guy—I can imagine what he was like when he was in his twenties. What a fantastic banjo player."

With two hands, he puts it on "Old Bessie" and it starts to spin. I am a bit embarrassed at my excitement: Could this be the ur-version, from which rest sprang? Will it have more verses? Will it mention the house of prostitution? Probably not, given that it was recorded around the time that the Hays Code was beginning to make Hollywood mind its Ps and Qs.

He puts the needle on, and after a few seconds the static gives way to music. It starts with a jaunty guitar riff that sounds sort of like a yodel—which doesn't fit the tone of the song at all. Bussard notices my puzzlement and tells me such things were common around that time and may have had nothing to do with Ashley. Jimmie Rodgers, whose trademark was a yodel, had died three months before the recording was made, and the tidal wave of popularity (and record sales) that engulfed his career had record executives hungry for that kind of market clout. So a lot of old-time musicians who came into the recording studio were given instructions to "try and sound like Jimmie Rodgers."

Then Ashley's unmistakable nasal voice cuts in, and accompanist Gwen Foster's harmonica trills in the background. Foster, who recorded several duets with Ashley, was so skilled on the mouth harp that he could make it sound like instruments that didn't exist, and he does so here; he doesn't *play* the harmonica so much as make the air around it *vibrate*.

"They are a house in New Orleans, they call the Rising Sun. Where many poor boy to destruction has gone, and me, Oh God, for one," Ashley sings just before offering another Rodgersian guitar riff. It sounds so . . . sunny.

This "Rising Sun" is about a man, rather than a woman, who went to his ruin because of excess and greed rather than the dark forces of coercion and intimidation. In Ashley's version, what happened to him is his own fault. "Just fill the glass up to the brim. Let the drinks go merrily around. We'll drink to the life of a rounder, poor boy, who goes from town to town."

Ashley offers a verse that I will hear only a couple times again during my search and still haven't been able to figure it out:

> *Now boys, don't believe*
> *what a young girl tells you*
> *Let her eyes be blue or brown.*
> *Unless she's on some scaffold high*
> *Sayin' "Boys, I can't come down."*

What on Earth could that mean? I suspect it's a floating lyric that was originally in another song. It seems a warning against the siren who will lead you down the wrong road, but the only references to "scaffold" I can find in the American folk tradition refer to hanging. Could it be advice to a wandering boy that the only safe woman is a dead woman? Or a woman on a pedestal so high that she's unattainable and thus powerless to do harm? A similar verse appears in an obscure Kentucky song recorded by Shortbuckle Roarke called "I Truly Understand You Love Another Man," but it lacks the puzzling presence of the scaffold:

> *I never will listen to what another woman says,*
> *let her hair be black or brown.*
> *For I'd rather be on the top a some hill*
> *in a rain a-pourin' down.*

The Ashley and Foster version shows, for certain, that one incarnation of "Rising Sun" was a rambler's song, and that the Animals' decision to make it about a man instead of a woman was not, as many believe, solely modern. Ashley's interpretation puts it squarely in the place I had suspected—the repertory of white Appalachian songsters and ballad singers rather than black country blues. And nothing in it indicates that it *originated* in New Orleans, just as I had surmised.

"So," Bussard says to me after I ask him to play it for me the third time. "You're pretty obsessed here."

I have looked into the vast maw of obsession, and it is Joe Bussard's face that stares out at me. And now he's telling me *I'm* obsessed. I could have a problem here.

Here's what Joe Bussard obsesses about most: the records he *doesn't* have. The time in War, West Virginia, where he missed a houseful of records by four months because they'd thrown everything out?

"Ohhh . . ." The little record company in the Midwest that, upon going bankrupt, took its stock out back for a skeet shoot? "Ouch!" The guy in Wisconsin who lined his roof with old Paramount Masters for insulation? "I can't even think about that." All that great music—gone. And all the chaff that replaced it.

"How can anybody listen to Benny Goodman and Artie Shaw when you've listened to Jelly Roll Morton? It's like coming out of a mansion and living in a chicken coop."

Bussard's purism is infectious. Every school of thought needs extremists to thrive. But while I can appreciate his purist bent, and my ears and my quest benefit, his mind-set warrants caution. Our journey is shaped like an hourglass: The top is where "House of the Rising Sun" came from, the bottom is where it goes. If I Bussardify my attitude, if I try to freeze the song in amber, I ignore the most exciting part of the quest: the trajectory and velocity with which the song moves through the hourglass.

Consider someone like Charlie Poole, a seminal string-band musician whose early Columbia recordings are sprinkled through Bussard's collection. Along with early performers like Ashley, the Skillet Lickers, Buell Kazee, Darby and Tarlton and the Carter Family, the hard-charging, hard-living, hard-drinking Poole, with his North Carolina Ramblers, emerged in the 1920s to become a first-generation country artist who carried the music of the hills to the rest of the land.

Listen to Poole today, and his songs sound like weathered postcards from the nineteenth century, from The Village. But it's simplistic to brand Poole a purist, a spear carrier of an age earlier than his own. We tend to do that with the earliest recorded performers simply because their music is the oldest available to us, so it's a natural conclusion that they are the wellsprings. Not Poole, who truly lived his music: He died in 1931 at age thirty-nine after a weeks-long bout of drinking. In his time he was a blender and an innovator, reaching backward into American yesterdays and harvesting them for the musical fuel he needed to charge forward. If Bill Monroe was the father of bluegrass, Poole was its grandfather.

His voice was fusion embodied, a blend of old Appalachian ballad tradition and the energy of 1920s modernism. And Poole's performances were just that—performed, musically and lyrically calibrated to audiences and microphones, making them different from true front-porch music. Some of his songs, like the long-unreleased "Mother's Last Farewell Kiss," are unabashedly sentimental parlor tunes. Others, like "Leaving Home," a take on the old "Frankie and Johnny" ballad, are raw and refined at the same time, managing to sound utterly white and rural while still incorporating black influences. And "Sweet Sixteen," writer unknown, bursts with Tin Pan Alley lyricism ("I loved her well, but it's sad to tell, she'd chew her chewing gum"). His magnificent take on W. C. Handy's "Ramblin' Blues" carries us to Paris, to Broadway and to Memphis, Tennessee, as Poole extols the joys of rambling around. "Talk about your whiskey and your bygone days," he sings, and his voice is sentimental and sarcastic all at once, an early equivalent to Springsteen's "Glory Days." The tug between traditionalism and modernism is embodied in him. Because it's embodied in "Rising Sun," too, and because "Rising Sun" is right up Poole's alley, I'm surprised that he never recorded it.

I remember discovering, years ago, that much of the American "Main Street" architecture we prize so much was, in its own era, considered pre-fabricated and mass-produced. The late architect and popular culture critic Steve Izenour once told me that "the measure of authenticity is time," and that goes for music as much as anything else. The songs that Joe Bussard adores stick with him because they seem like time capsules from a purer age, an age of possibility and magic, and in many ways they are. Music is different now, and many of those 1920s recordings are superior, rawer and more subjective than the majority of today's over-produced pablum. They tell stories of harsh realities. But to worship the ancestors and turn our backs on the descendants is unwise. We live in this world, not The Village, and ours is the music coming out of it. If you believe music reflects human experience, our modern music is as much the key to us as the "pure" stuff of the 1920s was to its people.

More than that, fusion culture crackles with possibility. Without Clarence Ashley, we would know far less of Doc Watson, who learned so much from him in the early 1960s—and adapted a lot of it. And without Doc Watson, none of the progressive music of Nickel Creek, perhaps no Alison Krauss and Union Station, and the *O Brother, Where Art Thou?* soundtrack would lack much of its texture. Without Charlie Poole, there might have been no Bill Monroe, no Flatt and Scruggs, no

Hank Williams, Hank Jr., or Hank III. These are speculations, but we build on the foundations we're given, and what was the entire house in the 1920s is now but a brick in a larger structure. That's as it should be. Venerate the foundation, but don't ignore the wondrous tower that rose from it—and the new wings that are constantly being constructed.

It's past 10 p.m. on Saturday night. Joe Bussard's neighborhood is quiet. His basement isn't. He is playing some old records that happen, accidentally, to have strange noises in the background. On one, recorded in the Victor studio on the top floor of the Charlotte Hotel in North Carolina, a truck rumbles by in the middle of a track. On another, a flubbed final note prompts an obscenity that made it into the record's final pressing.

This is Bussard's life. Arm him with a harpoon, aim him at Kelly Clarkson and you might well have a homicide on your hands. But show interest in his stacks of wax and you'll make a friend for life. "You'll get down here again, right?" he asks. Suddenly he looks like a little boy called away from the kickball game at sunset for dinner.

The phone rings. Bussard picks it up, listens a moment, then shouts into it from about three inches away, as if it's a soup can attached to a string. "We're still up here playin' stuff!" he booms.

He turns to me. "There's still records out there. You just gotta be in the right place. There's still a lot of really great records nobody's ever found." This statement is delivered not as an expression of possibility but as if the existence of a box of dusty 78s under a bed or in a closet anywhere in the land is an irritant to the Bussard immune system. It means that he has not yet prevailed, that there are miles to go before he sleeps. Forget your daughters, folks. Lock up your records. Joe Bussard's coming to town, and he's gunning for your songs.

His wife is gone. By most standards, he's alone. But his cat is doing well. And in his basement, folks long dead are singing—McMichen's Melody Men, Elder G. P. Harris, Ernest Stoneman, the Ozarkers, J. P. Nestor, Dewey and Gassie Bassett. And, of course, Clarence "Tom" Ashley and his "Rising Sun Blues."

Here, yesterday is not past and gone. It's loudly, vibrantly alive. Everything's Okeh. Joe Bussard's time machine—fueled by his records, his memories, and his unsentimental sentimentality—is still open for business. The past is ripe for the taking, three minutes at a time.

2 *Bubbling Up*

Yessir, the South is gonna change. Everything is gonna be put on electricity and run on a payin' basis. Out with the old spiritual mumbo-jumbo, the superstitions and the backward ways. We're gonna see a brave new world where they run everybody a wire and hook us all up to a grid. Yessir, a veritable Age of Reason.

—ULYSSES EVERETT MCGILL (GEORGE CLOONEY),
O BROTHER, WHERE ART THOU?

The map sings.

—ALAN LOMAX

DALLAS, TEXAS

"I was country-raised, cornfed and hand-spanked. We used hoot owls for chicken," Homer "Bill" Callahan says. He grins, and his eyes shine with the I'm-running-this-show intelligence of a veteran performer who knows his audience.

Callahan, eighty-eight years old on the afternoon I visit him in his bungalow on the edge of Dallas, is aware that, after so many years, people still love to watch him play the hillbilly and tell tall tales. No matter if the kind of performance that made him famous two generations ago plays to stereotypes that would make many of today's Appalachians bristle. It's his bread and butter.

Callahan was born in 1912 on a farm in Bear Branch, North Carolina, a hill community thirty miles north of Asheville. A photo taken when he was three captures the world he came from: Homer, his parents, an aunt, and six siblings standing in what appears to be thick

44

mountain woods. His father, a grocer, died a year later when he was four, and it made existence difficult for the large family. "I went to bed many a night hungry," he tells me.

Only when a family friend taught the Callahans to make corn whiskey did they earn enough money to stay together. Or so Homer Callahan says. Like most of his recollections—many of which involve taffy pulls, mules, and accounts of prodigious eating on his part—this one is accompanied by the grin, the wink, the brushing back of his white hair.

Like many other mountain families, the Callahans enlisted music to make those years bearable. And handmade music was everywhere in their neck of the Golden Triangle. By the time Homer was twelve, he and his brother, Walter, soaked it up whenever they could. Walter was a guitar guy; Homer started with the banjo and eventually added everything from mandolin to fiddle to ukulele. Opportunities to learn from older musicians were ample. Each year the family held a corn-shucking. They'd bury a five-gallon jug of corn whiskey in an enormous pile of corn, and the first neighbor to reach the bottom got the liquor. Then someone would pull out a fiddle and they'd move the furniture and dance into the night.

It was around 1928, "at one of those sing-ins one night," when a neighbor from across the mountain taught Homer the song that came to be known as "House of the Rising Sun." Callahan knew early on what it was about. "It's a gamblin' and prostitute house—I know that much," he says, "what you call a 'notch house.'" He loved the song immediately—the minor key, the intensity. "I've never heard anything that sounded like it," he says. "I wish I could remember the man that wrote the song down for me. I've tried for twenty-five or thirty years to find out. . . . He's dead and gone now. We can forget him."

For years, the Callahans studied early artists like Ernest Stoneman, the Skillet Lickers and, eventually, Jimmie Rodgers. When the brothers scored their first national recording contract, the song seemed a natural to record. My spider sense kicks in again, though, when Callahan tells of taking the train north in January 1934 to the recording session that produced "Rounder's Luck," the name that the American Record Corp. gave to his version of "Rising Sun." He's performing for the crowd of one—me. "We were thrilled to death—two little country boys barefoot and in overalls," he says. "We go out to eat breakfast, and people would follow us. We'd hardly have to buy a meal. They wanted to hear us talk."

Someone bought the brothers two pairs of dress pants, and Homer and Walter proceeded to Fifty-ninth and Broadway, to the ARC studios, and recorded thirty-two songs without stopping. They were paid $25 per song plus round-trip transportation.

Calling the song "Rounder's Luck" wasn't the Callahans' idea. Homer doesn't remember its original title; though he ended up calling it "House of the Rising Sun" himself, he's not sure if he picked that up after it became popular. As for "Rounder's Luck," says Callahan, "I have no idea why. I didn't like it too much. But they didn't ask me." Callahan figures the longer title wouldn't do commercially. In that context, he says, *house* was a loaded term that implied the word *whore* preceded it. This was, remember, the year that Hollywood began enforcing the Hays Code, making movies far tamer than they had been. The two other known versions recorded commercially in the 1930s—by Ashley and Acuff—reinforce this theory. They were called, respectively, "The Rising Sun Blues" and "Rising Sun" on their labels.

When the Callahan Brothers walked into that Manhattan recording studio, they were participating in a common ritual of the late 1920s and early 1930s: a moment when the traditional music of rural America was injected into the commerce stream of a rapidly expanding, twentieth-century mass culture. Though he may not have realized it (I think he did), Homer Callahan was a walking, talking connection between the hills and the highways—an evolutionary link with every verse sung in his nasal style, which both evoked old Appalachian balladry and exhibited clear influences of early blues.

Sung by Homer, with spare acoustic guitar accompaniment by Walter, "Rounder's Luck" sounds a step closer to our familiar "House of the Rising Sun" than Ashley's version of the year before. It is in a minor key, haunting rather than jaunty, and has an entirely different feel than the more conventional songs recorded at the same session. And though "Rounder's Luck" doesn't dart across the scale as dramatically as later versions of "Rising Sun," its music echoes real misery in a way that Ashley's version bypassed.

It starts in what today we would consider the middle of the song:

> *The only thing that a rounder wants*
> *is a suitcase and a trunk*
> *and the only time he's satisfied*
> *is when he's on a drunk.*

Like Ashley's, this is a song about a man ruined by his urges, not a woman forced into darkness. Later, Callahan asks the listener to "go tell my youngest *brother* not to do the things I've done," placing it squarely in the male column. Not until the fifth verse are the words "Rising Sun" mentioned. When they are, Callahan calls it "a place down in New Orleans" rather than a "house," lending more credence to the loaded-term theory. The lament aspect that made the song a cautionary tale may have made it more palatable, though; even Alan Lomax, who published the song with his father, John, after collecting it in 1937, was jittery about sexually edgy material. "If my father and I had included the so-called dirty songs in our 1930s anthologies of American folk songs, the books would have remained unpublished," he wrote. "It never occurred to us to endanger this goal by including erotic material."

Perhaps the most interesting part of the Callahans' version of "Rising Sun" is the third verse. It begins:

> *My mother, she's a seamstress*
> *she cuts and sews on jeans.*

Later renditions use something thematically similar—"My mother, she's a tailor; she sews my new blue jeans"—but the "seamstress" who "cuts and sews" is, as far as I can see, unique to "Rounder's Luck." It could conceivably be a floating lyric sucked up from the reservoir of rural blues stanzas: In his 1978 book *Blues from the Delta,* William Ferris chronicles an extended riff by two bluesmen that includes a similar line:

> *Well, my momma, she was a seamster,*
> *well, she learnt me how to sew.*

Who was this mother? Why a seamstress? Why jeans, which hardly occupied the cultural space that they do today? The mother-and-jeans reference has no analog in any other songs that I've found.

After their New York session, Homer and Walter Callahan became journeymen, performing for radio stations that would take them. They went to Kentucky, West Virginia, Missouri, and Oklahoma before landing in Dallas and, finally, Wichita Falls, Texas, where they became a fixture. Along the way, they changed their stage names to Bill and Joe Callahan, ramped up the vaudeville material in their hillbilly routine and moved, musically, toward the country-and-western and western swing styles that were becoming popular in the 1940s. They commercialized their heritage to make a living, and did it well. The songs they carried from the hills of Madison County, North Carolina, traveled with them.

How far did "Rounder's Luck" go? On paper, it's a cultural dead end. As eerie as the Callahan version is, none of the artists who would record the song in the 1940s, 1950s, and early 1960s—right up until the Animals' seminal take—riffed explicitly off Homer's and Walter's contribution. Tracing that is reasonably straightforward; lyrics are, in some ways, like fingerprints.

But the seamstress thing begs a bigger question: Did someone hear the Callahans, change "seamstress" to "tailor," add a verse and create, by hand, the version that would reach Georgia Turner in Kentucky three years later? Or did she hear it from the Callahans on a local radio broadcast? The brothers were, after all, based at Louisville radio station WHAS-AM in the mid-1930s and traveled throughout Kentucky in 1935 and 1936 as part of a music tour sponsored by a laxative company called Crazy Water Crystals.

Homer Callahan doesn't know if he helped spread it around. "I got standing ovations when I sang it, I know that," he says.

We talk for a while longer. He has so much to tell me. About how he did off-Broadway burlesque in New York. How he once worked in blackface in a minstrel show. About *Springtime in Texas,* the movie the brothers did in 1945. About how he teamed up with Mel Blanc years ago. He shows pictures: him with the cast of *Hee Haw!* His name on an old movie poster. Publicity photos from KWFT-AM in Wichita Falls, sponsored by Dr Pepper. "All of it came out of the mountains," Callahan says. "Every bit of it."

As he shows me to the door, he grabs my arm. It's a hearty grip for an eighty-eight-year-old. "I had fun all my life. I never was sad," he says. "I had a good life, son—and I'm still having a good life."

Homer Callahan died on September 12, 2002, at ninety. He lived to meet his great-grandchildren.

Deep in the mid-1930s, meanwhile, as the Depression deepened, our song was on the move along with tens of thousands of Appalachians. It had escaped the mountains, and people were passing it around in town. It was, though largely unnoticed, an exercise in early grassroots marketing. One man, a vigorous modernist who wore a traditionalist's coat, was about to carry "House of the Rising Sun" from the folkways to the highways. His name was Alan Lomax.

WASHINGTON, DC

John Philip Sousa, the most famous American bandleader and composer of the late nineteenth and early twentieth centuries, was deeply suspicious of the technologies that were starting to change the discipline he loved. In 1906, ten years after he wrote "Stars and Stripes Forever," Sousa took to the pages of *Appleton's* magazine for a bitter screed against the newfangled practice of recording music.

> I foresee a marked deterioration in American music and musical taste, an interruption in the musical development of the country, and a host of other injuries to music in its artistic manifestations, by virtue—or rather by vice—of the multiplication of the various music-reproducing machines. . . . Music teaches all that is beautiful in this world. Let us not hamper it with a machine that tells the story day by day, without variation, without soul, barren of the joy, the passion, the ardor that is the inheritance of man alone.

Sousa had a point when he said American music would be left with only professionals and recordings of professionals. "It will be simply a question of time when the amateur disappears entirely," he wrote. Today, far more of us consume music than produce it. A couple years ago, I took an informal poll of a dozen friends with small children; only one said he sang to his daughter. "Why would I sing? I got him a little CD player," said another. It reminded me of the illustration that accompanied Sousa's essay of a hundred years ago—an infant crying in a crib with an enormous Victrola towering over him.

Sousa's traditionalism was understandable. Yet he could not foresee what technology has made possible: capturing aural moments in time and freezing them as a photograph does with light. The recordings sit there, waiting for us to arrive, listen, and open doors to other ages.

I am seeking one of those doors as I walk into the Library of Congress's American Folklife Center one morning, my excitement barely hidden even in this home to so many Serious-Looking Texts.

The folklife center, formerly the Archive of American Folk Song, is one of the library's most storied departments. Here, preserved on everything from paper to acetate to reel-to-reel, from vinyl to cassette to compact disc, is the national songbook in all of its quilted tapestry. Most of these recordings aren't professional jobs produced by record companies; those are located, by the thousands, across the street in another building. At the folklife center, they are concerned with the rawer music that came directly from those amateurs for whom Sousa worried so passionately. The folklife center is located in the Thomas Jefferson Building. That pleases me.

All the strands of my search for "Rising Sun" have been pointing here, ever since I saw the name Georgia Turner atop a transcription of our song in *The Folk Songs of North America,* a compilation assembled by Alan Lomax in 1960. All roads meander back to Lomax: The first versions of the song to appear commercially in the 1940s were all by his friends, and his name is often mentioned in connection with the song's origins. Beyond that, I didn't know much. I knew Lomax was a collector who had traveled Appalachia and the Deep South in the 1930s, first with his father and then alone, collecting blues and prison worksongs and mountain ballads. Decades later, some of them would breathe life into the Coen brothers' 2000 film *O Brother, Where Art Thou?*—itself a film that straddles the cultural pivot point between the traditional and the modern in the American South.

The Folk Songs of North America has a full entry for what Lomax, upon its publication in 1960, was still calling "The Rising Sun Blues." He describes the song as "so far as I know, unique" and says he collected it in 1937 "from the singing of a thin, pretty, yellow-headed miner's daughter in Middlesborough [sic], Kentucky."

Pinpointing 1937 as the year of collection means that the Library of Congress will be pivotal in our search. That year, Alan Lomax, at twenty-two already a veteran songcatcher for the library, embarked on his first major solo excursion outside the shadow of his famous father.

In his trip proposal to his boss, Harold Spivacke, he advocated going into eastern Kentucky, to "the heart of the mountains that have protected for generations a rich heritage of Elizabethan song, manner, and speech, and at the same time have hidden the veins of coal that are leading to the disappearance of this tradition." And he identified the two types of people whose songs he sought, representatives of the ancient and the modern: "the mountaineer—the so-called mountain eagle—and the miner—a modern working man." Such a trip, he proposed, could produce three hundred recordings.

So in early September 1937, with an advance of $100 and his wife, Elizabeth, Lomax climbed into his Studebaker and headed south into hills that few outsiders visited. In his car was his 350-pound Presto "portable" reproducer, a needle-driven recorder that captured songs on heavy, fragile acetate disks.

The trip was bumpy, and not just because few of the roads were paved (this was nearly two decades before the Interstate Highway System). Even though Lomax had made arrangements in advance, some people wanted cash before they'd sing. In Hazard, a group of young men were making so much noise outside a hotel where Lomax was interviewing singers that he couldn't get a clean recording; he offered to fight them, one by one, in the lobby, and they backed down. "Perhaps," he quipped, "they did not know what weapons agents of the Library of Congress carried." One sixty-year-old man even attempted to stab Lomax, convinced the song collector was hitting on his wife: "I understood later that I should have received lead in my vitals from a gun if the irate husband had had his .44 in his pocket."

Technical challenges abounded. Some towns—indeed, some entire counties—lacked electricity. Bulky battery cells died and had to be replaced by mail. The Presto's parts failed. Lomax kept running out of blank discs. He caught the flu. Then there was the matter of cash. On September 28, Lomax cabled Spivacke: MACHINE RUNNING WORK BOOMING BUT POCKETBOOK EMPTY SPEED VOUCHERS OR WIRE MONEY.

Still, the material he collected from farmers and housewives, from preachers and laborers, was plentiful—even if the quality was spotty. The trip's first burst of recordings received a mixed review from Lomax.

He went back to Washington from Harlan, Kentucky, describing his songs—"some of them quite marvelous, some of them mediocre, but all necessary."

In the second week of September, the Lomaxes arrived in Middlesboro. Ringed by mountains, it was a rough-and-tumble coal town that sits in a basin smack in the heart of our Golden Triangle—just over the Cumberland Gap, where Kentucky, Virginia, and Tennessee meet and where thousands came west in the eighteenth and nineteenth centuries. English iron ore speculators had laid out Middlesboro in the mid-1800s. But for generations before that, mountaineers of English, Scots, and Irish stock built lives in the hills and, in their isolation, preserved a rich tradition of music and balladry.

By 1937, eight years into the Depression, coal and the railroad had made Middlesboro into a bustling little city with all the modern connections to the outside world and all the vices, too. By the time Lomax visited, some had dubbed Middlesboro "Little Las Vegas." Money and a population explosion from the mines had produced the familiar accoutrements of boomtown life: Gambling flourished, liquor flowed, and whores were openly available. "It was wide open," Tom Shattuck, the director of tourism for Bell County, where Middlesboro is located, told me. "Anything went."

Blend this with a town full of increasingly poverty-stricken miners and a transient population fueled by the trains rushing in and out of Middlesboro each day, and you have a recipe for rowdiness—exactly the kind of environment for which "Rising Sun," as a warning song, came into being in the first place.

Just west of downtown Middlesboro sits a poor neighborhood called Noetown. Part of it, along Cumberland Avenue coming out of downtown, consists of a series of houses on a lush hillside along one of the two sets of railroad tracks that carried goods and people into and out of Middlesboro. Today, the homes are well kept and clean. But in 1937, this area was barely a step above a shantytown, home to miners, day laborers, and their families. Some lived three, four, five to a room in shacks that offered little more in the way of amenities than the mountain cabins many had given up to come into town for work.

In one house, a log cabin heated only by an old kitchen stove, lived the Turner family, whose people had been in Bell County for generations. Gillis Turner, who worked for the coal companies, lived with his wife, Mary Mast Turner, who was known as Mary Gill, and their children—including Georgia, who was sixteen on the day Lomax came into town. She was shy and attractive; Lomax remembered her as having blond hair. Both mother and daughter were known around the neighborhood for their singing—Mary Gill for her religious songs, her offspring for more modern offerings. Their neighbors considered them good people—honest, hardworking, reliable.

Folks in Noetown rarely traveled. They had neither the means nor the reason. Sometimes, they'd watch the train rumble by and wonder about the people and things aboard—where they were going, what kinds of places sat down the line. That's why it's unclear where Georgia first heard the song that was known as her favorite. The neighborhood had no electricity; besides, the likelihood of such a poor family having a radio or a phonograph was slim. And yet here was this song. Neighbors would hear her singing it while she hung the wash outside the cabin, while she walked around the neighborhood, and at the times when people would get together to make music. Ed Hunter, an adolescent musician who lived a few houses away, said decades later that Georgia was the first person he'd ever heard singing about the girl who lost her honor beneath the Rising Sun. That suggests she didn't pick it up from someone in the neighborhood.

Hunter's uncle, a man named Tillman Cadle, had moved to Middlesboro from Tennessee as a young boy. He, too, had a home in the Turners' neighborhood, but he had a connection to the larger world, too: Through his friend, the singer Jim Garland, he met a woman named Mary Elizabeth Barnicle, who taught at New York University. Cadle and Barnicle married in 1936, though she remained in New York City at first while he stayed in Middlesboro. They were united by a love of folk music, and Cadle, a sometime coal miner, was also a fervent union activist and organizer; during the Depression and immediately after, the labor movement and folk music often walked hand in hand.

Lomax had been disappointed with the ballad fodder he found in many eastern Kentucky coal camps. He was scornful of outside influences. "Traditional material," he lamented, "has been ousted by the influx of records and radios, the ballad singer and the fiddler have been driven out by . . . the 'hill billy' singer who copies the broadcaster slavishly." He was hoping for something better in Middlesboro, and had, through Barnicle, contacted Cadle and asked him for help finding singers willing to contribute their songs. Afterward, Lomax would say that his visit to Middlesboro produced the best mining camp material he found on the entire trip.

On September 15, 1937, a group of people gathered at Cadle's house to greet Lomax, his wife, his Studebaker, and his Presto reproducer. Hunter was there, a teenager but already accomplished on the harmonica. Both Georgia Turner and her mother showed up. Her mother sang a few songs into Lomax's machine. After a while, Georgia's turn came and Lomax pointed the microphone toward her. He always loved this part. "Every time I took one of those big, black, glass-based platters out of its box, I felt that a magical moment was opening up in time," he wrote.

What did Lomax ask Georgia Turner to sing that day? Her favorite song? The saddest? Or did he leave it up to her? Lomax, who died in 2002, never said, and neither his published materials nor his files gave any hint. We know he was looking for unusual ballads, and this certainly was one. We can assume he had heard neither Ashley's version nor the Callahan Brothers', because he described the song, as he collected it, as unique. But he was about to record one of the most significant pieces of his career.

Sometimes pivot points in culture happen quietly and pass unnoticed at first. I have no reason to believe that this moment was any different. The ripples that this particular recording of this particular song would make were still in the future. It was nothing but an unknown song about a girl with a hard life behind her, sung from the heart by an unknown girl with a hard life ahead of her.

First, with Hunter playing the harmonica, Georgia Turner sang, in a high-pitched and chirpy voice, an old standard called "Married Life Blues." Then she brought her voice down to a throaty drawl, took a breath and began to sing her favorite song into the recorder.

Jennifer Cutting, a folklife specialist at the Library of Congress, has agreed to take me back into the humidity-controlled stacks where the recordings are held. The tapes we seek are stored down a dim corridor, behind a creaky wire door. As I marvel at the Egyptian-tomb feel of it all, Cutting informs me that the reel-to-reel tapes we're retrieving, while old, aren't the originals. Those are the acetate disks cut by Lomax in the field, and nobody plays them anymore; they're too fragile. From the top shelf, she pulls a white box of reel tape. We return to the reading room and she cues it onto a deck. I don padded headphones, flip a switch, and fast-forward to track 1404A1.

The voice of sixteen-year-old Georgia Turner fills my ears, unaccompanied and scratchy, sad and strong, and singing in a blues scale. For ninety-eight seconds, I travel through time back to 1937.

> *There is a house in New Orleans*
> *they call the Risin' Sun.*
> *It's been the ruin of many poor girl*
> *and me, oh God, for one.*
>
> *Go tell my baby sister*
> *never do as I have done*
> *to shun that house in New Orleans*
> *they call the Risin' Sun.*
>
> *My mother she's a tailor*
> *she sew those new blue jeans.*
> *My sweetheart he's a drunkard, Lord, Lord,*
> *drinks down in New Orleans.*
>
> *The only thing that a drunkard needs*
> *is a suitcase or a trunk.*
> *The only time he's satisfied*
> *is when he's on a drunk.*
>
> *One foot is on the platform*
> *and the other one on a train.*
> *I'm going back to New Orleans*
> *to wear that ball and chain.*

I sit silently for a moment, letting the song wash over me, trying to feel what it was like to be there, in that little house on a hillside by the railroad, so many years ago. To sing that song as though a life with a sad end was your inevitable destiny. I search for the feeling inside of me and cannot find it, though I want to very much. I feel for Georgia Turner, but the very facts of who I am and when I was born prevent me from feeling *with* her. I wonder if Lomax played it back for her after she was done singing, as he did with many musicians years later, and what it felt like for her to hear her own voice singing out of a mechanical contraption.

Jennifer Cutting is more interested in the style of the song as Georgia performed it. "She's singing in a blues scale. She's scooping. She's sliding," Cutting says to me. "That's a blues technique." The song sounds different from modern renditions, and Cutting tells me why: "The difference between her and the version everyone knows"—she hums the Animals' tune—"is she's not singing in a minor key. So who took it from the major to the minor? What I want to know is how it got to that minor."

I have just listened to The Moment—the nexus where generations of folk expression and oral tradition flowed in and the seeds of modern recorded, produced, marketed music flowed out. From the little cabin on September 15, 1937, we can chart a direct course into and out of the folk revival, to Bob Dylan and the definitive version recorded by the Animals—and everything beyond, across America and across oceans.

After the stop in Middlesboro, only two weeks into his journey, Lomax pointed his Studebaker north, deeper into the hills of eastern Kentucky. He recorded several dozen more songs in the next twenty-five days before, on October 9, he came across a man named Bert Martin in Horse Creek, a settlement near Manchester. It was fifty miles north of Middlesboro on today's roads, which meant probably twice that across mountain roads in 1937. Almost nothing is known about Martin today; Lomax kept no biographical material on him and occasionally misspelled his name as Bert Morton, and I was unable to track down anyone who knew him. But he, too, sang a version of "Rising Sun" into Lomax's Presto—albeit a less textured one. It showed that Georgia Turner's knowledge was not unique in this area and that the song was indeed kicking around. Manchester, in fact, is right between Middlesboro and another eastern Kentucky town called Daisy, where the song would bubble up on its own two decades later. Martin's version gave Lomax a couple additional verses—stanzas that had been in either the Ashley or Callahan versions but somehow didn't make it to Georgia Turner. Lomax would use these verses to fill out her version when he committed it to paper.

Here is Martin, as I heard the recording in the Library of Congress, accompanied by a banjo that he presumably played himself:

> *There's a house in New Orleans*
> *they call that Risin' Sun.*
> *Been the ruin of many poor boy,*
> *me, Oh Lord, for one.*
>
> *If ah'd a-listened to what Mama said,*
> *I'd a been at home today.*
> *Bein' so young and foolish, poor boy,*
> *let a rambler lead me astray.*
>
> *All that a rounder wants*
> *is a suitcase or a trunk.*
> *The only time he's satisfied*
> *[unintelligible] hobo [unintelligible]*
>
> *Fills his glasses to the brim*
> *passes 'em all around.*
> *Only pleasure he gets out of life*
> *is hoboin' from town to town.*
>
> *I'm goin' back to New Orleans.*
> *My race is almost run.*
> *I'm goin' to spend the rest of my life*
> *beneath that Risin' Sun.*
>
> *Go and tell my younger brother*
> *never do as I have done.*
> *Shun that house in New Orleans*
> *they call the Risin' Sun.*

Notice how Martin's version subtly summons details to match his own gender. It speaks of the "ruin of many poor *boy*," changing the song's purpose from the lament of an exploited girl to the regrets of an overindulgent rambler. Note, too, the mentions of filling the glasses to the brim, hoboing from town to town and his race being almost run. The first two would not have fit into a bad girl's lament; few people would be singing about girls filling glasses to the brim, and females weren't seen as hoboes or ramblers. In many ways, Martin's rendition is very similar to Ashley's recorded version of 1933, though Martin's adds the "go and tell my younger brother" warning verse that the Callahans used and introduces a new stanza entirely: the one about listenin' to what Mama said, a common lyric of regret that moves from song to song in the rural Appalachian folk tradition (as well as, occasionally, Delta blues).

But Martin's version lacked something that Georgia Turner's possessed: the verse about the tailor sewing blue jeans, and the one about one foot on the platform and the other on the train—itself a common lyric that migrated among rural folk songs in the early twentieth century. Both lyrics would end up in the Animals' famous version in 1964.

Lomax clearly thought less of Martin's contribution to the "Rising Sun" canon. In later years, he would credit Georgia Turner for the song and would try to track her down in an effort to send her royalties. On the occasions when Martin was credited, it was only for "other stanzas." Certainly Georgia's version—complete with tailor, blue jeans, a train platform, and a ball and chain—became the foundation for the most famous modern versions. But the Martin recording offers us several interesting nuggets in addition to the "other stanzas." It says that the song was on the radar of ballad singers in different regions of eastern Kentucky. It says that different versions were coexisting at the same moment in time. Most important, it shows the malleability of the narrative of "Rising Sun"—proving that, by balancing visual details with an equally compelling universal theme about the wages of sin, a song can resonate in different ways for a female singer and her male counterpart.

Before he ended his trip, Lomax would find one more singer who offered him "Rising Sun." Four days after recording Martin and a few miles away, in a remote part of Clay County called Billy's Branch that today is part of the Daniel Boone National Forest, Lomax found a man named Daw Henson. Details on Henson are scarce, though the liner

notes of a recent CD compilation called *Kentucky Mountain Music,*
which includes some of the Henson songs gathered on the 1937 trip,
say Lomax appreciated Henson's "mountain blues" style. What we do
know about Henson is that, at least in song, he casts himself as one of
the men with rough and rowdy ways to whom singing "Rising Sun"
might have come naturally. In one of the Lomax recordings, "Swafford
Branch Stills," Henson identifies himself by name as the protagonist:

> *My name is little Daw Henson*
> *A rounder boy, you know,*
> *I come from the state of Tennessee*
> *Not many days ago*

I don't take too much from the Tennessee reference; in another song
from the same session, Henson says he got to "Wallins Creek not many
days ago." Odds are, he was from right where Lomax found him. But
clearly he'd had exposure to bad-man ballads. Several of the songs Henson sang for Lomax include references to renegade moonshining, jail,
bail, men who "go from town to town," and women who were game for
hitchhiking and car rides and "belonged to the cigarette crew." When
Henson turned to "Rising Sun Blues," the harmonica he had used on
the previous song, "The Train," was pressed into service briefly, followed by an a capella rendition of four verses. The way he sang it, it felt
fragmentary—far less complete than other songs from the session. But
it was obviously our song, and he sang it from a female point of view—
particularly interesting since, as far as I can tell, there hadn't yet been a
professional recording from that vantage point.

> *There is a house in New Orleans*
> *they call the Rising Sun.*
> *It's ruined the life of many a poor girl.*
> *And it's me, oh Lord, for one.*
>
> *Go and tell my baby sister*
> *not to do as I have done.*
> *To shun that house in New Orleans*
> *that they call it the Risin' Sun.*

I got one foot on the platform
and the other 'un on the train.
I'm going back to the New Orlean
for to wear that ball and chain.

Ain't but two things a bachelor needs—
his suitcase and his trunk.
The only time I'm satisfied
it's when I'm on a drunk.

By this point in Lomax's trip, Henson's offering duplicated the Middlesboro teenager's entirely, so it would go ignored by Lomax when he put the song on paper. Thus did Daw Henson largely disappear from the history of "House of the Rising Sun."

Culture's spread is so unpredictable. You sing a song, then move on. But sometimes things echo. Sometimes momentum builds in odd ways. That is what happened in 1937 in the hills of eastern Kentucky: Three people sang the same song as it bubbled up from the folk tradition. One was forgotten, one became marginal. And then there was Georgia Turner. Only the quirks of scheduling that led Lomax to Middlesboro early in his trip permitted sixteen-year-old Georgia, amplified by Alan Lomax's recorder and reach, to be the inadvertent vector for a song that would soar out of the mountains and across the world.

MIDDLESBORO, KENTUCKY

Middlesboro today is far more sedate than it was in 1937. Part of this may be because Bell County is now dry, which I learn when I try to buy a six-pack in a convenience store. The area remains as beautiful as when the first settlers came through the Cumberland Gap two centuries ago; all is lush and green in the springtime, and the sun makes the landscape glow. No surprise that today, tourism brings in as many people as coal ever did.

Over in Noetown, a mile or so off U.S. 25 East and near the railroad tracks, I tracked down Ed Hunter, the harmonica player who performed at Lomax's 1937 session with Georgia Turner. Seven decades later, he still keeps a home just yards away from where her old shack was. He greets me in an undershirt and jeans—wary at first, then within five minutes completely enthusiastic. Hunter is seventy-eight, retired, snowy-haired but robust, and spends most of his days caring for his sick wife. He has kept up with the mouth harp and the fiddle, his two favorite instruments. "Music—I've been a slave to it," he says. He takes a sip from a can of Milwaukee's Best encased in a foam-rubber cooler with the slogan, "Jesus Is Coming—Everyone Look Busy."

When Hunter wants to show off his music, he doesn't produce an instrument; first he pulls out a cassette player, and plays a tape of him and two friends performing in 1982. This is exactly what Sousa feared, it occurs to me: Instead of playing for visitors, you play a tape for visitors. Fortunately, in short order, Hunter produces a Hohner harmonica and gives us a sample of his talents, playing "Green Valley Waltz" without a hiccup. "I've had youngsters say to me, 'That music's boring,' " he says. "It's good to know somebody's still interested."

Hunter has a personal stake in the neighborhood where he and Georgia Turner (he calls her "Georgie") grew up. After decades of assorted jobs in mines, tanneries, and factories, he spent the final fifteen years of his working life as a contractor, and he built the neighborhood into the pleasant, inviting hillside community it has become. He points to the houses around his—fourteen, all erected by him—with pride. Then he identifies a spot two hundred yards away where a house used to be. That was the Turner shack, he says, and singing was always coming from there. "Maybe they was tryin' to make themselves as happy as they could—singing away their blues."

When Lomax visited their neighborhood, Hunter says, it came as a surprise. It's not as if Lomax could have called ahead. "We didn't have any phones. He just busted in. I thought it was something different, and I loved it."

I ask Hunter if I can use his tape player, and I pop in a copy of the Library of Congress recording of his long-ago neighbor. He looks into the distance and nods in recognition. "Georgie, she's the first one I ever heard sing it," he says. "That was her theme song. I don't know how in the world she learned it. We thought this was the only world there was. . . . There weren't many visitors, and she didn't go nowhere."

Where did she get it, then? Clarence Ashley's daughter, Eva Moore, remembers that her father's medicine show circuit included eastern

Kentucky, mostly mining camps. Surely Ashley's performance could have been absorbed by someone in Middlesboro, then somehow made its way to Georgia Turner. Maybe she even once went to a medicine show herself, one that came to Noetown to separate the poor from their money with promises of health and vigor. Or did Georgia hear it on the train tracks near her house, from one of the ramblers or itinerant miners who rode the rails looking for work?

I hate it that I'll never know, but I have to admit: Considering all the possibilities may be just as exciting as actually figuring it out.

What Alan Lomax was doing, in Kentucky and across the South as he followed his father's footsteps, was, in a way, inherently contradictory. Like John Philip Sousa before him, Lomax fretted that the demons of technology—radio and, especially, recorded sound—would wipe away the folk-singing tradition. Who needs to sing when you can play a record, a record that may not have been local at all and may not have reflected people's lives? Thus would local traditions atrophy, the thinking went.

And yet as much as his father had a foot in both centuries, Alan Lomax was squarely a twentieth-century man. Whereas Sousa shunned the contraption he feared, Alan Lomax, like John Lomax before him, used it with no apparent sense of irony to accomplish his goals. The Lomaxes carried their bulky recording devices into places beyond the rural electricity grid, places where the folk tradition still thrived. Part of this may have been because technology was not yet widespread. But part of it was certainly that many carriers of oral tradition were the poor and the forgotten who couldn't afford a Victrola or a radio. So their ways of creating music, even in an age of invention, remained unplugged.

Even as Lomax lamented the effects of technology and popular culture upon the old ballads, he romanticized the same contraptions. "The collector with pen and notebook can capture only the outline of one song," he wrote. "The needle writes on the disc with tireless accuracy the subtle inflections, the melodies, the pauses that comprise the emotional meaning of speech, spoken and sung. In this way folklore can truly be recorded."

And it was. Because the machine, not the pen, was used, today we can, as Lomax put it, "confine the living song" and possess a sliver of yesterday. Thus it comes to pass that Georgia Turner, wherever she found "The Rising Sun Blues," sings it from the cassette deck of my rented Chevy Cavalier as I drive north on I-66 in Virginia, headed back to New York from Middlesboro in a manner far faster and far more removed from the landscape around me than Alan Lomax did in his beat-up Studebaker all those decades ago. I have a few CDs in my car that contain hundreds of songs; he carried pounds and pounds of heavy discs, each containing pieces of the lives he had walked into, sampled, then left behind.

Alan Lomax was a romantic figure, an Emersonian force in the modern world. Some thought him arrogant; some criticized his methods and accused him of piggybacking on the talents of others. I see it differently. Lomax was a conduit between two Americas—an interpreter who knew how to visit The Village, find the things worth saving, and return with them so they could make their way in a modern world. The subtleties of his methods can be debated. To chase down history as he did, to walk in and out of distant communities while realizing that your life is far more prosperous than the people you are studying, requires more than a bit of arrogance.

But modern American music owes a debt of gratitude to the Lomaxes. To most, their names are unknown. But for every "Rising Sun Blues," there is an equivalent: "Home on the Range," "Good Night, Irene," "The Midnight Special," "Bonaparte's Retreat." All were slivers of the folk tradition that were collected, retooled, popularized, and canonized in the popular culture by the Lomaxes. Without them, we would be a very different musical nation today.

And what of Georgia Turner? What happened to her family? All Ed Hunter knows is that they went north, following the trail of jobs and American industrialization toward Michigan.

"They left," he told me, "and I never did see her no more."

3 *From the Folkways . . .*

When I'm singing in this microphone
my voice comes out over there.

—KATE CAMPBELL, "STRANGENESS OF THE DAY"

Listen to the songs of the fathers and mothers
and the many friends gone on before
. . . get in touch with God, turn your radio on.

—TRADITIONAL SONG

Alan and Elizabeth Lomax returned from their 1937 Kentucky expedition with 228 recordings on 12-inch acetate discs. Lomax gave his own effort mixed reviews but was clearly excited. "I have learned things and seen people whom I should never have known existed otherwise," he wrote.

After some months, he set to organizing his finds. He enlisted Ruth Crawford Seeger, matriarch of a famous musical family, to help him do musical arrangements and prepare dozens of the newly collected songs for a book to be called *Our Singing Country*. While the father-son team's 1934 book *American Ballads and Folk Songs*—spearheaded by John A. Lomax, a member of a less media-saturated generation who came of age in the nineteenth century—focused largely on the stuff of yesterdays, *Our Singing Country*, with Alan's coming of age and subsequent influence on the family obsession, seemed more geared toward folk songs that reflected modern life. "These are the people who are making new songs today," the two said in a preface that, given its tilt toward modernism, seems written by Alan. "These are the people who go courting with their guitars, who make the music for their own dances, who make their own songs for their own religion. These are the storytellers, because they are the people who are watching when things happen." The Lomaxes also acknowledged the dynamism of twentieth-century genre blending even as, like before, they robustly glorified the old ways. "New songs grew up inconspicuously out of the humus of the old," they said, "thrusting out in new directions in small, but permanent, fashion."

That was certainly the case in 1938, the year after Lomax's Kentucky trip. While the arrangements for *Our Singing Country* were being cataloged and assembled, our song thrust out in another new direction— toward Nashville, where the traditional and the modern were being united in the exploding new country music industry there. At the vanguard of this was the man who would come to be known as the king of country music.

Roy Acuff (1903–1992) was from Maynardsville, a town in eastern Tennessee that sits on the edge of the Great Smoky Mountains. According to his biographer, Elizabeth Schlappi, the Acuff household during his childhood was a gathering place for old-time musicians. A skinny boy who grew into a skinny man, Acuff was a hell-raiser in his early twenties; he became a professional musician only after several instances of serious sunstroke proved that his body couldn't take being a baseball player. So he kept singing and learned to fiddle.

For much of 1932, Acuff traveled around eastern Tennessee and Virginia, earning a couple dollars a day playing with a medicine show operated by a neighbor, Doc Hauer, who liked Acuff's fiddling. He asked Acuff to join his multistate effort to use music to sell Mocoton Tonic, which purportedly was "the cure for everything." Hauer's medicine show players formed a small band. "You sang to several thousand people in the open," Acuff told Schlappi, "and you couldn't get to them if you didn't put your lungs to the fullest test." The show included none other than Clarence "Tom" Ashley, whose grandparents had taught him "Rising Sun."

The medicine show persuaded Acuff that music was his destiny, and he set to making it happen with a group called the Crazy Tennesseans, whose name he later changed to the Smoky Mountain Boys. Six years after his medicine show travels, Acuff went to South Carolina to record some songs for Vocalion (Ashley's label, recently acquired by Columbia) on portable equipment. Among the titles he cut was one he called simply "The Rising Sun," recorded on November 3, 1938. The session was convened ten months after he began appearing regularly on the Grand Ole Opry on WSM-AM Nashville, which in turn was five months after Lomax recorded Georgia Turner in Middlesboro. That makes it likely that even if Georgia did have access to a radio—which Ed Hunter insists was not the case—she could not have heard Acuff singing it over the airwaves.

Acuff's version opens with a dobro guitar that sounds positively Hawaiian and strangely placid. The verses, though in a different order, will by now sound familiar. He sang it in a major key with a melody similar to those sung by Georgia Turner and Bert Martin but with a soft, lilting voice that suggested none of the desolation or misery of its lyrics.

There is a house in New Orleans
they call the Rising Sun
It's been the ruin of many poor boy
and me, oh Lord, for one.

Go tell my youngest brother
not to do as I have done
to shun that house in New Orleans
they call the Rising Sun.

Go fill the glasses to the brim
and let the drinks go merrily round
we'll drink to the health of a rounder, poor boy,
hoboes from town to town.

The only thing a rounder needs
is a suitcase and a trunk
for the only time he's satisfied
is when he's on a drunk.

So shun that house in New Orleans
they call the Rising Sun

It's been the ruin of many poor boy
and me, oh Lord, for one.

Acuff didn't say where he learned the song, and it never became a famous part of his extensive repertoire, which helped define the course of country music from the 1940s to the 1970s and was built upon such songs as "Wabash Cannonball," "The Great Speckled Bird," and "Wreck on the Highway." It seems likely that if Acuff didn't actually learn "Rising Sun" from Ashley, at least they played it together at the medicine show in 1932. The Callahan Brothers were also playing in the general area during that time, and the writer of the liner notes for a Time-Life Records Acuff compilation in 1983, John R. Rumble, said Acuff "may have learned this number from such neighboring Smoky Mountain artists as versatile entertainer Clarence Tom Ashley or the Callahan Brothers."

Acuff would record "The Rising Sun" once more, in 1962, after he had been a country music superstar for two decades. The melody is the same, but his voice sounds far more confident, and the effects of the emergent Nashville Sound are clear in the production values. By that time, the more haunting, minor-key version of the folk revival had become the dominant text, and as far as I know no version after 1962 riffed off Acuff's takes even though the song was included on an LP of his greatest hits. It was Lomax's version, through his friends and emissaries in New York, that was about to take wing.

The Lomaxes sent *Our Singing Country* to their publisher in March 1941. It is an exciting, somewhat melancholy musical snapshot of a nation on the eve of changing forever. The forces of mass culture had been gathering since before the first World War, and World War II and its aftermath would entrench those pathways—phonograph records, radio, and eventually television—in the American psyche. In the process, many of the old ways would be lost or subsumed or changed forever; as Marshall McLuhan put it years later, the medium was becoming the message.

Many have criticized the decision by the Lomaxes (and others) to stitch together verses from various informants to create patchwork versions of songs that may never have actually existed in the folk tradition.

It's a valid point: Educated cultural anthropologists working their "magic" on the people's music undoubtedly obscured the raw message that came from the mouths of those who actually lived raw lives (Lomax, Guthrie, and Pete Seeger later collaborated on a book called *Hard Hitting Songs for Hard-Hit People*). Father and son justified this decision as something that would benefit the general audience: "We have in certain cases created composite versions of the texts of ballads or songs . . . so that the non-ballad student among readers may quickly survey all the choicest lines that any group of song variants contains." This was not a new practice for the family. John Lomax had been doing it since 1910, when he published with an eye toward popularity as much as anthropological accuracy. Roots-music historian Benjamin Filene described the Lomaxes' joint 1933 excursion through the South this way: "Their collecting methods and attitude make the trip, from today's perspective, seem part talent search, part sociological survey, and part safari."

Thus, the version of "Darling Corey" or "John Henry" or "Look Down That Lonesome Road" that wound its way into the folk revival may have less to do with individual renditions sung in field recordings than we think. It may, on the surface, seem richer and more textured. But it is inevitably a product of the instinct to popularize, for to enable the "non-ballad student" to "quickly survey all the choicest lines" is the printed-word equivalent of producing a commercial record—removing rough edges to ensure mass appeal. "A lot of people miss this," Matt Barton, the archivist at the Lomax Archives, told me. "Above and beyond going out and collecting things for the sake of preservation, Alan and his father were very interested in popularizing these things— getting them into the mainstream, getting them recognition and trying to bring things to life."

With "House of the Rising Sun," the Lomaxes' decision to construct a composite version also created an indelible cultural footprint that, with one publishing decision, made the song they called "The Rising Sun Blues" much easier to trace into the folk revival and through the half century beyond it.

Lomax took Georgia Turner's distinctive field recording and used it as the cornerstone of his *Our Singing Country* version. Her verses were all included, including the one about the mother and the tailor—though Lomax heard Turner singing about how her mother "*sold* those new blue jeans," when in fact what she sang, if you listen closely, was "*sew* those new blue jeans." Also present was the "one foot is on the platform, and the other one on a train" verse that is, for "Rising Sun," unique to hers and Daw Henson's renditions.

But Lomax also included a couple pivotal verses from the Bert Martin recording. He referred to them as "other stanzas," but it's worth noting that they were verses that had already been recorded commercially in the Ashley and Callahan Brothers versions of 1934 and 1936.

Verse two became:

> *If I had listened what Mamma said,*
> *I'd 'a' been at home today.*
> *Being so young and foolish, poor boy,*
> *let a rambler lead me astray.*

This was inserted as verse six:

> *Fills his glasses to the brim,*
> *passes them around*
> *only pleasure he gets out of life*
> *is hoboin' from town to town.*

And this became the final verse of the text:

> *Going back to New Orleans,*
> *my race is almost run.*
> *Going back to spend the rest of my days*
> *beneath that Rising Sun.*

The Daw Henson field recording was not credited; it was the final one of the three that Alan Lomax collected, and it offered nothing new.

The inclusion and positioning of those Martin verses created a more coherent, Lomaxified narrative of the Rising Sun ballad. The details now unfold in a cinematic way: The singer introduces the song and her ruin, says she'd have been okay if she had listened to her mother; talks about what the drunkard sweetheart needs for his ramblings and then has him filling his glasses, passing them around and going from town to town; describes herself boarding the train to return to her personal hell; and then sums up with her race almost run. The song is at once more detail-rich and more universal. If you endorse the methodology, it's a magnificent piece of patchwork quilting; if you don't, it's cultural corruption. I see it as a bit of both.

Lomax included "The Rising Sun Blues" on page 368 of *Our Singing Country*. In an introductory paragraph, without citing sources, he wrote a bit about what he believed to be its history:

> The fact that a few of the hot jazzmen who were in the business before the war [World War I] have a distant singing acquaintance with this song, indicates that it is fairly old as blues tunes go. None of them, however, has information at his fingertips about the mother who ran a "blue-jean" shop, about the "house they call the Rising Sun" or about the young lady it proved the ruin of. We have heard it sung only by Southern whites. "Rising Sun," as a name for a bawdy house, occurs in a number of unprintable songs of English origin.

Lomax's assessment here is cryptic and more than a bit frustrating. He doesn't say where the "hot jazzmen" were or whether they *knew* it before World War I, only that they were "in the business" at that time. What's more, if those singers familiar with it didn't know about the "house they call the Rising Sun," what exactly, then, were they singing? The verse about the Rising Sun is the salient element that makes "House of the Rising Sun" the song that it is; without it, you have little more than a collection of migratory verses. And what of the unprintable English songs? What was he referring to? Other than the Harry Cox recording of years later that mentioned Lowestoft, I've found no evidence of "Rising Sun" as a name for an English whorehouse. Pubs, yes—Rising Sun pubs are all over the place in the United Kingdom. But not bordellos.

Without being able to ask Lomax, who died in 2002 and was incapacitated by several strokes by the time I began poking around, I was left to speculate. I think this is what must have happened: Lomax asked around about the song and found a few people who knew about it vaguely, including one who mentioned a British connection, and the rest was extrapolation. Lomax's vague wording—and an examination of his other writings, in which vague wording often means he was discussing things he didn't know much about—suggests that he had a nugget of information and was looking for some context. Still, I'd love to know just what he meant by "hot jazzmen," especially given that this song reveals, as we've seen, virtually no connection to the black blues or jazz tradition in its ancestry. It would build its own links to that genre later on.

Whatever its merits, the *Our Singing Country* version of "Rising Sun Blues" became the basic text for folk musicians of the time. Over the decades, it would become easy to figure out whose versions came from Lomax by looking at what verses they included. If someone sang, "My mother was a tailor," it went back to Lomax. If the second verse was "If I had listened what Mamma said," as Lomax inserted it, same story. As the folk revival began to spread, that arrangement of verses provided a fingerprint to track who was using the Lomax version and who was inspired by others—namely by Ashley (a few people), by Acuff (one person) or by the Callahan Brothers (none that I've ever found).

It's difficult to overestimate the influence of *Our Singing Country*. What Harry Smith's *Anthology of American Folk Music* would do for recordings more than a decade later, *Our Singing Country* did in terms of sheet music. It brought songs to the voices who could amplify them.

Lomax had gone to Kentucky, caught a musical virus and become the vector. With *Our Singing Country* and his omnipresence in the liberal, folk-singing community of New York City in the 1940s, he was deliberately spreading it to others—his friends and protégés, the people whose work he both collected and contributed to. "He purposely tried his best to infect us," Pete Seeger told me. These were musicians who came from their own traditions and had their own repertoires but were looking to diversify (and stay relevant and fresh; this was, after all, their way of making a living) by taking Lomax's work in the hills and incorporating it into their own worldviews.

These men would become national legends and end up on postage stamps. But in the early 1940s they were part of a tight-knit, multiracial, sometimes activist musical community that met in Manhattan apartments and small clubs to drink, eat, and talk music and politics. They also became the arbiters of authenticity for the New York folk music scene, which saw itself as sophisticated and curatorial. Woody Guthrie was there, and a young, earnest Pete Seeger too. The black bluesman-turned-folksinger Josh White and his guitar were ever present, and it's hard to imagine the scene without the imposing presence of the singer and guitarist Lead Belly, whose path to this moment had led in and out of Louisiana's harshest prisons. They all swapped lyrics, shared songs, and piggybacked each other's musical styles, honing their own and cross-pollinating in a musical environment that has never been duplicated. Robert Cantwell, in his seminal folk revival history *When We Were Good*, said many of these once-rural musicians effectively "reinvented themselves by their passage into New York, converting their difference into an ideological, cultural, social, psychological and commercial resource."

If "Rising Sun" was the gospel, these were the disciples who received the Word and would carry it throughout the land.

Few Americans occupy the place in the national mythology that Woody Guthrie does. In life, he was a rambler in both the better and worse senses of the word. He was committed to noble causes and spreading the voice of the people, but he was also a larger-than-life shunner of responsibility, a man who—in the time-tested American tradition—hit the road when the going got tough. In plainspokenness he found grandeur; in puffery he found targets; in music he found a place where he could be his most exuberant, most delightfully nonsensical, most angry, and occasionally most irritating self.

The American psyche needed, and still needs, Woody Guthries. Americans have been very particular about who we elevate to the highest spots of our mythology, at least until recently (*American Idol, Survivor*). We like to think of ourselves in certain narrow ways that fit the national identity we have built for ourselves. We roll up our sleeves and get the job done, knocking down the obscene, cartoonish figures of irrational authority while making sure The People always have a voice. We are stouthearted and vociferous (life, liberty) but also narcissistic (the pursuit of happiness). We cherish our family and friends ("There's no place like home") but adore the road, too ("I reckon I got to light out for the Territory"). We preach about justice and morality but prize humility—or the elastic definitions thereof. And in the end, we carry a streak of the martyr inside us for what we inevitably have to give up. This character has taken many forms over the decades. In old movies, it was embodied in characters played by Jimmy Stewart and Gary Cooper. On TV, think Marshal Matt Dillon or Captain James T. Kirk. The city and the frontier, at odds but working together. A little bit country, a little bit rock and roll.

Woody Guthrie embodied that at a pivotal time in the nation's musical and technological history. He had the chops of authenticity: born in Oklahoma, a childhood streaked with tragedy, an adolescence of confronting authority and finding new backdrops against which to tell his story. But he also possessed the savvy of a Hollywood performer. In an age when the "authentic"—the Music of the People—was being produced and marketed for rural and urban audiences alike, Guthrie was a mediator and a moderator. He was a more musical, more hardscrabble version of Alan Lomax. He could take the rough edges of a rural ballad, add his guitar and make it an amiable song suitable for radio and live performances. His presence in the clubs and on the union stages of New York City said two things: I am one of them, but I am one of you, too. It was a masterly balance, and he never quite let on how conscious it was. But in bringing the music of some of the people to the *rest* of the people, Guthrie was the charismatic sales guy who staffed the storefront of a factory that was operating in the back room, brought to life by rural musicians who worked on an assembly line of music and song, with people like Alan and John Lomax as the shift supervisors.

That made Guthrie, with his influential early-1940s group the Almanac Singers, the perfect second-generation interpreter of what, suddenly, was being called "House of the Rising Sun."

In 1941, the year after he scribbled the lyrics to what would become "This Land Is Your Land" in a looping hand on a piece of three-ring notebook paper, Guthrie was traveling in and out of New York City, talking to and singing for workers and union organizers and early folkies. He and several other like-minded musician-activists formed the Almanacs, named after the house in Greenwich Village in which they all lived and practiced. The group also included the gangly young banjo player Pete Seeger, son of musicologist Charles Seeger and stepson of Ruth Crawford Seeger, who was doing the musical notations for *Our Singing Country;* Lee Hays, a fervent performer of union songs; Millard Lampell, a writer from New Jersey; and, occasionally, others, including Alan Lomax's sister Bess and Guthrie's fellow Oklahoman and political singer Agnes "Sis" Cunningham.

At a series of sessions in July 1941, the four core members of the Almanacs—Guthrie, Seeger, Lampell, and Hays—recorded enough material for two 78 rpm albums. The sessions were arranged by Alan Lomax and were done quick and dirty. The Almanacs already knew all of the material they were recording, and, according to the liner notes of a 1996 reissue of the material, Lomax was the source for some of it. Also, the year before, when Lomax and Guthrie had spent several days together in Washington, Lomax took the Oklahoman through the Archive of American Folk Song and regaled him with recordings from recent songcatching field trips. Was the Georgia Turner recording among them?

From these sessions came the group's take of "House of the Rising Sun," which starts with a brief harmonica and banjo intro followed by Guthrie singing. It hews closely to the vocal style of Georgia Turner's and is sung from a girl's point of view, traits that offer strong clues that it came from Lomax. But here's the ultimate tipoff: The lyrics that Guthrie sang, with a few tiny changes for rhythm, were *exactly* those that Lomax had created for his composite version of the song in *Our Singing Country.* The Almanacs' version made only three changes of any substance: In the second verse, it became a "gambler," not a "rambler," who led the singer astray; in the final verse, "my race is almost run" became "my time is almost done"; most significant, the warning verse—"Go tell my baby sister"—is moved from the third verse down to the sixth verse, where it makes more sense from a narrative standpoint. And that's exactly where it would stay when the Animals recorded it twenty-three years later.

Seeger learned from both Guthrie and Lomax during his Almanac days about how to take a traditional song and make it your own through a unique blend of arrangement, rearrangement, and soul. It was Seeger who, years later, took an African folk tune and turned it into

"Wimoweh" (which became "The Lion Sleeps Tonight"), and who borrowed from the Bible's Book of Ecclesiates for his song "Turn! Turn! Turn!" He remembers Lomax consciously injecting "Rising Sun" into the mix, teaching it to all the people around them who were making music. " 'House of the Rising Sun' was one of Alan's gems," said Seeger, who learned it from him. "He knew he had a great song there."

Imagine the scene in those Manhattan apartments in the early 1940s. War was near, and these amazing musicians were trying to retrench, to move away from the pro-union and sometimes overtly socialist activism that would land some of them in serious trouble in the 1950s. They were edging toward a different brand of relevance that would include wartime patriotism, and they were struggling to incorporate, into their growing personal songbooks, raw material of the kind Lomax had collected. In photographs of those song sessions, you see so many of them sitting around, watching each other play. Lomax is often there, sleeves rolled up, looking on and looking satisfied. Lead Belly is often dressed in a suit. Josh White is holding his guitar and appearing somehow more suave and polished than the rest of them combined. Stare into those pictures, and you can feel the folk revival's foundation being laid brick by brick with each rendition, each verse, each modification to each folk song. "Lawyers rearrange old laws to fit new circumstances, chefs rearrange old recipes to fit new stomachs," Seeger told me. "It is the same way with music."

Lead Belly, born Hudson "Huddie" Ledbetter in Mooringsport, Louisiana, probably in 1885, did not have an easy life. He was an itinerant laborer and musician—a genius on the twelve-string guitar—who spent time in prison in both Texas (for murder) and Louisiana (for attempted murder) before being "discovered" by John and Alan Lomax in 1933 at the Louisiana State Prison at Angola. Alan was barely eighteen at the time, and he and his father were collecting songs from southern prison inmates when they came across Lead Belly, whose singing prowess and mental song catalog enchanted the elder Lomax. When Lead Belly was released (not because of the intervention of John Lomax, as lore often has it), he accompanied the Lomaxes back north to great fanfare and played at colleges and conferences—sometimes in a striped prison outfit or sharecropper clothes—before he fell out with the elder Lomax and tried to strike out on his own. In that brief moment when literary

New York celebrated his arrival, William Rose Benet published a poem in
The New Yorker, "Ballad of a Ballad-Singer," that both glorified Lead Belly
and revealed the urban condescension with which he was viewed:

> *He was big and he was black*
> *And wondrous were his wrongs*
> *But he had a memory travelled back*
> *Through at least five hundred songs.*

Though he had been a violent man at times, Lead Belly's friends in the
urban music scene of the early 1940s remember him as a dignified gentle giant respected for both his music and his life experience, ugly and
otherwise. Despite the impasse that his friendship with the politically
conservative John Lomax had reached, Lead Belly stayed close with the
more liberal Alan, and the two haunted the New York folk scene of the
early 1940s together. It was there, most likely, that Lead Belly picked up
Lomax's "Rising Sun Blues" and retooled it into a rollicking song that
he first called "In New Orleans." The earliest recording I can find dates
to February 1944 and sounds like a ghost, imported straight from a raucous barrelhouse in the last decade of the 1800s. No feeling of lament
here; the guitar is upbeat and insolent and teases slyly as it opens the
song. "Way down in New Orleans, house called the Rising Sun; now,
been the ruin of many poor boy, and me, oh God, for one." Lead Belly's
voice is strong, robust, a contrast from his famous "last sessions" when
it sounds like a tightly strung guitar string being jabbed. He punctuates
the song with spoken-word interjections like "go 'head and tell her"
and "rock me." If you weren't listening to the words, you wouldn't
know it was our song.

But in a subsequent version called "New Orleans (The Rising Sun
Blues)," Lead Belly slows it down a bit and moves a few steps closer to
the more familiar rhythm and tune, though it remains in a major key.
The recording date is unknown for this version, which was captured
on an acetate disc and found in the collection of Moses Asch, founder
of Folkways Records. By the quality of Lead Belly's voice, it appears to
be from about 1947. It follows the lyric order of the Lomax text and,
indeed, is credited "J. Lomax, A. Lomax, G. Turner/TRO-Ludlow Music,
Inc." That would be the earliest that Georgia Turner's name appears as

a credit for a "Rising Sun" recording, though it's possible that the CD version of this recording contains a modern credit that did not appear originally.

The final existing Lead Belly recording of our song comes in the fall of 1948, when Frederic Ramsey Jr. spent three nights with the ailing singer and made the high-quality recordings that would be stitched together into *Lead Belly's Last Sessions*. By this time, it's simply called "House of the Rising Sun." You can tell that Ledbetter's voice is fading; he sounds strung tightly, almost like a woman—reminiscent, in fact, of how Georgia Turner sounded eleven years before when she sang for Lomax. It wasn't the best song of the session, or the most noticed. But by including "Rising Sun" on his final musical offerings to the world, Lead Belly, whose reputation was already melting into legend in the months before he died, helped push the song toward a permanent presence in the folk canon.

The fact that Ramsey, a jazz scholar, sat with Lead Belly for these final sessions and used equipment that was cutting-edge for its time offers an interesting glimpse into the shifting notion of performance for folk musicians in the 1940s. As Anthony Seeger points out in liner notes for the Smithsonian Folkways issue of the *Last Sessions* recordings,

> These recordings are also significant as historic documents because they present music in the way it is often made—by people sitting around their homes, in bars, or elsewhere, talking about the songs, relating them to their lives, singing one after another. But Lead Belly wasn't just any person singing in someone's home: He was a master. And the home wasn't just any home: It belonged to a jazz scholar who had one of the new tape recorders.

This is an intermediate step between recording directly from the folk tradition, as Lomax did, and engineering professionally produced music. On one hand, a production like *Lead Belly's Last Sessions* is not simply music performed for the benefit of the guys sitting around with you, though it has elements of that; on the other, it's not truly professional, not chosen and curated for business purposes, though it has elements of that, too.

When Ramsey wrote about the sessions five years later in *High*

Fidelity magazine, he had already begun propagating the myth of the man whose voice he captured for the final time. "In the United States, not so long ago," he wrote, "we had a giant of a man with us, a singer and adventurer whose exploits, if we did not know the actual facts of his existence, might one day have been amplified into a sort of Paul Bunyan legend." Despite the qualifiers, that's exactly what Ramsey was doing with that statement—amplifying Lead Belly into legend. But Lead Belly lived in a modern age of technology, where the facts of his life were captured by the written word and the recording device, and that prevented the man from becoming a legend as entirely as he might have in the past. His songs became the legend.

This is what mass culture and recorded sound do. Maybe, for example, there once really was a John Henry, a steel-driving man who died with a hammer in his hand. But we're not sure, and the legend, the song, has become more real than the reality. If Lead Belly had lived a century earlier, he might well have been remembered as a foggy myth, because stories in the folk tradition were preserved as tall tales—the very kind that Lead Belly himself liked to tell so much.

Hearing Lead Belly sing about the "Rising Sun" myth seems natural because he lived much of the misery. When he sings, "If I had done like Mamma said, I wouldn't be here today," he has the experience to back it up. And though he skipped the verse about one foot being on the platform and the other on the train, he really *had* worn the ball and chain in his life, and it came out in his voice. Lead Belly may not have infused a recognizable lamentation into the sound of "Rising Sun," but he brought every moment of his travails to bear when he sang the song. Anyone who knew anything of Lead Belly's life could not listen to a song like that and miss the message it was delivering.

Figuring out which black musician began singing "Rising Sun" first— Ledbetter or Josh White—is a toss-up. They were both in the middle of that Manhattan musical mix in the early 1940s. But as much as Lead Belly adapted "Rising Sun" and made it his own, White's embracing of it was much more influential in the song's march toward the folk revival. Not only did White's interpretation take a significant step in sound and feel toward the Animals' version, but it reconceived the piece as a personal cautionary tale. In Josh White's hands, "House of the Rising Sun" sounded like a song that was meant to be mouthed into the microphone in a smoky, big-city club rather than on a front porch somewhere in the South. Not only was it intimate, it felt overtly sexual, too—a perfect fit with the persona of White, who had the reputation of ladykiller.

Josh White (1914–1969) was in his late twenties and performing in New York when he first recorded "House of the Rising Sun" in either late 1941 or early 1942—several months after the Almanacs had cut the first version under the now-common title. White, from Greenville, South Carolina, was a young boy when his father was sent away to an asylum after an altercation with a white bill collector who had spit on the floor of his house. He spent his late adolescence working as an assistant to blind bluesmen who needed help getting around Southern cities during the late 1920s and early 1930s. Among them was Blind Lemon Jefferson, one of the most famous early folk-blues guitarists. In this way White was exposed to all kinds of music at a pivotal time when white Appalachian balladry was blending with black blues and creating an early fusion of American music.

Like Guthrie, White became an interpreter who translated the rawness of rural music into something smoother and more palatable to urban audiences. There was a key difference between the two, though. Guthrie liked to affect a hick persona, whereas White had no problem embracing smoothness and, later, a pop mentality as he whittled away at songs' hard edges. He was an effective translator of songs and an adept blender of racial traditions.

White's milieu was the smoky cabaret, where he could sit onstage, on a stool with his guitar, and hold the attention of a well-lubricated audience—particularly its female members. His silken voice, coming through the microphone, was a potent sexual tool, no small matter in the early 1940s if you were a black performer and many of your female customers were white. Through his music, White became a fervent advocate of racial justice (the antilynching ballad "Strange Fruit"), economic justice ("One Meat Ball"), and patriotism ("The House I Live In"). Those stances, which seem congruent today, were less so in that era, when advocacy of justice could be seen as socialist and communist. White would learn that the hard way a decade later in the 1950s, when some of the groups for whom he performed were used to call his loyalty into question, and he was forced to defend himself against charges that he had links to American communists.

When you listen today to White's songs from the early 1940s, even the most innocuous of them—the whimsical Australian ballad "Waltzing Matilda," for example—seems charged with defiance. His combination of confidence, melancholy, and vague anger comes through clearly in versions of "House of the Rising Sun" he recorded between 1941 and 1945. The deliberate, minor-key version performed by White is the first that carries a melody truly similar to the one familiar today. He introduced a polished sensibility that captivated a Café Society audience very different from those who listened to Guthrie. In one recording, he introduces it as "a song about the red-light district in New Orleans— wine, women and song."

In White's care, with a subtle guitar accompaniment, "Rising Sun" took on the sheen of sophisticated urban blues—slow, mournful, pitying, bitter, and very much in keeping with his masterly blending of black and white traditions. Stylistically, there is no echo of Georgia Turner in it, no flavor of Appalachia. And White sang it so deliberately, enunciated it so clearly, kept the voice of the woman so intact that there was no doubt what the song was about. That was his hallmark: to claim a song and make it his own.

"He would say to all of us, 'If you're going to sing a song you have to believe it. Because if you don't believe it, those people you're singing to won't believe it,' " Josh White Jr., who sings the song regularly in performances, told me. "With 'House of the Rising Sun,' you believed every word. 'House of the Rising Sun' with my dad was one of the first songs he took on as first person. It was a girl's song, but he didn't try to change it around to another perspective. He *was* that woman, and that's what you felt."

Where did the elder White pick up "Rising Sun"? All evidence except for the tune itself points to the Lomax version that had already been sung by Guthrie and, possibly, Lead Belly. White's 1944 rendition follows Lomax's almost to the letter for three verses, then skips four more verses—including the "My mother was a tailor" verse that Georgia Turner had added seven years before, an interesting one to drop given that White's own father was a tailor. Eventually White comes back to Lomax's final verse about "my race is almost run." Pete Seeger, who was there, says flatly that Lomax taught the song to White.

What's clear is that White engulfed the song, made it his own. His version is unequivocally in the minor key, much more similar to the tune we know today than anything previous to it. He also registered at least one joint copyright to his arrangement, in 1941–42. It lists his co-arrangers as folk music promoter and radio producer (and future movie director) Nicholas Ray and Libby Holman, a white singer and actress with whom White performed in the early 1940s.

In *The Josh White Song Book,* published in 1963 six years before he died, White maintains he came by "Rising Sun" on his own in his early years, "from a white hillbilly singer in either Winston-Salem or High Point, North Carolina." The book goes on to say: "A few years ago he had to 'convince' a folklorist that he hadn't learned it from one of his books or recordings." That folklorist is obviously Lomax. But it's worth noting that the notes for White's songbook were written by Robert Shelton, the same music critic who insisted around the same time, without citing sources, that "Rising Sun" was an example of "early city blues." And White's own biographer, Elijah Wald, notes that he often dissembled about his sources: "He could certainly be cavalier about such matters and over the years he often took credit, or at least tacitly accepted it, for introducing songs that had previously been done by other artists."

With folk songs, of course, the lines are blurrier. The whole point of such a composition is to put your personal stamp upon it, to make it relevant to your audience, whether they're on a Kentucky front porch or in an intimate Manhattan café. White acknowledged this in an interview quoted by Wald:

> You take a song, and if the story just doesn't run true to form, then you sort of write into it; you add, and you subtract. And that's one thing about folk songs, you're at liberty to do this kind of thing. You don't have to sing them word for word. If the story doesn't make it, then you sort of make the story. You write into the story what you want.

And yet . . .

Both White's son and Oscar Brand, a musician and radio host who spent a lot of time with White in the 1940s, told me that they, too, heard White say he got it from "some country singer" (even though, says Brand, "he never named a person. He never named a date or a time"). And of the earliest versions recorded in the 1930s, the tune that

White uses in his interpretation sounds the most like the one done by the Callahan Brothers in 1934 as "Rounder's Luck." And Homer Callahan was certainly a white hillbilly singer in North Carolina.

Clearly Lomax's composite of Georgia Turner and Bert Martin in *Our Singing Country* influenced White; the words and verse order of the two versions are simply too similar. What mattered was the way that White interpreted it—like no one else before him, in a way that would ripple through to the 1960s and catch the attention of Eric Burdon. In one White rendition from the 1940s, he ends with a little acoustic guitar riff that sounds just like the famed beginning of the Animals' song two decades later. Like Guthrie and Lead Belly, White had feet planted in both American yesterdays and American tomorrows. And, like the other two men, he was in a position to amplify "Rising Sun"—to ensure its berth in the musical tradition that would preserve it through the 1950s and into the 1960s.

Obviously, White cared about his stewardship of the song. " 'House of the Rising Sun,' just like 'Strange Fruit,' took on a very haunting presence with the old man," Josh White Jr. says. I find it interesting that the two songs that resonated the most with his father are about a woman and a black man going to their respective dooms. "It sticks with you," the son says. "I'll have people saying they heard it, maybe it's Cafe Society 1948 or at a college, and it has stuck with them." And then, when requested, the son plays the father's song and makes it *his* own. When he does, he makes sure they know where it came from for him: "I tell people who ask for it: This is the White version of the song."

Just after White died in 1969, Oscar Brand was in Italy with his son. They happened upon a piazza, where a Scandinavian man was sitting. He had a guitar and was singing "House of the Rising Sun." Brand mentioned to his son that "Josh sang that." Suddenly, the man noticed the two passersby.

"The guy kind of woke up and said, 'Josh'? I said, 'Yes, I knew him.' The guy just let loose a line of Norwegian excitement," Brand recalls. "It was as if I had touched God on my travels."

By the end of the 1940s, "Rising Sun" had taken firm root. It was a Josh White standard and would remain so until the end of his life, years after the Animals had recorded their definitive version. Lead Belly's specific versions largely died with him in 1949, because they were rarely emulated, though other songs that soared through him—"Goodnight, Irene," "The Midnight Special," and "Rock Island Line"—became household presences during the coming decade. Pete Seeger's new group, the Weavers, with his old Almanac Singers cohort Lee Hays and fellow musicians Fred Hellerman and Ronnie Gilbert, had formed in 1949. They committed themselves to reinterpreting folk songs that included but weren't limited to the kind Lomax had brought back from Appalachia more than a decade before. "Our name meant that we were weavers of songs," the group wrote in a songbook issued in 1960, after they had been playing together for a decade and endured the 1950s anticommunist crusade. "We did not want a name that pinned us down to any one kind of song, like cowboy or hillbilly songs. We wanted to sing music of such wide range that no specific name could describe it all."

Pete Seeger was becoming the dean of American folk musicians, and the Weavers were the gold standard for his kind of music. Seeger was still five years away from being subpoenaed by the House Committee on Un-American Activities, and his musical word carried formidable weight. Many obscure folksinger wannabes—the equivalent of today's garage bands—studied the Weavers' song repertoire closely to find inspiration. The Weavers, meanwhile, openly cited Lead Belly and Guthrie as chief influences. "My own biggest thing in life was simply being a link in a chain," Seeger says, "going from college to another college, singing a batch of songs and saying, 'Aren't these good songs?' and telling them about Woody and Lead Belly."

In their songbook, the Weavers offer their take on the "Rising Sun" arrangement they had played regularly since 1949—the one that sent the song powerfully into the coming revival. The muted arrangement, credited to Hellerman and Gilbert, is sung by Gilbert. She tackles it in a minor key reminiscent of Josh White's but with more dramatic flourishes that take her voice from the bottom of the scale to the top and back.

The Lomax–Georgia Turner version was spreading. Each musician brought a new interpretation, a new sensibility to the material. And somehow the story, with its deft balance of specifics and universal themes, was elastic enough to take all comers without losing its oomph. "You bounce a song off an experience of life the way a basketball bounces against a backboard," Pete Seeger told me. "Think of the young girls who sang it, the mothers who sang it, the cynical piano players. It gets new meanings as different people sing it."

Some meanings it didn't need. Consider Libby Holman. A well-known torch singer in the late 1920s, she was married briefly to the heir to the R. J. Reynolds tobacco fortune. When he died of a gunshot wound, she went on trial for murder, but the charges were eventually dropped, though the saga inspired a Jean Harlow movie. Holman vanished from view. When she met Josh White in New York a decade later, the two began a tumultuous, years-long friendship and professional relationship. Holman recorded her own version of "Rising Sun" a few years later, apparently with White's assistance and endorsement. It mimics his arrangement loosely but features a melodramatic piano backing. It's three minutes and thirty-five seconds of sheer purgatory that is a challenge to endure. She also sees fit to analyze the song, missing the point entirely in the first part of her assessment and pointing out the obvious at the end.

> There is something so architectural, so straightforward about "House of the Rising Sun." It's as if it had been carved out of granite. The piano interprets the feeling I have in my bones. And because it deals with pain in a house of pleasure, there's a great deal of dissonance in the setting.

Hardly. The song has lasted only because it is *not* carved out of something as unyielding as granite. If anything, it is fashioned from putty and can be remolded at will. As Holman did. To its detriment.

Before we leave the 1940s, let's pay a visit to one version that had nothing to do with Lomax but is worth mentioning for its obscurity and its presence in the emerging Tennessee country music scene.

Esco Hankins's 1947 "Rising Sun" is nearly a beat-for-beat re-creation of Roy Acuff's still-to-come 1962 version, and thus undoubtedly cribbed from what Acuff was playing consistently in those years after his 1938 recording. The melody and the fiddle playing match, as do the pauses and the verses. This is in keeping with the career of Hankins, a talented performer little known outside the Smokies, where he took Acuff's place as a hometown boy once Acuff made good at the Grand Ole Opry.

The rare Hankins version was recorded on the King label in 1947 but disappeared until a recent compilation CD of Hankins's work put out by the British Archive of Country Music—and also called "Rising Sun." It features a photo of Hankins—who resembles the archetype of every 1940s country-western singer with guitar and cowboy hat—set against the backdrop of a sun rising over trees. Remember, this was an era when modern country music was just taking shape. For every star, and Acuff was the biggest, dozens of talented imitators made their musical marks by grabbing fame's coattails.

Kevin Coffee writes in the liner notes that Hankins "did his best to fill the departed man's shoes in East Tennessee." Coffee also points up a weird fact about the Hankins-Acuff symbiosis. Acuff changed the name of his band, which he called Roy Acuff and His Crazy Tennesseans, to Roy Acuff and the Smoky Mountain Boys because, according to biographer Elizabeth Schlappi, a radio station manager told Acuff that "the name Crazy Tennesseans was a slur to Tennessee." But according to Coffee's sources, Hankins had a group in the 1930s called Esco Hankins and the Smoky Mountain Boys. When a fast-rising Acuff decided he wanted the name, they swapped, so the Smoky Mountain Boys went on to Opry stardom while Hankins's group rode off into obscurity as the Crazy Tennesseans. Schlappi credits Hankins with being a virtual Acuff doppelganger. "His records," she wrote, "even fooled Roy's mother."

Hankins's "Rising Sun" offers us a useful puzzle piece. It affirms that, though Acuff may not have been recording the song as regularly as he was rerecording his top shelf standards, he was performing it enough for someone like Hankins to profit from an Acuff knockoff. And at the end of the 1940s, Acuff was to country what Seeger was to folk: the king, the dean, the man who set the agenda. If he was still singing it, it's no wonder "House of the Rising Sun" would, in coming decades, embed itself in the country music scene and emerge in distinctive ways as the Nashville Sound came into its own.

NASHVILLE, TENNESSEE

"The District" is the part of Nashville dedicated to the kind of country fan who ranges from street to street, snapping pictures, buying large portraits of Faith Hill, and listening to Vince Gill wannabes in shadowy bars. But I should not be critical; before I began this quest, I thought country music was merely the purview of dutiful dogs and rusty pick-ups and the breaking of various roadhouse waitresses' hearts. How much we think we know, how little we actually do.

Smack in the middle of the District is the Ernest Tubb Record Store. The late Ernest, I had learned from someone in an internet newsgroup, allegedly once recorded a little-known version of "Rising Sun." So I stride in and ask the clerk whether that is the case. "I doubt it," he says. "But if he did it, we have it."

He proceeds to consult the definitive Ernest Tubb discography, and it confirms his notion. No "Rising Sun." (Clerks here call Tubb "ET," as in, "That would have been pretty early in ET's career there.") However, it turns out the shop has two versions I haven't yet come across—one by the Country Gentlemen (with Ricky Skaggs), and one by a country chanteuse named Jody Miller. I pick out a few more CDs and leave after securing a promise from the clerk to call me if other obscure versions turn up.

Next up is the Lawrence Record Shop, down the street. There, I am greeted by two men. The sedate one, a gentleman with an almost pro-fessorial demeanor, is Paul Lawrence, son of the man who founded the store in 1949. His manic counterpart and brother, who adopts us imme-diately, is Ted Lawrence.

Lawrence's is exclusively LPs, 45s, and cassettes, which gets me to thinking that I might find some versions unavailable on CD. Paul con-sults his catalog and comes up with one that I don't have: Ronnie Mil-sap. He leads me to the Milsap section of the 45s area and hands me a fistful of the thirty or so Milsap 45s in stock. "You take half, I'll take the other half," he says. We flip through them. Nothing.

A few moments later, I am examining the Milsap albums when Ted Lawrence approaches. Ted is gangly and wiry, jerks around like Gumby and talks a mile a minute. On the belt above his blue jeans is a leather snap case containing a Zippo lighter. His black T-shirt bears this slogan: "My Two Best Friends—Charlie and Jack Daniels."

"He comes in here a lot," Ted says, and I realize he is referring to Mil-sap. At that moment, I come across the LP that does indeed have "Rising Sun." I grab it so that no one else can (not that anyone is anywhere near me), and Ted continues. He is talking about visits from Nashville's stars.

"A lot of 'em come in here. Once they get past the counter, they're just like any other customer. That's how we treat 'em. They come in here to buy their own stuff. Sometimes they're surprised at how much it costs."

It dawns on me that the Roy Acuff 1962 version might be on an album here. I walk toward the front, toward the Acuff section. Ted is still jabbering. "All over the world, we get 'em from," he says. I ask him why people from as far as Germany and Japan like American country music. He ignores me—sort of.

"One German guy came in, and you won't believe this," he starts off. Seems the guy had a camcorder and, when he realized he couldn't buy everything, started videotaping album covers. He took the tape back to Germany, made a movie out of it and started showing it at theaters. Or so Ted Lawrence says. "My friend calls me up and says, 'Hey—there's a movie about you in Germany.' "

Lawrence insists his stories are true. "We get orders from a king in Africa," he says out of the blue.

"What country?" I ask.

"Africa!" he snaps, as if that clarifies matters.

Despite such outbursts, I suspect his stories about country stars are true. After all, there are pictures all over the counter of Lawrences mugging with Dolly Parton here, k.d. lang there.

"Acuff, he used to come in here when he was alive. One time he was in here and got talking to a guy who said, 'That Opry's an impressive place. You ever been up there?' "

"Roy, he said, 'Oh, a few times.' "

"Guy said, 'I've been up there. I've seen 'em all and met 'em all.' He even said he'd met Roy Acuff."

"Then the guy said, 'You like it?' Roy Acuff, he said, 'Um, let me introduce myself.' The guy's jaw dropped about to the floor. He got out of there fast."

I come across an Acuff album with a picture of a barn on it, priced at $24.99. It has the 1962 version of "The Rising Sun" on it. I snap it up. Lawrence sees my grin. "Found it, huh?"

As Paul Lawrence slits the shrink wrap of the Acuff LP to play "The Rising Sun," I ask his brother once again: Why do so many people from so many places like country music? Once again, he doesn't answer. But this time, his non-answer has something I'm looking for.

"You know where country came from? It came from jazz and the blues. They just slowed it down, made it more deliberate-like," he says. Well, not really, but a case could be made for part of that. "And now, right here on this street"—Lawrence gestures out toward Broadway's honky-tonk strip—"they're putting in jazz and blues in the clubs."

"Is that a good thing?" I ask.

"I don't know if it's good. It just is. That's music—that's what it does."

We pause to listen to Acuff singing about the poor boy's ruin. It's different from the 1937 version—less dobro, more polished in the way that a twenty-five-year veteran of the Grand Ole Opry can pull off. Paul Lawrence smiles. "Not bad," he says.

I walk out of the Lawrence shop, and my eyes are immediately scorched by the blistering midafternoon Nashville sun. When my pupils adjust, I see a family walking by in full country regalia. The father is wearing a black cowboy hat and carrying a guitar in a black case with a bumper sticker that says "Nashville." They are grinning and speaking in excited tones.

In Japanese.

That's music. That's what it does.

4 ... *To the Highways*

I bid farewell to old Kentucky
The place where I was born and raised.

—"MAN OF CONSTANT SORROW"

By the late 1950s, "House of the Rising Sun" was a folk standard. Young musicians who were styling themselves as second-generation Woody Guthries and Lead Bellys were singing the song. Though some in the folk community had turned their backs on Josh White because of the perception that he had caved to the House Committee on Un-American Activities, his musical influences and his unique take of "Rising Sun" were rippling out to a wider audience, too. The influential Weavers, even after their guru, Pete Seeger, left the group in 1957, continued to perform the song. Sometimes they called it "House of the Rising Sun," sometimes "House in New Orleans." It kept sucking in bluesiness and taking on the shape of the urban blues it had never been. The liner notes of a 1958 Ronnie Gilbert solo album say that her rendition "borrows something of the 'feel' of the blues and gives it an entirely appropriate home in the old 'House of the Rising Sun.' "

A pivotal event took place in April 1957, when the music and lyrics to "House of the Rising Sun" were published in *Sing Out!* a freewheeling music journal that functioned as a combination bible and instruction book for folk-music aficionados of the day. The text that *Sing Out!* ran was almost word for word the Lomax composite version from *Our Singing Country,* with a few minor orthographic changes and the "Go tell my baby sister" verse moved further down in the song. It ran under a short description that said, without sourcing, "No one knows the exact origin of this famous Negro folk blues." Again with the Negro folk

89

blues: Was this still because of the erroneous report that bluesman Texas Alexander had first recorded the song in 1928? Was it because Josh White's iconic version, so popular in the 1940s, had linked it to black tradition? Or did they know something we don't?

It's difficult to overestimate the influence of our song's presence in *Sing Out!* at that early moment in the folk revival. Well-thumbed copies of *Sing Out!*—not to mention mimeographed sheets of its contents—were passed around from musician to musician as raw material. Folkies performing in bars, clubs, and the fast-emerging hootenannies were ravenous for content, and *Sing Out!* was a prime source. If you were a folk musician who didn't know "House of the Rising Sun" before the spring of 1957, odds are you had at least heard of it after that.

One group that emerged in 1958, right at the cusp of the revival's (and our song's) acceleration into high gear, was a trio called the New Lost City Ramblers. The Ramblers were in some ways a prototype for many folk groups of the early 1960s: They looked with dedication back to the roots of American folk music, but hewed closer to original arrangements rather than modernizing them into popular chart-toppers as the Kingston Trio had done with "Tom Dooley." The Ramblers were liberal easterners who saw, in Appalachia and its music, a direct path toward some of the better things about America. Their raw material was music from the late 1920s and early 1930s—both field recordings and commercial music from such old-school labels as Vocalion.

The big-ticket name in the Ramblers was Seeger—Mike Seeger, Pete's half brother, who as a boy had listened to the 1937 Lomax field recordings that his family was transcribing for the book *Our Singing Country.* But we're more concerned with another founding Rambler who would find a pristine, untouched, and utterly unique version of "House of the Rising Sun" in the remote mountains of Perry County, Kentucky. John Cohen was a thoughtful musician and photographer from New York City who saw, in the rural tradition that suffused the songs he sang, an antidote to the postwar modernization that had pushed America toward what he considered a cookie-cutter existence. Cohen viewed the world in both images and music. When he picked up a camera and got behind it, what came out was so lyrical that his photos and his music fit together like puzzle pieces.

In 1959, not long after the Ramblers began performing together, Cohen licensed some of his photos to *Life* magazine to fund a music-hunting trip to Appalachia. He didn't have a car, so he took a Trailways coach through Washington, switched buses a few times, passed the house of still-living ballad legend Dock Boggs without even knowing it and finally wound up in Hazard, a hard-bitten Kentucky mining town with a reputation for roughness. He took a room and bought a car; it broke down immediately and he traded it in at a gas station for one that cost $75 more. The second one had sand in the fuel lines, and as he got it fixed he began to build a list. "I'm here looking for banjo players," he'd say, this red-haired Jewish boy from Queens. Folks responded, though, and he began to make some good recordings. "For me, this was a chance to experience something similar to what Lomax did—going out and looking around," he says today. "I wanted to get out there."

One Saturday night, at a roadhouse called Russell's near where the ballad singer Jean Ritchie grew up, Cohen watched a square-dance band that featured two local musicians named Lee Sexton and Odabe Holcomb playing breakdowns. This performance energized Cohen, who had run out of people on his list to record. The next day, he drove into the woods and decided to turn onto the first dirt road he saw.

He crossed a little railroad track and, without knowing it, pulled into Daisy, population less than one hundred, which even today shows no evidence that it's actually a town. He ran across some kids and pulled out his spiel: "Any banjo players here?" They pointed to a house that turned out to belong to Odabe Holcomb, the man he had seen play the night before. Odabe's wife, Mary Jane, was there. She played a song she called "Charles Guitar," which was, of course, "Charles Guiteau," the James A. Garfield presidential assassination ballad. Then she looked past Cohen and said, "Here comes Rossie."

Cohen turned to see a wiry, middle-aged man coming up the hill, ambling along like Chaplin's Little Tramp. On his face he wore the expression of the "worried man" he always said he was. He sported a porkpie hat and the kind of rimmed glasses that almost every near-sighted American man wore in the late 1950s. Mary Jane Holcomb handed him a guitar and he started playing the old song "Across the Rocky Mountain." It made Cohen's hair stand on end.

Though Cohen didn't know it yet, this man would become one of the finest Appalachian musicians ever recorded. And for Cohen, who would do the recording, "he changed my life."

The man's name was Roscoe Holcomb, though anyone who knew him called him Rossie. He was forty-eight years old and lived in a plain wooden house on the far end of a holler just past a lumber camp near Daisy. To get to his home, Cohen recalls, "You crossed a stream and then climbed a steep hill . . . there was a vegetable garden in front of the porch and a few sheds behind the house." Rossie Holcomb was a laborer, a man whose rutted face and hands told silent tales of a difficult life of odd jobs and years of struggles to get by. When Cohen met him, he was working on and off pouring concrete for the new Interstate Highway System even though the nearest interstate, I-75, was more than two hours—and, psychologically, entire worlds—away.

Unlike his cousin, Rossie didn't perform in roadhouses; he played his music for himself and those few who wanted to listen. There weren't many. Cohen recalls that when he first visited, "there was a sense of tension in Roscoe's home. He was tolerated, but there was little feeling for his music." Often he played on his front porch, where a wooden swing hung from the ceiling on chains. Still, in a landscape of devout Old Regular Baptists, Holcomb was an oddity even among his own people—a man who sang music that wasn't gospel hymnody, who had the audacity to accompany his songs with a guitar, an instrument whose existence was sacrilege to his Baptist brethren. And, oh, how he played that guitar—the unusual tuning, the weary fingers gliding along the strings and creating melodies that sounded sometimes as if there were two people playing at once.

Rossie's voice was equally nimble, dancing up and down the scale and venturing into a nasal falsetto to make a particularly bluesy point. For a lifelong chain smoker, his vocal cords were in amazing shape. His voice sounded organically bonded to the guitar that accompanied it, like a seventh string. The seamless combination of voice and instrument that Holcomb offered was a skill that captivated Eric Clapton and that Bob Dylan, years later, would famously describe as an "untamed sense of control." Cohen would visit Rossie often during the decade after they met, and often he'd encounter the music before he'd encounter the man. "Sometimes," Cohen told me, "I'd be coming up that hill to see him, and you'd hear the guitar."

Rossie had been absorbing music since he was a kid and had been heavily influenced by the blues—particularly Blind Lemon Jefferson, whose records he listened to in the 1930s (the story goes that railroad conductors brought them into the predominantly white hills and sold them at a significant profit).

Rossie knew more than four hundred songs by heart and professed to have learned them within a year after asking God "to give me something I could do, that I could make a little money." It was his own, more pious version of Robert Johnson's devil dealing down at the crossroads in Clarksdale. "I say it is a gift," he told Cohen, "and I believe God gave it to me." He also had his own rather romantic views about what made music magical. It was clear he thought about it a lot. He once told Cohen, "You can take just a small kid, I've noticed it, that can't even sit alone, and you pull the strings on some kind of instrument—a fiddle, or a banjo, or something or other like that—And you watch how quick it draws the attention of that kid. . . . And it draws the attention of the whole human race."

Shortly after meeting Rossie, Cohen invited him to New York to record some tracks that would be issued as part of an album called *The Music of Roscoe Holcomb and Wade Ward* (the latter was a musician from Virginia whom Cohen also recorded). Holcomb had never made a commercial recording. Among the songs he finally recorded for Cohen, in 1961, was "House of the Rising Sun." It's lost to history what Rossie called it. He may not have had a title; that was true of many of the songs he sang, and Cohen affixed his own titles to the songs unless Rossie gave him a name. This was called, simply, "The Rising Sun," though later compilations of Holcomb songs would refer to it as "House in New Orleans."

Cohen already knew the song, though the Ramblers never performed it. "I would have known it from Guthrie and Josh White. Mike [Seeger] would have known it from Ashley and we would have gotten in a fight about it," he says. But regardless of what Cohen thought he knew about the song, he had never heard it like Rossie Holcomb sang it.

It begins with that complex guitar that makes you wonder whether Rossie had more than five fingers on each hand. Then his voice cuts in. It sounds like it actually *contains* the hills. The tune is nothing like any other version of the song, and unless you listen intently, you can barely tell it's English. At times, it sounds like the music of Tuvan cowboys in western Mongolia who sing their songs from the back of their throats. At other times, it sounds like the Muslim salesmen I would hear rolling their carts along the streets of Kabul, Afghanistan, in 2002, hawking plastic containers and roasted mutton during the months after the Taliban fell. The first time I heard Rossie sing it, I spent several minutes cueing and reviewing, making sure to my own satisfaction that it was actually the same song.

"Ah, way on down in New Orleans . . ." he sings. The song comes from the male rambler/drunkard point of view: The Rising Sun, he sings, is a place where "many poor boy has stretched his arm, and me, oh Lord, for one."

He also uses a variation of the verse that Ashley used:

> *Don't ever listen what another girl says*
> *let her hair be dark or brown.*
> *Say, unless she's on that old scaffold high*
> *sayin' now boys I can't come down.*

Holcomb never said where he learned "Rising Sun." He may not have cared; Cohen says he rarely recalled how he learned a piece. "Sometimes, you know, you feel like playing certain songs," Rossie told Cohen. "It's just according to how a man feels, to what he's got on his mind when he takes a notion to play one. That's the way I feel. It's just to satisfy me, to pass the time away. . . . I don't care if it suits anybody else or not, just so it's done me good. I'm getting it off me, see."

Rossie Holcomb's voice, guitar, and banjo express pain. Through his fingers and his vocal cords, the riffs and words carry the life he experienced, even if it is not direct. Once, in his early sessions with Cohen, he trailed off in the middle of the old standard "Man of Constant Sorrow" and couldn't finish. "He felt it was 'too true,' " Cohen reported, "too revealing of his own feelings about himself."

At the end of "House in New Orleans," after a roller-coaster ride in which Rossie takes his voice across the scale and screeches the familiar verses of ruin and melancholy, he introduces a stanza that has made a practice of migrating from song to song and is particularly associated with "In the Pines," another Holcomb standard. It is, perhaps, the most basic Appalachian musical image—that of the desolate road and the final choice between survival and death.

"Look up, look down that lonesome road. Hang down your head and cry," he sings. His voice cracks. "If you love me as I do you, you'll go with me or die."

In 1962, John Cohen took time away from the Ramblers to make a stark film called, appropriately, *The High Lonesome Sound.* It is impressionistic, filmed in high-contrast black and white, equal parts Walker Evans's documentary photographs and Rod Serling's *Twilight Zone.* It is a biography of some men and the land that shaped them—a land of railroad tracks and thick foliage and the beginnings of the modern world descending upon a twilight region unaccustomed to fast ways. Its unlikely star was none other than Roscoe Holcomb, unemployed construction worker and musician. "Life is hard here," Cohen says in his voice-over, "and music is a celebration."

What unfolds is a surprisingly intimate examination of the lives of a few people, Rossie among them, and how he and his music fit into their rural Kentucky community. It also offers up Rossie in his own words. He is far more articulate and insightful than I'd expect—a reflection of my own middle-class northeastern preconceptions.

The film makes a viewer today feel like a time-traveling astral projection, moving silently through the hills and looking in on lives. We see Rossie as he shows the bare bedroom of his bare house, illuminated by a bare lightbulb and a bare oil lamp. A banjo hangs on the wall. Nothing with a brand name is visible. We see him sitting on a front porch swing playing guitar and singing. Before him are the mountains, the beautiful mountains being tapped out by the mining that sustained so many eastern Kentucky families. Every home that Cohen lets us see, no matter how threadbare, has a front porch. Those porches were launching pads for the music that would travel so far and make such a difference. Where would Appalachian music have been without the front porch on which to play it?

As with any arresting image, it is contrast that makes the most impact. The scenes of miners emerging from the blackness of underground into the sunlight, smoking and chatting and going about their business, coupled with scenes of mountains sheared off by mining, say what the narration can't: that the way of life represented by the Roscoe Holcombs of the world is on its way out, traveling, inexorably, down the lonesome road to the horizon. Men like Holcomb are flies caught in a spider's web; indeed, Cohen finds a web and zooms in on it silently to characterize Rossie's existence.

Cohen's film is chockablock with the imagery of an encroaching modern world. In one scene, in the comparatively metropolitan county seat of Hazard, miners looking for work congregate on street corners and try to steer their lives toward some level of prosperity. In another, Bill Monroe and his immaculately dressed Bluegrass Boys—traditional, from today's vantage point, but the vanguard of modern in their hey-day—sing about John Henry on the steps of the courthouse in Hazard in front of an American flag. Their polished sound, an archetype of early bluegrass to most of us today, is everything that Rossie's personal and solitary music making isn't.

The most gripping image is one presented in passing—though, knowing Cohen, it is deliberate. The camera focuses on Rossie tilling the land that produces just enough to feed his family. Cohen pulls away, leaving Rossie in the background, and in the foreground a girl dances feverishly to Sam Cooke's "Twistin' the Night Away." A toddler, holding a tiny shovel, dances to the tune and walks toward a seemingly baffled Holcomb, his hoe in his hand.

"It is this music which joins them to the generations before," Cohen's voice-over says. "Their ballads and church songs are the old traditions from which the new music has come. Now hillbilly bluegrass and country rock and roll are heard alongside the old-time music, and are just as much a part of the mountains."

Rossie had moved around a bit in his earlier life; he hadn't been sealed up in one place all those years. During World War II, he picked vegetables in southern New Jersey until asthma forced him home. Later, he worked at Coney Island in Cincinnati. But because of his meeting with Cohen and the fame that the subsequent recordings gave him, Holcomb would end up traveling even farther from his Kentucky hills. He sang and played his guitar in New York and, eventually, Europe. He never got much money out of it, but he spread his songs and became a living archetype for folk purists.

Identical themes surface in another black-and-white film made by Cohen five years later. *The End of an Old Song* is even more melancholy than *High Lonesome*. It follows Dillard Chandler, an unaccompanied balladeer and lonely itinerant worker from Sodom, North Carolina, through his silent, sobering realization that the old times aren't coming back.

Chandler was a slight, taciturn yard worker in his late fifties when Cohen captured him on film in 1967 and 1968. The camera trains its lens on Chandler in two situations—in his bare-bones shack in the thick hills of northwestern North Carolina and in the comparatively modern city of Asheville, where he is a barely noticed interloper in a world that is moving far too fast for men like him. "I recall back instead of going forward," he says at one point. Cohen, in a title card, calls Chandler "one of the marginal men of the mountains" who happens to have a major talent singing ancient ballads as his father did before him.

Over and over, the film reminds us that Dillard Chandler is a stand-in for many Appalachian men, each scrabbling to survive and hang on to his tenuous spot in the world. "My mail address would be Route 3, and I ain't even got a box here or nothing. But I don't ever fool with any mail, and when I get mail I can't read it no-how," Chandler says. "There's a good many of 'em in the same shape that I'm in around here."

It is excruciating to watch as Chandler realizes, with no visible emotion, that he and his ballads are relics. "I feel sometimes that I'm sort of like that song: 'All my good times done passed and gone. All my good times are over.' " He gazes blankly into a diner jukebox that plays modern country and pop. At the very end, he's sitting at a booth in the diner with a woman, a beer, and a cigarette. The woman gets up to drop another dime and hear another record. It comes on—upbeat, sugary, polished, modern, everything that the Dillard Chandlers of the world and their music aren't. "T-O-B-A-C-C-O," the speakers blare, "yeah, that's the stuff for me." Chandler walks over, kisses the woman on the cheek, and dances awkwardly to the music that is making him obsolete.

Watching Chandler on film, you realize it was probably inevitable that the old songs would fade. Whether you call it cultural pollution or evolution, they became droplets in the ocean of mass culture. They were surrounded, and some were absorbed. They became part of something bigger. They still existed, still recognizable as part of the bigger sea, but as individual drops no longer. That's the message that Dillard Chandler and his unaccompanied ballads send us from a generation ago.

Months after I first saw *End of an Old Song,* I ordered Chandler's only album from Smithsonian Folkways. It contained an unaccompanied ballad called "Sport in New Orleans," which turned out, to my surprise, to be "Rising Sun." Does everybody sing this thing?

Like Rossie Holcomb, Chandler is dead and I cannot ask him about it. He picked up his repertoire, he told Cohen, by "just learning songs from somebody else that I've heard sing 'em. I ain't never took up the habit of singing new songs."

Chandler's version is significant because it is the most recent one I've found that came directly out of the folk tradition. It was clear from the lyrics that he hadn't picked them up from the Animals or any of the popular recorded versions that he never listened to anyway. The lyrics use the word *sport*—a quaint euphemism for prostitution or prostitute— making this version incontrovertibly about a whorehouse rather than a gambling den or a prison.

> *There was a sport in New Orleans*
> *they call the Rising Sun*
> *She's broke a heart of many poor boy*
> *and mine, oh God, for one.*

The rest of this abbreviated version is a hodgepodge of familiar lyrics. But it shows that as late as 1968, there were still musicians who sang "Rising Sun" with no visible influences from the "outside" world, where our song's post-Animals trajectory was increasing and turning it into a globally recognizable piece.

The earlier movie, *The High Lonesome Sound,* ends with Roscoe Holcomb singing a cappella. His instrument is his voice, and it plays like an insistent guitar string as the credits roll. You are left with the feeling that things are possible, even amid the hardship—that this is being piped out to us from deep in The Village, a pocket of the world where spells can still be cast, where things that can't happen do happen. Where, despite the unremitting pressure of the modern and the disposable, the eternal can still hide safely.

Today Rossie Holcomb is nearly three decades dead, and John Cohen is an old man, though his eyes still look as young as they did when he cut those first songs with the Ramblers in the 1950s. He has managed to blend his New York roots with his Appalachian affections: He lives on a lush patch of land in a place called Putnam Valley an hour outside of Manhattan, which feels light-years away. Walk up Cohen's driveway toward the pond at the back of his property, and within a few steps you could easily conclude you are in the middle of the Kentucky hills. Even his home, though stacked with books and records and bedecked with a modern stereo system and computer, somehow feels as if it's turned its back on the millennium.

Cohen thinks often of Holcomb—the man who he says had "one foot in the blues and one foot in the old Baptist singing"—and wonders how they affected each other's lives. "Here's the disquieting thing," Cohen tells me as we walk around his pond in the sun. "Would Roscoe Holcomb exist if I hadn't thought him up? He speaks for me. He embodies what I'm trying to say. And if people hear him, I don't have to say it."

Speaking, and singing, through other people. There is wisdom in that notion. It's what keeps "Rising Sun" moving around. Each person passes it to the next, and each singer builds on the words and notes of the previous one. In the last century, recorded sound has helped that notion multiply. Rossie Holcomb the man existed, of course. Yet in one odd cultural way, Rossie Holcomb the maker of music that transcends generations didn't exist until Cohen found him, recorded him, and made us able to hear his music. Better to say that John Cohen *amplified* Roscoe.

I can't help but wonder: What of all the Roscoe Holcombs who don't exist because no one found them? What of all those who are silent because no machines captured their words and their songs before they vanished from the Earth? I don't mean to suggest that an Appalachian singer who elevates only his family or his community with his music is irrelevant unless an educated easterner records him. But how many songs died with the men and women who sang them because the music, instead of being captured by a recorder, simply drifted into the ether and disappeared?

In 2001, while my wife and I were on our song-seeking honeymoon, we walked into a bar in Nashville called Jim and Layla's Bluegrass Inn. We entered because it was the only one into which we poked our heads and did not hear someone singing a song about a pickup truck, a dead dog, or a cheating heart. In Nashville, unsurprisingly, country music clichés are everywhere.

The Bluegrass Inn on that day was cool, dark, almost empty. A five-piece string band called Mixt Company was enthusiastically playing old-time bluegrass—including an insolent women's prison song about "turning big rocks into small rocks." The front woman, a fiery redhead, mentioned something about her people back in Hazard, Kentucky. After their set, I went up to her.

"Did I hear you say Hazard up there?" I asked. The woman, who identified herself as Virginia Lee, nodded. Then I asked her: "Have you ever heard of Roscoe Holcomb?"

The answer she gave surprised me into silence.

"My daddy was a Holcomb," she replied, pronouncing it Halcomb. "Roscoe Holcomb was my uncle."

Suddenly, with no warning and just a few minutes of conversation, we became Virginia Lee's close friends—and would, it turned out, remain that way for years. She was enthusiastic about the old songs and adamant about passing them to her grown children; one, Letitia, a girl with a haunting, angelic voice, was in the band. So was Virginia's husband, David Blood, who grew up in Philadelphia but became Appalachian by transplant, musical inclination, and marriage. She gave me her number, and we agreed to talk music soon.

That is the backstory that, ten weeks later, leads us to Slemp, Kentucky. Virginia—her entire family calls her Monkey, and she insists we do as well—wants to introduce us to her people and her music, so we are invited to the family's summer pig roast. But I get the feeling something else is at play, too: I think Monkey wants us, as urban northeasterners, to see that she and her people have transcended the misery and pain that defined her childhood in the hills. "I hate the word *hillbilly*," Monkey hisses during one of the few times I see her genuinely angry. "It's an insult, and it has no place being used."

I am struck by Monkey in a way that no one else has ever affected me. Here is a woman who lived through some of the darkest experiences that the Southern Highlands can dish out, and she emerged tempered by her crucible into one of the most caring human beings I have ever met. "If anyone had told me just how poor we were, I wouldn't have believed," goes a verse in one of her songs. In her music and in her life, Monkey balances a musician's emotional intensity with the pragmatism that daily life requires. The result is someone who lives with her eyes open, ready for good things to happen—not because they always have, but because she feels that by persevering and doing the right thing and playing music with passion, she can somehow will goodness into existence.

To get to the pig roast, we meet Monkey and David on a July Saturday morning in a Wal-Mart parking lot in Hazard. This is a couple dozen miles away from our destination, which is her uncle Kermit Asher's house in a place called Beehive Hollow. Virginia insists we follow her there in our rental car; we'd get lost, she says—and besides, outsiders poking around in the hollers aren't always welcomed. She is smiling, but I detect a seriousness beneath it.

We make our way south on State Route 7, a serpentine two-lane that, while completely rural, is the only main road through southern Perry County. We pass through the dust speck that is Daisy and pull into an equally tiny town called Slemp, where we finally turn onto Beehive Hollow Road, a lush, winding path that meanders into the woods at the foot of Beehive Mountain. This is the home place of Virginia's people—the Ashers and the Halcombs, as they spell the surname.

We pull into a driveway that traverses the vast lawn of a well-kept ranch house that belongs to Uncle Kermit and his family. It is late morning, and the lawn is already bustling with Halcombs, Ashers, and their guests—three dozen people in all. Children run around the lawn, playing with each other and with a scattering of barnyard tabby cats with abbreviated tails. A few folks are gathered around an aging man in red suspenders and a white T-shirt that says "Lee Sexton," the name of the popular old-time musician that John Cohen had seen play in that roadhouse in the late 1950s. The man is alternating between a banjo and a fiddle as he sings the old standard, "Whoa, Mule!"

"Who's the guy with the Lee Sexton T-shirt?" I ask Monkey.

"Lee Sexton," she deadpans.

She and David approach him, watch for a few seconds, then pull out their instruments—Monkey her guitar, David his mandolin—and join in. A front lawn jam session.

"Can you play a fiddle?" Sexton says to David.

"Nope."

"Bet you can," Sexton says. "Never met a mandolin player can't play a fiddle."

"You met me now." David is grinning.

Various family members and friends come up, dance, sing, and wander away into other conversations. We hear life stories, condensed: the Vietnam vet, the miner, the woman on her fourth marriage. As noon arrives, an enormous grill shaped like a charred Quonset hut is beginning to belch forth smoke. Melissa and I walk over for a closer look, and the man tending it pulls it open. Inside are the chops, loins, and various other parts of what must be at least three well-fed pigs. The grill master takes a swig of his Coke, then pours some over the pig meat. It hisses appealingly. "Coca-Cola," he says. "Can't barbecue without it."

Monkey walks up with an elderly man wearing a newsboy's cap and striped suspenders over a striped shirt. When he smiles, he reveals two gold bicuspids. She introduces him as Fess Halcomb, one of the family patriarchs, who lives over the ridge in Little Leatherwood Hollow. Fess is seventy-six, retired from a mine foreman's job after twenty-six years at Blue Diamond Coal Company. In between mining shifts, he built houses in the nearby hollers—thirteen in all, including his own. He is also a fiery Church of God preacher whose sermons are known to get the tears flowing.

"So it's Halcomb. Not Holcomb?" I ask.

"We only had one spell it Holcomb," he says, referring to Rossie. "His marketers got it wrong."

I'm still trying to figure out exactly who's related to whom and how. Roscoe Holcomb was not, as it were, Monkey's uncle—at least not technically. Fess Halcomb thinks for a few moments, then offers that Rossie was Fess's dad's second cousin. This clears things up only a bit. Fess remembers Roscoe as tall and lanky, with a little house that he describes as "over in Cornettsville," even though Cornettsville is less than four miles away.

I try to picture this holler in the 1950s, when John Cohen visited the area and heard Rossie sing. The images in my head are, of course, black and white, because they are conjured from Cohen's film. But the color-drenched scene around me, the lush greens of the brush and trees and the deep yellows of the shining sun, suggest nothing dark or desolate on this day. I can understand why Rossie was reluctant to leave this place and go to the cities to sing his songs; there is something utterly comforting about it. Spiritual, even.

Fess Halcomb couldn't be more welcoming and friendly, but there is a wariness about him as he talks to the earring-wearing, notebook-wielding, New-York-rental-car-driving writer who is me. It's obvious he is sensitive about how Appalachians have been portrayed in the mass media. Understandably so: The classic image of the "hillbilly"—undereducated, inbred, playing the fool—is a persistent one in American culture.

A few years ago, J. W. Williamson of Appalachian State University in North Carolina wrote an entire book on that image called *Hillbillyland: What the Movies Did to the Mountains and What the Mountains Did to the Movies*. In it, he explored the dual nature of the hillbilly myth—a laughable, pitiable figure on one hand (*The Beverly Hillbillies*) and a menacing, backwoods presence on the other (*Deliverance*). "The distance between the hillbilly as comedy and the hillbilly as threat is amazingly short," Williamson lamented. Many Appalachian performers—from the Callahan Brothers, at one point in their career, all the way to some of the sketches on *Hee Haw*—did their region no favors by adding vaude-villian comedy into the mix beginning in the 1930s and 1940s. In such acts, rural singers, looking to lend texture to their acts, helped to develop a modern gap-toothed, moonshine-swilling, rubbery-faced caricature that suggested all hill folks were dullards.

Which is, of course, utter bullshit. When I worked in West Virginia in my twenties, I spent some time with the highly humorous and, sadly, now deceased Jim Comstock, who edited a popular, iconoclastic newspaper called *The West Virginia Hillbilly* ("A newspaper for people who can't read, edited by an editor who can't write"). Comstock, famed for his tall tales, once told me a joke about a young man from the hills who came across a traveling salesman near a crossroads.

"Hey, kid," said the salesman, trying to show how stupid the boy was, "how far is it a mile or so up the road?"

"Well," replied the boy, "I reckon it's about fifty times as long as a fool, so you better lay down and start measuring."

Such humor was a backlash; Comstock was reclaiming some of the bite from the ugly urban dog that had been nipping at Appalachia's heels. A lot of the sting remains, though, as Fess Halcomb is quick to point out. "We've been classified," he says. "We had a Kennedy girl come down here, and she degraded mountain people just about worse than anybody ever."

He's talking about *American Hollow,* an acclaimed 1999 documentary by Rory Kennedy, RFK's daughter, that some said perpetuated Appalachian stereotypes. "I'll drop a thought in your mind," Fess Halcomb says to me. "I've never seen a man go to bed hungry here when another man has food. I've never seen a man sleep at the side of the road here. . . . A lot of our people aren't educated, and they come in here and go right to the slums."

He finishes up: "Give us the good with the bad."

Fair enough. It's hard to see anything that's bad from the vantage point of the Halcomb-Asher family pig roast. Because Monkey knows why I have come, she turns the conversation to Rossie Holcomb and his music. Memories start emerging of the man, of the songs he sang—and of "Rising Sun."

"I don't know who made it or how it came about. It just fit him," Fess Halcomb says of Rossie. "Roscoe, he's the only fellow I ever heard sing it. It was important to him. Why, I don't know." Ed Hunter had told me almost the exact same thing about Georgia Turner.

"He never was a man who would fuss and fight," Fess says of Rossie. "He had a drinking problem—not a gambling problem, but a drinking problem. He'd have some to drink, and everybody loved him. . . . You talk about a man who could dance, buddy." He smiles. "His voice, he had a voice that would break glass. We'd go work all day and then have dances—bean stringing, corn hoeing. We'd clear out all the furniture and dance. Roscoe played the banjo for us."

As we talk, Kermit Asher approaches. Not surprising, since we and the pig roast are on his lawn. "This is Uncle Kermit," Monkey says. Fess Halcomb married Kermit Asher's sister in 1958, and the two have been co-patriarchs ever since. Their clans account for much of the population of Beehive Hollow. "Roscoe was with 'House of the Rising

Sun' kind of like Bill Monroe was with 'Muleskinner Blues,' " Kermit says.

Monkey has been talking up Uncle Kermit, saying he knew Rossie way back, so I am excited to ask him if he knows where "Rising Sun" came from. He doesn't, alas. But he remembers a night in 1935 when he first moved to what probably will never be called the Daisy-Slemp metropolitan area. He had gone to a square dance because he had nothing else to do, and "there was Rossie. It was pitch-black, he's walking up the road playing the banjo." Sounds like the day John Cohen first met him.

I have brought my laptop, which contains my absurd assortment of digitized versions of "House of the Rising Sun." I beckon Fess and Kermit up to the trunk of our rented Mitsubishi Mirage, get out the laptop and boot it up. They stand there, looking . . . not uncomfortable, but tentative. The afternoon rain hasn't come yet, and the bright sun makes the laptop screen difficult to see. I launch Musicmatch and begin to play: Holcomb, Roscoe. "House in New Orleans."

The two men stare at my computer as if it's human, as if looking away from the performance would be impolite. As if somehow, logic be damned, it's *him* in there—it's Rossie, singing again, echoing through trees reforested after years of strip mining, reaching into falsetto as he sings about the house in New Orleans where many poor boy has stretched his arm. And who's to say it isn't him in there? Couldn't there be a tiny part of the essence that was Roscoe Holcomb trapped inside my machine—a *deus ex machina* in the most literal of senses? "It's like he's here, walking up this driveway," Fess says. Kermit says nothing. But he's smiling.

We spend the rest of the day enjoying exactly what people who live around here enjoy—activities that relate to, or at least evoke, the magnificent natural world around us. We go four-wheeling into the hills at breakneck speeds. We traverse narrow roads named for real people and real landmarks that our hosts remember. In the woods, it is so quiet that I can't help but wonder if folks here made music simply to combat the silence.

We eat lots of Coke-saturated barbecue, talk of families that lived here and there, listen to a constant stream of music as handmade as the coleslaw that accompanies the pork. We meet various family members, and each accepts us as if our last name, too, was Halcomb. The Vietnam vet, a man named Rick who is related to someone or other, tells me of his idea for a T-shirt. It would feature the Grim Reaper playing a guitar, and it would say, "God has the best band." Then he picks up his Fender Strat and, without an amp, plays me the opening chords of the Animals' version. At one point, Melissa is in the kitchen with some Asher and Halcomb women and emerges with Monkey, grinning. She had been offered, somewhat furtively, moonshine from a jar. It burned, she said. She felt like she had been accepted.

Outside, Fess Halcomb is telling me about Rossie and the difficult life he led. "He never got nothing out of his music," Fess Halcomb says of his cousin. But I must disagree. When you listen to Roscoe Holcomb sing, you can hear the exuberance. Oh, it's hidden pretty well in lyrics of misery and guitar and banjo riffs saturated with old pains. But this was a man who needed to make music. What's more, the ability to echo across generations and sing to your friends and their progeny long after your death—because you sang well enough for someone to record you and sell it—is priceless.

As the sun sinks and the mist settles over the mountains behind Uncle Kermit's house, Melissa and I bid Monkey and her family farewell and drive back toward Hazard by ourselves. We stop at a roadside Long John Silver's, and as we order our chicken planks, John Cougar Mellencamp comes on the radio with a song from my high school years that I never thought much about. Now, although it's more poppy than what we've been hearing, it seems to summarize the day.

> *I was born in a small town*
> *and I can breathe in a small town.*
> *Gonna die in a small town*
> *and that's probably where they'll bury me.*

A few minutes later, we pass a Sunoco station. There is a huge sign posted in its window with a message, a corporate slogan.

"Follow the Sun," it says.

SPRINGFIELD, MISSOURI

Stay in the late 1950s, but now we sweep west for a few moments—through Nashville (listen for the guitar twangs of Chet Atkins), across the Mississippi River, into the woods of northwestern Arkansas and southwestern Missouri—the Ozark Mountains, so much like the Appalachians in their flavor, their people, and their song-marinating isolation. Some six hundred miles from where Rossie Holcomb spent his life and sang his songs, a man named Max Hunter was discovering and refining what would become his life's work.

Hunter was a traveling salesman in his late thirties who sold refrigeration products from his home base in Springfield, Missouri. His route, a 150-mile loop that he ran every four weeks, took him in and out of backwoods and mountain towns across the insulated Ozarks, a region just as storied—and, sadly, just as denigrated—as the Appalachian hills we've left behind.

Hunter's peregrinations read like a gazetteer of The Village's most tucked-away corners. His stops included places like Hog's Scald Holler, Hemmed-in Holler, Skunk Holler, Lost Valley, and Eureka Springs. Like many Ozarkers, Hunter's family had moved west from the Appalachians in the nineteenth century, a migration from one set of mountains to another that carried the culture of eastern Tennessee, eastern Kentucky, and western North Carolina into an entirely new region.

In 1956, as his musical interests grew, Hunter got to know Vance Randolph, the Ozarks' premier folklorist, and Randolph's eventual wife, Mary Celestia Parler, who taught at the University of Arkansas in Fayetteville, in the heart of the region. Randolph, who had been collecting northwestern Arkansas's traditions since before World War I, was the author of a seminal four-volume collection published in the late 1950s called *Ozark Folksongs*. He had been collecting in the field for decades by then, not only on his own but also for the Federal Writers' Project in Missouri and, in the early 1940s, for Alan Lomax as a Library of Congress field worker.

The Lomax approach to collected songs, though, was not for Randolph. He was suspicious of popularization and felt he should protest what educated easterners were doing to traditional mountain culture. He called 'em "Brooklyn hillbillies" and insisted that they "wouldn't know a folk tune if they met it in the middle of Broadway."

(Randolph collected folklore as well as songs. His personal papers include such gems as a snippet entitled "To Cook Eels." One of the no-nonsense instructions for this activity is rendered as "cut up the goddam eel and season it.")

Randolph frequently ran into trouble with the songs he collected because they were honest, which meant they were often in conflict with the aesthetics of the age. Most songs about vice—even those warning against the evils of it—were an impossible sell. Even as he was compiling *Ozark Folksongs,* Randolph held out hope that he could publish a volume of bawdy songs once the four-volume set established his credentials. That wasn't to be; the State Historical Society of Missouri, Randolph's sponsor, said no. Randolph's problems with such material "never ended in his lifetime," wrote G. Legman, who edited parts of his work.

Still, Randolph recognized the importance of such songs, and he continued to collect and compile them through his life. That led, after he died, to the 1992 *Roll Me in Your Arms: "Unprintable" Ozark Folksongs and Folklore,* edited by Legman. Published twelve years after Randolph's death, it included sexual material of all stripes—including a rather lengthy section on "Rising Sun."

It turns out Randolph had turned up versions of our song that, according to his informants, dated to the beginning of the twentieth century, almost as early as the one that Clarence Ashley had learned from his grandparents. The Ozark versions possessed one key difference, though: some of them were a lot dirtier.

The folks who sang those versions for Randolph were, understandably, reluctant to have their names appear in print and attached to such improper songs. Or perhaps Randolph decided to protect them. Either way, he recorded their identities using only initials and towns, so their descendants are impossible to track.

One version came from a woman identified only by her location— Benton County, an area of northwestern Arkansas near the Missouri border that is now home to the global headquarters of Wal-Mart. On November 6, 1949, she sang a variant of "Rising Sun" to Randolph that she said she had heard her brothers sing in about 1920. This version is starkly different, rich with details that make it obviously about a bordello. What's more, the woman told Randolph that there were additional "nasty" verses that she couldn't (or wouldn't) remember.

Hers starts and ends with the classic "There is a house in New Orleans . . ." verse. But between those bookends sit three more verses—two entirely new to us, one a very different take on the warning verse—that bring "House of the Rising Sun" into focus like no other version.

Beware the red light out in front
An' the pictures on the wall,
An' yellow gals dressed in purple shoes
Without no clothes at all.

Shun the red light an' flowin' bowl,
Beware of too much drink,
Them whores will take an' lead you on
To hell's eternal brink.

Tell brother Jim at home alone
Bad company to shun,
Or it will surely lead him on
To do what I have done.

Yellow gals? Were these Asians? Could the Rising Sun be linked to Japan, the nation whose very name, in its native language, actually means rising sun? Or do the lyrics refer to a little-known, archaic American definition of "yellow"—slang for mulattos or partially black women? And "hell's eternal brink"? This implies syphilis or gonorrhea. The intriguing verses above leave no doubt about the subject that the singer intends to convey, and it's not a gambling hall or a prison. I suspect that not only the immorality implied in the phrase "without no clothes at all" but the explicit use of the word "whore" helped this version disappear. But I wonder, too, whether the very use of specifics is to blame for isolating this version. Here, details—a red light, a flowing bowl, yellow gals in purple shoes, a brother named Jim—are conveyed much more cinematically than in the typical version of "Rising Sun." And if the haziness of the narrative that we usually see—a vision blurry enough to be virtually anything imaginable in the pantheon of sin—is replaced by specifics, perhaps the song becomes less effective as a warning. Perhaps too many details spoil our song's broad appeal.

Barely four months later and fifty miles north, in the rough-and-tumble mining town of Joplin, Missouri, a man identified as Mr. R.S. sang a fragment for Randolph on March 19, 1950. He told Randolph that "similar verses were sung by miners around Joplin as long ago as 1905." If true, that's one of the earliest references to the song existing in the folk tradition anywhere.

> *There is a house in New Orleans*
> *They call it the Rising Sun,*
> *An' when you want your pecker spoilt*
> *That's where you get it done.*
>
> *They drink all day an' fuck all night*
> *Until your money's gone;*
> *They kick your ass out in the street*
> *When the second shift comes on . . .*

A note, presumably written by Legman, posits that these are the "nasty" verses that the woman in Benton County, Arkansas, could not remember. That's unlikely. Mr. R.S.'s rendition tackles "Rising Sun" from an entirely different perspective. It's a man-as-whorehouse-patron version that describes dispassionately, sarcastically, even enthusiastically, the workings of a bordello. Sure, there's a bit of grousing about the price and the lack of loyalty by the hookers, but there's little lament here save annoyance that when the money runs out, so do the girls. The common "don't do what I have done" message would be highly out of place in this variation; no warning against such activities, whether as provider or consumer, is implicit with Mr. R.S. I picture coal miners taking a lunch break between shifts in the dark underground tunnels near Joplin, singing about the Rising Sun and laughing uproariously, knowing it's the kind of tune that probably wouldn't go over too well outside the mine shaft.

A year later, in 1951, Randolph encountered one more version from a Mrs. D.S. in Fort Smith, Arkansas. It's just a few verse fragments from the familiar lament—so familiar that it's possible this woman didn't plunder the song from the Arkansas folk tradition at all but instead was repeating it from a Guthrie or Acuff recording. It's worth mentioning only because of the woman's view of the song she was performing. "She would not sing it into a tape recorder," the authors wrote, "as she said she had heard there was a law against singing songs about 'bad houses.'"

The northwestern corner of Arkansas and southwestern Missouri, where Randolph encountered these "Rising Sun" offshoots, is intriguingly near Baxter Springs, which is just a few miles across the Missouri border into Kansas and barely fifteen miles from Joplin. Baxter Springs, you'll recall, is the rough-and-tumble prairie town where Ray Bohanan of Sevierville, Tennessee, placed the Rising Sun in a version collected in 1929 ("There's a girl in Baxter Springs . . .). Mentions of Baxter Springs appear nowhere else in the history of our song, but to have it just sitting there, so near to other places where the Rising Sun was entrenched in the folk tradition, stretches the fabric of coincidence.

To dip into Ozark lore is to realize quickly that it's a natural place for "Rising Sun" to have lurked. A solid dose of dark-holler loneliness, coupled with new experiences in new mountains, had created a corpus of folklore not unlike, yet distinct from, that of upper Appalachia several hundred miles east. Other songs collected by Randolph, in fact, contain fragments that mirror "Rising Sun" lyrics. One, a lament that he took down in 1941 from Charles Ingenthron of Walnut Shade, Missouri, was called "I'll Never Get Drunk Any More." It featured the following "Rising Sun"–like lyric:

> *Oh once I had a fortune*
> *All locked up in a trunk,*
> *I lost it all in a gambling hall*
> *One night when I got drunk.*

Another the same year from Gladys McCarty of Farmington, Arkansas, contained material strikingly similar to part of "Rising Sun":

> *Oh if I had a listened to what mama said*
> *I would not have been here today*
> *A-lyin' around this old jail house*
> *A-weeping my sweet life away.*

And Hunter, late in the 1960s, would collect a song called "The Saw Mill Boy" from a woman named Kay Ohrlin of Mountain View,

Arkansas, which in tune and material is unrelated to "Rising Sun" yet contains doppelgangers of two of its verses:

> *Go fill th' glasses to th' rim*
> *Go pass them early around*
> *We'll drink good luck to th' saw mill boy*
> *Who works ten hours around.*

And:

> *The only time that he's satisfied*
> *Is when he's on a drunk*
> *An' all he has in this whole wide world*
> *Is a suitcase or a trunk.*

"Rising Sun"–related verses have popped up in other compositions—the platform/train verse and the suitcase/trunk reference most commonly. In fact, every verse in Alan Lomax's composite version of "Rising Sun" has appeared elsewhere, with two notable exceptions: the "my mother was a tailor" verse and the introductory "There is a house" that defines the song. The shared lyrics make it even likelier that our song coagulated from pieces of other songs in the second half of the nineteenth century.

Randolph's future wife, Mary Celestia Parler, became his protégée after she came to Arkansas in 1948 to collect mountain ballads. She loved the irony of folklore's presence in an increasingly modern culture. Once she told an interviewer: "It always strikes me as being humorous when someone turns off a program being televised from New York to sing a song for me that's been all but forgotten by most of the world."

Soon Parler, too, was sending batches of students out from the sprawling university campus in Fayetteville to interview aging Ozarkers and preserve their stories for a modern age. This moment—the end of the Eisenhower era and the dawn of the 1960s—was pivotal in developing connections between young university students and the older parts of the culture around them, and courses like Parler's were petri dishes for the creativity fueling the rising folk revival.

Parler herself found a version of "Rising Sun" in the folk tradition in 1958. It was collected as "House in New Orleans" by one of her assistants, apparently a student, named Billie Lou Ratliff, from a smooth-voiced man named L. D. (Jack) Franklin in Dutton, Arkansas, not far from where Burnett learned many of his songs. The text seems straight from the Lomax tradition, with a couple of minor variations. There's no evidence he had heard any commercial versions, but neither is there any indication of where Franklin might have learned it. His rendition got filed away in the University of Arkansas Library.

While not an academic, Max Hunter shared with his University of Arkansas friends a passion for the region's folklore. He had grown up singing at the dinner table, picking up old folk songs from his mother, and it stayed with him. He married a woman whose aunts were known for orchestrating one of the earlier incarnations of the all-request hour. "When the telephone began to be used," Hunter recounted, "my father-in-law can tell how two of his sisters used to crank the handle and all the people who were on their line would listen in. The sisters would sing into the mouthpiece and the neighbors would listen over their own phones. If the neighbors had a favorite song they would request it."

Hunter's line of work and its challenges also pushed him toward music. During the early part of his sales career, he would hole up in motel rooms at night, alone, singing and playing his guitar. "People who don't travel day in and day out just don't know how lonesome a motel can get," he told an interviewer in 1979.

Before long, Hunter realized that he had another calling very different from selling refrigeration products—an abiding interest in his fellow Ozarkers and their music and culture. His regular sales route offered him access that most songcatchers would envy: He could establish relationships with people on repeat visits and win their trust gradually; if one attempt at capturing a song didn't pan out, he could try again the next time his route brought him through town.

Hunter's field work contained an elegant symmetry. The traveling salesman is an American archetype, yet the Willy Lomans of the land are cast in our popular culture as leading lives of quiet desperation. They spend much of their lives apart from their families, on the road in anonymous hotels, trying to develop connections that will help them sell just one more widget. Rarely does the archetype see them capturing something eternal from the communities they canvass. Hunter was the opposite of the anonymous suit who entered a town and built only the relationships he needed to sell his wares. He wanted to know the people in these communities, to understand their lives and the way they told their stories. He was sowing enthusiasm—not merely for refrigerators but for folks' own culture, too.

Hunter began to carry a recorder in his car, and for most of the thirteen years between 1957 and 1970, he filled reel-to-reel tapes with the sounds of aging Ozarkers singing and telling stories. He'd do his sales job during the day and visit singers in the evening in their homes and their yards, at filling stations and country stores. He'd come by after dinner, when they'd be most likely to be primed to perform. He was a purist, and he could be picky. If an Ozarker sang a song that contained verses from outside the region, he'd purge it from his tape.

Unlike collectors such as Alan Lomax, Hunter considered song composites to be a betrayal of tradition. He wrote 'em down the way he heard 'em. "No one," he said, "has a right to change a person's speech." Some things he never preserved at all; he considered his friendships with his informants too important to betray their trust (economics may have been a motivator, too; some of them, probably, were his clients).

Hunter made a habit of lecturing about his collecting at local clubs and meetings around the region, and he wasn't shy about telling audiences where he stood. He followed Vance Randolph's creed strictly: When you ask someone to sing into your recorder, realize that they're doing *you* a favor, not the other way around. Collect the entire person, he'd say, not just the song. Above all, he preached respect for hill people, who he believed were getting a bad rap in the media. "Don't try to imitate what you think these people might be wearing," he said in one speech. "You just wear something clean, something comfortable, and let them wear what they want to. Don't put on overalls and gingham dresses and things like that because you think you are going to see a hillbilly. He's liable to fool you and show up in a suit."

Hunter's collecting tapered off in 1970. He was reaching his fifties, and many of the oldest musicians who sang for him had died. But his research continued, sporadically, through the decade. By the time he was done, he had recorded more than twenty-two hundred songs and nearly fifteen hours of old stories collected from across southwestern

Missouri and northwestern Arkansas. He had "songs written on tablet paper, notebook paper, backs of calendars, posters, wallpaper, and anything that was handy and useable."

Contained in his collection was everything from Elizabethan-era English ballads to songs about specific events that happened in the Ozarks. There were renditions of old Appalachian tunes like "In the Pines," several variants of the fabled ballad "Barbara Allen," and many examples of the musical tales that gave The Village its identity—"Pretty Polly," "Little Omie," "Frankie and Johnny," and "Charles Guiteau." I even found "Dunderbeck," a variation of the cheerfully gruesome song called "Johnny Verbeck" that my father sang to me about a butcher whose wife had a nightmare and, sleepwalking, ground him up in his own sausage machine. *She gave the crank a heckuva yank, and Johnny Verbeck was meat.*

My favorite nugget in the Hunter collection, though, is a ditty called "John Thompson's Dog" that he collected in 1959 from Fred High, the only resident of High, Arkansas:

> *I'll sing you a song*
> *it ain't much long*
> *it's in th' case of murder.*
> *John Thompson's dog*
> *he bit my frog*
> *an' th' song don't go no furder.*

Hunter collected sixteen songs from a man named William Harrison Burnett, who went by his middle name. He was a night watchman at the University of Arkansas in Fayetteville, so he and his music were readily accessible to Hunter, who would probably have met him through Randolph and Parler.

Burnett had already contributed some of his knowledge to the term papers Parler's folklore students were writing. He sang for Parler as early as 1954, a tune called "The Arkansas Song." In a 1958 class project, a Parler student named Doyle Fulmer has pasted in a snapshot of Burnett and his wife sitting on their front porch swing and, in a caption, calls him " 'Red' the singing night watchman."

On August 18, 1960, Hunter, accompanied by Parler, visited Burnett in Fayetteville. It was a good opportunity for Hunter, who already was aware of Burnett's singing ability and repertoire. "I believe Harrison is one of the finest singers I have ever visited and collected from. . . . Harrison has a quality that you very, very seldom run into," Hunter said on one of the tapes. "Harrison has been written up in the various papers, so others not too well hep on what's going on realize there is a quality here that is hard to find and should be preserved."

Burnett sang a passel of songs for Hunter that day. Among them, delivered in a sad, almost moaning voice, was "Rising Sun," which he sang a cappella. Though the words he used are familiar to us, they are punctuated by a less common verse about the travails of the rambling man and an ending verse that had surfaced nowhere else.

Burnett said nothing about the history of the song—or, at least, he didn't while Hunter's recorder was rolling. Let's jump to a scene two years ahead, also in Fayetteville, when collector Sandy Paton stopped by and Burnett sang "Rising Sun" again in an almost identical way—apparently directly out of a songbook, and this time with a bit of background afterward.

Burnett's version never mentions New Orleans. Instead, it begins, "There is a house in yondos town . . ." In the middle of the song, Burnett offers this verse:

> *Oh mama, oh mama, what makes you treat*
> *that ramblin' gambler so?*
> *I'd rather be that rambling man*
> *than anyone else I know.*

Then comes Burnett's final verse, an exhortation for kindness toward a man that is living on the fringes:

> *Dear friends take care of that rambling man*
> *to him be nice and kind*
> *you'll never know what trials you'll meet*
> *you may travel the same old line.*

There is a silence for a moment after Burnett finishes. Then Paton speaks. "You didn't have that last verse written down there, did you?" he asks.

"That's my version," Burnett says.

"You wrote that last verse yourself?"

"That's my verse that I put in there."

"Where did you say you learned it?"

"Oh, I learned that, ah, from . . . let's see, I forget just who that was that sung that song," Burnett says.

"Where was it?"

"It was back here on the hill from Wesley, back there." Wesley sits about fifteen miles east of Fayetteville, at the intersection of state routes 74 and 295 in northwestern Arkansas. It's a place where Burnett spent many of his younger years doing odd jobs.

Paton is insistent. "When, about?"

"Oh, it's been about nineteen, twenty years ago," Burnett says. That means he learned it around 1940, just three years after Alan Lomax recorded Georgia Turner in Middlesboro, but before wide distribution of any of the early versions from Guthrie, White, and Lead Belly.

"Is that right?" Paton says. "You just heard it one time?"

"I just heard it one time." Burnett snaps his fingers to indicate how quickly he learned it. "That's all I heard it."

Burnett's version is unusual in its lack of a New Orleans mention. It keeps the location of the Rising Sun quite generic—"yondos town," using a variant of the word "yonder" that was heard often in the Ozarks. It has all of the images that commonly bind the song together into its fuzzy narrative: the warning verse, this time aimed at the singer's youngest brother; the toast to the rambling man, this time an exhortation to "drink a health"; the suitcase and trunk image, followed by the suggestion of alcohol troubles.

And, finally, Burnett's own verse tacked onto the end, something quite gentle to leaven a song that has spent much of its life bathed in darkness. In this version, because of his improvised lines, there is hope for the next guy—hope that goes beyond a *pro forma* ballad-style warning to a younger brother or sister. There's always been that hint in "Rising Sun" that this could happen to you, too, but in Harrison Burnett's hands it's said explicitly. And here's a way out, too: Be nice to the rambler, the gambler, the rounder. You never know what trials you'll meet, after all. You may travel the same old line.

On February 9, 1960, Hunter drove into the small but vaguely bohemian town of Eureka Springs, Arkansas, and stopped by a tavern run by a barkeeper named Paul Edy. Going inside, he saw that a seventy-year-old man named Joe Walker was there. Walker was a farmer who lived with his wife, Ruth Ann, on a hillside outside Berryville, a handful of miles east of Eureka Springs on U.S. 62 (Berryville, it's worth noting, has, at its edge, the Sunrise Motel).

Though Hunter knew Walker as a man who could belt out a worthwhile song or two, the pair's previous encounter took place at a time when Walker was, in Hunter's words, "a little bit too inebriated to keep his words distinguished." This evening showed more promise, so Hunter decided to go retrieve his recorder and bring it back, in hopes the second attempt will be more fruitful. "Some of the songs that Joe knows, if I can get him to sing, are pretty bawdy," Hunter said into his recorder before the session, "so we'll see what happens."

People in the tavern are laughing and talking and a radio is playing as Hunter turns on his recorder and Walker begins to tell stories and sing songs. It definitely sounds as if he's a little lit. A woman named Eileen, who works in the bar, is helping Hunter coax Walker to sing more, more, more. He demurs, saying they're just songs "nobody cares for." But she keeps saying, "How'd this go?" "How'd that one go?" Walker relents: He sings a song called "The Whore Set in the Parlor." Eventually, he gets to a song that Hunter will transcribe simply as "The Rising Sun."

"Let's see," Walker says. Someone is whistling in the background. Voices are encouraging him: Go ahead! Go ahead! "It's not going to be what you think it is," Walker says. "You got that goddamn thing going?" he asks Hunter. Then he begins.

Th' whore house bells are ringing
an' a man stood in th' door
all day long with a big hard-on
tryin' to fuck a whore.
She had a dark an' rolling eye
she belonged to th' roguish crew . . .

Well, I rustled her, I tustled her
till I got her heart's content
I slipped five dollars in her hand
an' off t' bed we went.

She had a dark an' rolling eye
she belonged to th' roguish crew . . .

Well, I teased her, I tumbled her
till I got my heart's desire
in about ten days, after that
my ass was set on fire.
She had a dark an rolling eye
she belonged to th' roguish crew . . .

As he delivers his rendition, you can hear Walker smirking and some-times laughing. When I hear these verses, though, I am confused. The song is, after all, called "The Rising Sun." But this tune, in subject and melody and cadence, is nothing like our song. Then Walker inhales and delivers the payoff—the final verse.

Well, now, when you go down to New Orleans
just stop at the Rising Sun
there'll you'll see
three pretty French whores
an' that damn bitch is one!
She had a dark an' rolling eye
she belonged to th' roguish crew . . .

At that, Walker stops. "That's all I'm gonna do," he grumbles. But—encouraged by his companions, his drinks or both—he continues through three more songs, laughing throughout much of their off-color material.

Though Hunter calls Walker's song "The Rising Sun," it has much more in common with two dirty ballads that appear frequently both inside and outside of Ozarks folklore. In the 1950s, Vance Randolph col-lected at least two versions of what he called "The Whorehouse Bells," both in Eureka Springs, where Walker sang his. Though most verses are different from Walker's, the first is almost identical. Here it is from "Mr. R.C." of Eureka Springs, who sang it in 1955 but dates it to 1914:

The whore-house bells were ringing clear
A man stood at the door.

> *Stood all day long with a big hard-on*
> *A-waiting to screw a whore.*

The second related song, often called "She Had a Dark and Rolling Eye," also appears in the 1950s around Berryville, Joe Walker's hometown. In this, the chorus that's repeated is simply "She had a dark and rolling eye." It appears as if Walker blended the two songs, using "The Whorehouse Bells Are Ringing" for his verses and the latter as his chorus.

Things get more interesting from there. Randolph notes that "Rolling Eye" is descended from a sixteenth-century bawdy ballad called "The Fire-Ship," which rails against the effects of venereal disease and the prostitutes who spread it. Historian Ed Cray, in a section on "The Fire Ship" in *The Erotic Muse: American Bawdy Songs,* offers an obscure verse of "Fire Ship" from a song in the Utah State University Archives. It was written down (under the title "The Dark and Rolling Eye") by a singer named M. Stubblefield, who said he learned it sometime before the 1930s from another man in Enterprise, Oregon.

> *As you go down in Brooklyn town,*
> *they call her the Rising Sun,*
> *And many a chap she's given the clap,*
> *and among them, me for one.*

No subtlety there. No metaphor. No euphemistic mention of "hell's eternal brink." It's pretty straightforward: Here's the Rising Sun, and here's gonorrhea.

This is what I love about this journey. It keeps serving up surprises; you poke at something small, something local, and it becomes wider. Joe Walker sang of the Rising Sun in New Orleans in a song that had little to do with the one we're chasing. This M. Stubblefield, way out in the northwest, placed the Rising Sun in Brooklyn, of all places. And yet their two renditions are connected across the miles by the "dark and rolling eye" verse that seems to be linked to "Rising Sun" nowhere else.

Listening to Max Hunter's tapes of Joe Walker letting loose, I can't help but think of Harry Cox, the old Englishman who had sung the bawdy version of "Rising Sun" to Alan Lomax seven years before ("If you go to Lowestoft, just ask for the Rising Sun / there you'll find two old whores, and my old woman's one"). Not only are the content of both the song and the Rising Sun verse similar, but here are two men who, despite the miles and ocean that separate them, are not that dissimilar. Though much evidence suggests Cox's repertoire was more varied and included many more serious songs, both men did their best work in the public setting that a tavern offered, and each clearly appreciated the social lubricant that a nasty song could serve up.

"Well, I got Joe to sing," Hunter says into his machine after Walker is finished. "But as I said, some of his songs were pretty bawdy." Particularly, perhaps, for the son of a minister that Walker was.

Joe Walker died in 1967 and is buried near his old farm. I learn this when I visit Berryville and stop in at the Carroll County courthouse, which has been converted into a quiet historical museum and genealogical research center ("Shhh! I'm hunting forebears," says a sign near the entrance). I am fortunate enough to run into Lucy Kell, a native of the area who is working on her family history. She grew up on "the country road" and remembers Walker, albeit only vaguely. She doubts many others do. "I just knew him as being one of the farmers along the road," she says. "I just knew him as Old Joe Walker, though he probably wasn't old. You think anyone over thirty is old when you're young."

The visit gets me to considering the life of this farmer who, it appears, lived largely off the grid and is remembered today by only a few people. Unlike Harrison Burnett's singing, Walker's didn't captivate people in a college town who put his name and his songs in the paper and remembered him as a character in the community. He didn't end up in any University of Arkansas files. From what I can see, the Max Hunter recordings were the rare instance, other than the human milestones of birth, marriage, and death, that Joe Walker ever put in an appearance in the kinds of recorded history that we use today to discern whether people actually existed.

Yet he, too, is a thread in this tapestry. Ribald, grouchy, and probably feeling good from the liquor on a February night in 1960, Walker sang a song and moved on. Years later, it is a clue in a larger cultural mystery of which he has become a part.

SILVER DOLLAR CITY, MISSOURI

If you don't have a time machine, pushing backward in history requires a robust imagination. You can read the documents, listen to the field recordings, view the sepia-tone pictures and assemble the scaffolding of another age, but to *feel* it requires something else: closing your eyes and letting your mind summon images of worlds long gone. Listening to all these old songs for so long makes me hungry to touch the past. What was life like for the people who sang these songs? What did it *feel like* to be there?

I decide to channel the mountains of yore and see how they informed today's Ozarks. What better place to do so than Silver Dollar City, the Ozarks theme park in the hills of southeastern Missouri? It promises, after all, to reveal a taste of the 1880s in this corner of the land—that is, of course, the 1880s with safety-checked roller coasters, plastic tureens of Coke, and $41 admission tickets.

When I arrive in the parking lot, a few miles from the music theaters of Branson, row after row of church minivans are disgorging young people for their afternoon of fun. At the tram pickup area, a sign in thick type forbids alcohol and firearms on the premises—which, of course, kind of undermines any notion of an authentic feel. Not that I'm advocating battalions of pistol-packing park goers fighting it out over the last serving of $3 frozen lemonade, but the irony is inescapable: the gritty ugliness of frontier history has been sanitized for your protection. What would the House of the Rising Sun be if it were depicted here? A cheerful, sexless bordello full of whores with hearts of gold and jocular men smoking cigars?

Inside the park, it's the same unsordid story at JJ's Mine Restaurant, which you enter through a terraformed cave entrance off the "town square." JJ's is dimly lit, presumably so you can see less of the food on the $8.99 all-you-can-eat barbecue buffet. What do we gain, exactly, by pretending we're eating in a coal mine? I imagine the miners of Joplin, Missouri, who sang "Rising Sun" not far from here a hundred years ago would have killed to eat their lunches out in the midday sun.

As I sit east of the 1881 Hotel and listen to banjo music pumped at me through loudspeakers, I become aware that, despite the ribs and sauce-laden brisket upon which I have just gorged, there is a hollow feeling in my stomach. It is the same feeling I get walking through Walt Disney World or watching *The Simple Life* or hearing about how tasty the new iteration of Pepto-Bismol is. It is the feeling of losing my own story, of being sucked up by corporate narratives and becoming a cog in the churning machine of story-driven capitalism that has consumed our country.

This is part of why I have come to Silver Dollar City. "Rising Sun" contains a kernel of authenticity that got me up off my seat to find the real amid the artificial, and this weird blend of the historical and the synthetic seems a land between. It feels purgatorial. I buy myself a chilled bottle of something called Sioux City Sarsaparilla to cool off. The label says it was bottled on Long Island.

When our natural frontier ran out in the late 1800s, we began to build synthetic ones—lite, safe—and when our buying power was exported abroad, naturally, the way capitalism works, our preferences were exported, too. That's why Japanese and Germans come here to drive old Route 66, why pirated DVDs of American movies go for $1 each on the streets of Beijing—and why people are recording "House of the Rising Sun" and singing it in Vietnam, China, Finland, and France.

There is no shortage of clichés within the confines of Silver Dollar City. Its "bookstore/print shop" sells *Granny's Beverly Hillbillies Cookbook*, an ode to the 1960s television show that made Ozark mountain folk look like blithering idiots. Alongside it is "The Last Supper: 1,000-piece Puzzle." At the Ozarks' Farmer Gift & Clothing store, half of the merchandise is branded John Deere.

I wander into the "general store" on the "town square," which has a "post office" that, jarringly, is an actual post office. I buy a postcard for my son and several others that purport to illustrate "Hillbilly Livin'." They contain depictions of backwoods people aimed at the irony of urban sensibility. The ugliest, called "Home Improvement," shows a rattily dressed family painting the side of an outhouse. Another, "Springtime," features a mother washing two urchins in a stone tub while a shiftless, bearded father sits around watching. I ask the clerk, a middle-aged woman, if locals don't get offended at such portrayals. "I guess if you live here, the jokes are okay," she says. But aren't visitors the ones who send most postcards?

Finally, right on the "town square" I see something that bills itself as real—a log cabin built in 1843 by the Levi Casey family, whose members moved here from Tennessee. Could they have imagined that their backwoods existence would be anecdotalized in a theme park, surrounded by other "log cabins" that put themselves forward as examples of what life was like? This kind of stuff is considered harmless fun, but it tells American consumers, through repetition, that history is only a well from which new excuses for fun can be drawn. Tribulations? Forget 'em. Just have some funnel cake. Black lung? Pshaw. Let's wear our hillbilly hats and queue up for the Fire in the Hole ride.

On the old log cabin's front porch, traditional musicians sit telling jokes and playing guitar, banjo, harmonica, hammered dulcimer, flute. They sing some old mining songs and some funny folk tunes, and they are talented, but nevertheless I have the suspicion that this music, like the architecture around it, is carefully calibrated to seem frozen in time.

Max Hunter was aware of this after he helped Silver Dollar City produce a show called the Mountain Folks Music Festival in 1976. He wrote a blistering letter to the park's special events coordinator objecting to the "great confusion" that resulted from what he considered the festival's irresponsible mixing of musical traditions. How, Hunter wondered, could a festival designed to showcase music from the 1860s and 1870s include in its performances songs that emerged only decades later? Hunter said that the musical carelessness turned the festival into "a joke with excuses like, 'the musicians were there to entertain the guests.' " Some of this was in defense of the musicians, but the notion also personally offended Hunter.

"With a very few exceptions, what the guests heard was what they can hear on radio and records, anytime," he wrote. He attached two lists of songs that should not have been used in the festival because they were copyrighted or composed after 1900 (among them were "Deep in the Heart of Texas," "Goodnight, Irene," "This Land Is Your Land," and "Wreck on the Highway") and a third list of songs that were okay ("Frankie and Johnny," "Streets of Laredo," "Pretty Polly," "Oh, Susannah").

This outlook fit Hunter's worldview: Just as he would erase songs he collected that didn't reflect pure Ozark tradition, he also didn't want historical authenticity sacrificed upon the altar of commercial performance. "The influence of the tourist, the city people coming here to retire, the radio, the television, are corrupting us all, especially our younger folk, toward our heritage," he wrote. That's how I felt walking the "streets" of Silver Dollar City—that the commercialization of a particular historical period insults the people who lived through it. It seems unreasonable to teach history, be it geographic or musical, by adulterating the raw materials that produced it in the first place.

Yet isn't the journey of "House of the Rising Sun" a case study in exactly that? It began as a narrow, specific piece of a particular culture, then spread and became more emblematic. The only reason for its dissemination was its commodification: So many performers adulterated it, changed it around, shaped it to their own circumstances that it grew into something modern. The same forces that make the anecdotalization inside Silver Dollar City seem so unsettling are the ones that propelled "Rising Sun" on its odyssey. The measure of authenticity is time.

These are difficult questions, particularly when the twenty-first-century mass-culture machine encourages us to accept and digest prepackaged stories. But from television to amusement parks to the silliest of theme restaurants (the Rainforest Cafe), we're dealing with these issues each day. Each representation of American culture, even those that seem crass and commercial, is of us. Trying to figure out which ones are oversimplifications and which are productive parts of the cultural collage like the one that produced "House of the Rising Sun" is one of the major challenges of our era.

FAYETTEVILLE, ARKANSAS

William Harrison Burnett's daughter lives in a one-story bungalow just up the street from the North Street Church of Christ, where her father's funeral services were held in 1974. I find her through an elaborate chase of data snippets that begins at the community library, takes me to a funeral home at the edge of town, then propels me to a church's retired minister, who susses me out for purity of heart before producing a phone number. When I get Dortha Bradley on the phone and tell her I was hoping to track down one of Harrison Burnett's kids, she responds, cheerfully: "I'm the only one. So if you ain't got me, you ain't got anybody."

She invites me over. I am greeted more enthusiastically than I expect. At seventy, Dortha Bradley is a bit frail but very much still part of the world. Family photos hang everywhere; I learn that this daughter of a man who sang sad ballads is no stranger to the blues herself. She had a sister who died after one day in this world ("Her heart never beat right"). Her husband, Marvin, has been dead four years; two years before that, her adult son committed suicide. I feel a bit intimidated in the presence of such heavy memories, but she seems pleased at my visit.

Since I first heard him sing and listened to Max Hunter rhapsodize about him, I have wanted to learn more about Harrison Burnett. This was an unusual man. While so many old-time folksingers were "rediscovered" and brought onto college campuses during the folk revival in the 1960s, here was a musician in a different situation: He was already working on a university campus, and college kids looking for folk authenticity needed to go no further than his office to find what they sought.

"Making music was just part of life," his daughter says. "I never remember there not being an instrument in our house. If my dad wanted an instrument and couldn't afford to buy it, he'd make it." He'd fashion his own banjos and guitars, and even, once, made an electric guitar from scratch.

Like so many Ozarkers, the Burnetts were originally from the mountains of Tennessee. They settled here because the hills, the weather, and the ways of life reminded them of home, and they brought their traditions with them. Perhaps one of those traditions was a proto "Rising Sun," given that this region seems the only place other than our Golden Triangle where our song has emerged from the folk tradition directly.

Harrison Burnett's mother, Mary Elizabeth Mattingly Burnett, started him on traditional music. She sang songs to him and his brothers when they were little, and he'd memorize them. Sometimes he'd forget them for years, but when he did his rounds as a night watchman around the university campus decades later, he'd review them in his mind and write them down the next morning. It wasn't uncommon for folks on the University of Arkansas campus in the late 1950s and early 1960s to see the gangly security guard making his rounds through the darkness, singing old songs as he walked.

At fifteen, Burnett left his family when his father whacked him one time too many. "Granddad took a tree limb this big"—Dortha Bradley makes a circle the size of a large coffee saucer—"and hit him with it. So he never did go home to live after that. He was doing a man's work anyway, and so he did it elsewhere."

He became a rambler, moving from town to town in rural Madison County, Arkansas, east of Fayetteville, doing migrant farm work. He went to Washington state for a couple years to chase apple-picking work during harvests. When he married Dortha's mother, he was twenty-one and she was thirty-three. His brain absorbed all sorts of miscellany, whatever was useful. Once, he took apart a 1930 Chevrolet, laid all the parts around the house, found what was wrong, fixed it, and put the whole thing back together again. He was drafted for World War II but excluded because of varicose veins. So he packed up the family, moved to Fayetteville and worked at a chicken-processing plant and a grocery supplier before landing his night watchman job.

All the while, he was accumulating a remarkable collection of old ballads in his head. "Whenever he got on one of those binges, he'd just go over and over them. Whoo. Didn't stop," Mrs. Bradley says. "And then he'd pull out another verse. I don't know how he did it. He had a place back there in his mind where those songs still lived."

By the time Dortha was college age, in the mid-1950s, Burnett had developed a reputation around campus as a folksinger. He was popular because most of the people who knew the old songs were extremely elderly and didn't have much voice to sing with anymore. Burnett's voice was nasal and strong, and he loved to oblige. "A few of the girls at church were getting pretty upset because there were all these boys coming over to our house," Mrs. Bradley remembers, laughing. "But they weren't coming to see me. They were coming to see him. . . . Those university boys had a knack of finding it out. They also found out my mother was very good at making beans and cornbread."

Later in life, Burnett compiled his own handwritten songbook, but most of it came straight out of his brain in exactly the form it had gone in. That was the case with "Rising Sun."

"He sang it considerably differently than what the more modern version of it is," Dortha Bradley says. She has always known the song was about New Orleans, despite the absence of the city's name in Burnett's version. Remember, he refers only to "a house in yondos town."

"It was viewed as a sinful city," she says. "That's what this song's about. Let's face it. It's about a"—she pauses—"whorehouse." I laugh when the word comes out of her mouth. So, I ask, why isn't prostitution mentioned more explicitly? It's a relic of the age the song came from, she proposes—a time when such things weren't talked about in churchgoing circles. "Words get changed when songs are passed down from person to person," Mrs. Bradley says. "Back then, a lot of the people, especially the young men who grew up in the mountains, they wanted to see part of the world. When they left here, they were innocent people. But when they came back, they most certainly were not."

Dortha Bradley had a hard time when her father died. For the first few years, she didn't want to hear the recordings he made. She just couldn't. She has some old tapes, but they've been socked away. She still fears them a little. "What I have of my dad's music is what he recorded for me," she says. "And I'm sort of afraid . . ." She tears up. "I'm sort of afraid that when I play it, it won't work."

After nearly two hours of marshaling sometimes difficult memories, Dortha Bradley remains energetic and amiable. She leaves me with this: "I went to New Orleans a few years ago. I loved every minute of it." When I return home, I burn a CD of the songs her father sang to Max Hunter, print out a photo of her parents from the University of Arkansas library as the cover and mail it off to her. Before I do, I play it to make sure it works.

BRANSON, MISSOURI

Branson is called "America's Hometown," and that makes sense in a way. Today's "hometowns"—the term has become generous in many cases—are often subdivisions acting as ribs of a large retail spine that's filled with Ruby Tuesday and Denny's and Wal-Mart and Jiffy Lube. That's exactly what Branson is, except it adds to the mix colorful theaters and musical performers of varying fame, ability, and genre. So naturally, people feel at home here because this is not something special that's out of their frame of reference, like New York City, but rather something special that's actually stamped onto their frame of reference. If you're going down Highway 76 in Branson, and you make a turn off the road, you could just as easily turn into the Krispy Kreme as you could Yakov Smirnoff's theater, Dolly Parton's Dixie Stampede, or Tony Roi's Elvis Experience.

It's not quite as cartoonish as Orlando, Florida, America's theme park capital, though there are elements of the outsized attraction here—water slides, Ripley's Believe It or Not. But there's also something of a sweetness in Branson. It's not as big as Orlando or Vegas. Most of the motels appear independent and are filled with that kind of entrepreneurial exuberance that says, "Maybe, if our sign is bright enough and unusual enough and our rates are low enough, you'll turn off and decide you're going to stay here." And that is the core of American capitalism.

Though I find no evidence of "Rising Sun" performed live anywhere in Branson, the town is an excellent place to examine the status of our song because, like "Rising Sun" on the verge of the 1960s, Branson blends the modern—the postmodern, even—with fragments of a fanciful, countrified American past.

Like Silver Dollar City a few miles away, Branson is about yesterday. But while the theme park is designed to hand you a prepackaged experience, the town is more complicated. It aims to use the notion of "country"—an imagined way of life with key pieces of reality seeded in—to reinforce perceptions of a past that didn't really exist and to propose, through music and showmanship, that the same past still exists in our culture today.

Branson is Broadway for Red America. It's a repository of the dramatic and musical narratives that keep the nation going, drawn from the same pool as "Rising Sun" and, like the song, carried off in countless directions. Mongrel.

After driving the strip several times, I choose a show called the Ozark Mountain Jubilee. It is held at the Grand Country Music Hall, a multiplex-like establishment that brings the glitz of a theater to the parking lot of a strip mall. About two hundred people—many of them Canadian, curiously—are in attendance. A man in a "traditional" mountaineer hat leads folks to their seats. As he ushers two young men and an elderly lady to their second-row spots, he points at me. "One of you is going to have to sit next to *that,*" he says. They laugh.

After a round of call-and-response hellos ("Howdy, everybody!"), the show begins with an ensemble performance of "Play Me Some Mountain Music." This is followed by "Rocky Top," the 1967 song that was composed to sound Really Old and has become one of the state songs of Tennessee. It's musical jiu-jitsu, playing to mountain clichés and making them a point of strength rather than derision. *Corn don't grow at all on Rocky Top, it's too rocky by far. / That's why all the folks on Rocky Top get their corn from a jar.*

The next two hours unfold on a stage awash with gaudy costumes and purple and turquoise sets. The show brims with self-deprecating sketches, silly songs, constipation humor, and gentle religious jokes like the one about the new Baptist minister who preaches too long: "The Lutherans beat us to the Hong Kong buffet."

The Bacons, members of the multigenerational musical clan that runs the Ozark Mountain Jubilee, are keenly aware of the power of family in the rural narrative. This is the same power that "Rising Sun" and other warning songs exert. It's the notion that by remaining within the family unit and following its moral code—*go tell my baby sister not to do what I have done*—will lead to earthly and spiritual salvation. Amid their music, they offer a slide show of Bacon family photos from the 1970s and 1980s that's also interspersed with nostalgia-saturated snapshots of Pac-Man, Rubik's Cube, *Star Wars, The Dukes of Hazzard*, and the *Challenger* disaster, all dosed with an I-wish-I-could-go-back-to-those-simpler-days sensibility. Even though the 1980s are recent, it appeals to one of Branson's key demographics—parents with growing children.

Again, it's also very country: invoke yesterday fondly. Look back. Forward is disruptive. Forward interrupts the Country Narrative that holds the key to wisdom and purity of heart. Moral cleansing lies in examining our yesterdays, when, ostensibly, things were better than the current modern conundrum of complexity and spiritual decay. *If I had a-listened what Mama said, I'd a been at home today.*

The show ends with a dedication to all veterans. The house lights rise so every vet in the audience can stand and be recognized. This comes after a burst of gospel songs leading to the big finish, including some Bacon children brought out to sing a countrified "Amazing Grace" and a poem about the flag that equates religion with patriotism. It goes over well; after years of near-daily performances, the Bacons know their audience.

After the show, the Bacons do a curious thing. They emerge, immediately, to mingle with the departing audience in the theater lobby. Part of this is to sell more CDs—when the performer's there to sign autographs, the product moves faster. But as I watch them interact comfortably with their audience, it occurs to me that they are participating in something that folk music contained but that modern professional performance has largely abandoned: the notion of the performer as part of the community.

Somewhere in modern music, the performer became separate from the audience. That coincides with the time when music became a commodity, another article of consumption. That became more pronounced toward the end of the 1950s and the beginning of the 1960s when rock and roll, Elvis, and eventually the Beatles and the British Invasion changed the landscape of music sales.

During this period, as it shaped itself into the form we know so well, "Rising Sun" was a standard in the folk repertoire. The *Sing Out!* version was being played everywhere. Blues singer Nina Simone had taken a slower, Josh White–like take and made it her own, carrying it squarely into the clubs of Manhattan. A Texas singer named Hally Wood, an Alan Lomax protégée with a voice that sounded like a violin, was singing a haunting, ethereal version she adapted from the *Our Singing Country* text, and it was getting attention in folk circles.

And as the 1960s dawned, a Jewish boy from Minnesota, barely twenty, who lived at the northern end of the fabled Highway 61, was about to latch on to "Rising Sun" and send it on its way.

5   *Blast Off*

The jester sang for the king and queen
in a coat he borrowed from James Dean
and a voice that came from you and me.

—DON MCLEAN, "AMERICAN PIE"

The calendar may have said January 20, 1961, but John F. Kennedy's inauguration marked the moment the 1960s began. Kennedy calibrated his inaugural address to evoke two Americas—the tradition-rich, gradually awakening nation of the early 1900s and the future-is-now, post–World War II land that belonged unequivocally to the twentieth-century man. Generations were changing hands in an acute way, even for America.

The cultural critic Lewis Mumford was watching. He called Kennedy's address "a fresh wind from the high slopes of an older America."

A president sets the tone for a nation, and Kennedy's determination to build tomorrow by leveraging the best of yesterday spread through the land. Nowhere was this truer than among young people who had been captivated by the old songs. After nearly a decade, the folk revival was spreading into the mainstream.

Old-time musicians were being "rediscovered" by educated urbanites hungry for something authentic. The Delta blues master Mississippi John Hurt resurfaced. Appalachian death-ballad singer Dock Boggs made his first recordings in three decades. Clarence "Tom" Ashley came out of musical retirement, played the banjo and sang "Rising Sun Blues" on the campus folkie circuit. Texts by John and Alan Lomax, Cecil Sharp, the poet Carl Sandburg, and other ballad hunters were plundered for fresh material. College students went on musical expeditions into Appalachia, hunting for songs and the people who played them. The Eisenhower 1950s had left them cold; they needed to reach back further and find rawer materials.

Nineteen-sixty-one was important, too, for a young musician named Bob Dylan, who had been studying the state of the world during the first two decades of his life. Of the year he was born, 1941, he said this: "You could feel the old world go and the new one beginning. It was like putting the clock back to when B.C. became A.D."

Dylan seized upon this seismic shift of the culture. He had watched, from the northern reaches of Highway 61 in Minnesota, the dying gasps of the minstrel shows and the rise of the Beats. He found a dying Woody Guthrie, the man who had inspired him, in a New Jersey sanitarium and played him guitar, all the while idolizing and imitating and learning. He embarked upon a wholesale ransacking of the American musical past and, genius that he was even at that tender age, used it to assault the present in a way no one ever had. Later, reflecting on the earliest parts of his career, Dylan would come up with an apt term for what he was then—a "musical expeditionist."

"A song is like a dream, and you try to make it come true," he wrote. "They're like strange countries that you have to enter."

Dylan's first years coming out of Hibbing, Minnesota, and ensconcing himself in the Greenwich Village folk music scene are well documented. So let's move directly to his relationship with a lesser-known but influential Greenwich Village musician, Dave Van Ronk. Even in his younger days, Van Ronk, who died in 2002, cut a fatherly figure with his barrel chest, booming voice, and papa-bear demeanor. "Van Ronk seemed ancient, battle tested," Dylan wrote years later. "Every night I was sitting at the feet of a timeworn monument." Van Ronk sang an acoustic "Rising Sun" at various clubs through the late 1950s and into the 1960s. He used Hally Wood's low-key version of Lomax's text. Van Ronk's male take on Wood's feminine rendition became part of his repertoire.

"I put a different spin on it by altering the chords and using a bass line that descended in half steps—a common enough progression in jazz, but unusual among folksingers," Van Ronk wrote in *The Mayor of MacDougal Street,* his posthumously published memoir. "By the early 1960s, the song had become one of my signature pieces, and I could hardly get off the stage without doing it."

I tried to catch up with Van Ronk about "Rising Sun" before he died, but I never received a response. Through a third party, I heard he didn't want to talk about it because of all the fuss that had surrounded his and Dylan's alleged dispute over the song. But I was pleased when I screened Martin Scorsese's 2005 Dylan documentary, *No Direction Home,* and saw both Dylan and Van Ronk discussing it—separately.

"I'd never done that song before, but I heard it every night 'cause Van Ronk would do it," Dylan says. "I thought he was really on to something with the song, so I just recorded it."

Then an aging Van Ronk elaborates on the "Rising Sun"–related "feud" that either did or didn't erupt.

"Bobby picked up the chord changes for the song from me. It really altered the song considerably, although the lyric was pretty much the straight 'House of the Rising Sun' lyric and so was the melody," Van Ronk says. Then, one night, Van Ronk was sitting at his regular back table in a bar called the Kettle of Fish, right next to the popular club Gaslight, when Dylan "came slouching in." He'd been busy in the Columbia studios recording the songs for his eponymously titled first album.

"He asked me if I would mind if he recorded my version of 'House of the Rising Sun.' And I had some plans to record it. So I said, well, gee, Bob, I'd rather you didn't because I'm going to record it myself soon. And Bobby said, 'Uh-oh.' "

Turns out Dylan had already recorded the thing, assuming Van Ronk's approval in advance. And why not? Bob Dylan was all caught up in the intense moments of his first sessions. He was plundering. He was an expeditionist. Did it matter whether the expedition was to the reaches of Appalachia, the Mississippi Delta, or Dave Van Ronk's songbook? "The mystery of being in a recording studio did something to me, and these are the songs that came out," Dylan offers in explanation.

It's difficult to tell whether the friendship was cleaved because of this. Van Ronk called the whole thing "a tempest in a teapot." But the one inevitable trait of folk music—the haziness of authorship—reared its head. Before too long, Van Ronk found himself accused of copying the compelling arrangement of "Rising Sun" . . . from Dylan's album. "I had to stop singing the song," Van Ronk says. "Now that was very, very annoying. But I couldn't blame that on him."

Step back a moment and consider this cultural transaction that took place in the smoky cafés of Greenwich Village as the 1960s dawned. Jewish boy from small-town Minnesota, at the very uppermost reaches of the North Country, arrives in New York wanting to sing. He visits an ailing Woody Guthrie, plays for him, imitates him. He changes his name, makes up a backstory or two, then finds a friend who becomes something of a mentor. Then the boy learns from the older singer—learns so well that, in short order, he takes his place alongside the elder man as an equal.

"I remember," Dylan wrote in a prose poem in 1963, "Dave singing 'House a the Risin Sun' with his back leaned against the bricks an words runnin out in a lonesome hungry growlin whisper that any girl with her face hid in the dark could understand."

During this friendship, something passes between the two of them—something rather ancient, rather mystical, sung into Lomax's machine by sixteen-year-old Georgia Turner two decades earlier. Dylan was only twenty years younger than Georgia Turner, but they belonged to different worlds. She belonged to The Village. He was from our world, though a bit of him was *of* hers or at least desperate to reach it. The jester sang, for everyone, in a voice that came from you and me.

Dylan almost certainly heard other performers do "Rising Sun" before he himself recorded it. Before New York, he visited Denver and was influenced by Judy Collins, who was playing it. Dylan also hung out in Lomax's loft in his early New York days, and met his future girlfriend, Suze Rotolo, through her sister, who was Lomax's personal assistant. And we know he saw Clarence Ashley play at least once before *Bob Dylan* was recorded. I doubt he ever heard Lomax's Georgia Turner field recording, though one of his Minneapolis friends, Harvey Abrams, told Dylan biographer Robert Shelton that Dylan, when appropriating a song from yesterday, "had to get the oldest record and, if possible, the Library of Congress record."

Unless Dylan ever decides to discuss it, we'll never know how much he considered non–Van Ronk interpretations when he did his own—particularly Woody Guthrie's earlier, more traditional rendition. Guthrie's, pulled straight from *Our Singing Country* with barely a modification in the early 1940s, sounds much more like Georgia Turner's than the minor-key version that the Weavers, Van Ronk, and others spread around the folk revival.

"Dylan clearly knew the other arrangement—the Guthrie arrangement, the more traditional American arrangement, the version that's in Lomax," Dylan biographer Clinton Heylin told me. He says Dylan performed the Guthrie version at least once in a New York folk club. But mostly, and in the studio, Dylan did Van Ronk. In fact, he outdid Van Ronk.

With that transference—Van Ronk to Dylan—"House of the Rising Sun" gains speed. When Dylan recorded it on Columbia 08579, *Bob Dylan,* it was as if he sent it shooting out of one of those circus cannons that fires a man skyward. No more would "Rising Sun" be "kicking around" or "passed along" or "spread." Like so much else in the 1960s, it was suddenly hurtling toward the moon.

The kicker of the Dylan–Van Ronk story is the best part. Here's Van Ronk: "Later on, when Eric Burdon and the Animals picked the song up from Bobby and recorded it, Bobby told me that *he* had to drop the song because everyone was accusing him of ripping it off of Eric Burdon!" Then he laughs uproariously.

Four decades after the Animals' rendition became the definitive version, Dylan's 1962 reading (called "House of the Risin' Sun") remains impressively haunting. Part of it is Van Ronk's novel arrangement, which ratchets up the drama. But there's more to it. Van Ronk's version, committed to tape years later, is screechy like Dylan's, but the voice is clearly only Van Ronk's, the time clearly only the 1960s. It does not echo of other places, other eras as Dylan's does. "A folk song has over a thousand faces," Dylan wrote in his autobiography, "and you must meet them all if you want to play this stuff."

In Dylan's "Risin' Sun," though he appears to mimic Van Ronk, something epic is afoot, resonating behind what Robert Shelton, evaluating Dylan's version in a September 1961 review, called "a scarcely understandable growl." You can hear the tension moving around inside Dylan like a pinball bouncing on the table's upper bumpers. Even the guitar is impatient. You want to jump up, not to dance but to scratch some primeval itch that has somehow always been there but now must be attended to. He sounds possessed by the musical forces he was about to unleash, pinned between the ancient and the modern, between tradition and progress. He sounds at once old and beaten down, like a nineteenth-century mountain singer, and hip and current like the coffeehouse folkie he already is. He sounds guttural and whiny, like a goosey five-year-old told to sit still at the table even though he's bursting with nervous energy that cannot be contained. *Go tell my baaaaaaaabbbbby siissssterr not to dooooooooooooo whutttt I have doonnnnnnnne.*

And somehow, though I can't begin to explain how, Bob Dylan sounds like a poor girl gone wrong who will never get her life back, who's doomed to spend the rest of her wicked life beneath the Rising Sun. Wherever or whatever or whenever it may be.

SALTVILLE, VIRGINIA

After more than two decades of traveling along bumpy roads, the old-time musician Clarence "Tom" Ashley found some good times in the 1960s.

He had done pretty well during the 1920s and 1930s when he was traveling with a medicine show at the height of the "hillbilly music" golden age. In those years, Ashley recorded more than seventy sides with such labels as Columbia, Okeh, and Vocalion, including, with Gwen Foster, the earliest known recorded version of "Rising Sun" in 1933. But when the Depression overtook Ashley's corner of the world—the mountainous pocket where Virginia, Kentucky, and Tennessee meet—things grew harder. His extensive traveling with the medicine show ended when his son fell ill, bringing Ashley home to his farm in Shouns, Tennessee, where his wife Hettie and their children, J.D. and Eva, were living.

The ensuing years were consumed with attempts to get by. In addition to farming his land, Ashley worked in coal mines, hauled goods for the government, raised cattle and tobacco, and worked at sawmills and lumberyards. He quit the medicine shows for good in 1943. Around that time, while working at a lumberyard, Ashley cut his left index finger, and it went through a rough recovery. He concluded that he could no longer play. He maintained his affection for the old songs, though. In the 1950s, he began teaching them to his neighbors and his grandson, Tommy Moore.

In 1952, unbeknownst to Ashley, Harry Smith's seminal *Anthology of American Folk Music* introduced some of his early music to a new generation. The collection included his signature song, "Coo Coo Bird," and the classic ballad "The House Carpenter." But the industry hadn't kept up with Ashley, and no one knew where he was. Smith's liner notes even mention both a "Clarence Ashley" and a "Thomas Ashley" with no indication that they were the same man.

As folk music resurged through the 1950s and into the 1960s, more ears heard Ashley's early music and were inspired by it. It was probably inevitable, then, that the world would eventually come to his door.

Like many old-time musicians, he was widely believed to be lost to the mists of time. He and his music were, after all, a part of The Village—that place that had been swept away by the Depression, World War II, and the rise of American mass culture. Really, who could tell whether the Clarence Ashleys of the world had ever been real? Their obscurity was part of their allure; they belonged to another age. But it was a civilization that the musical movement of the 1960s was determined to excavate. Thus did Ashley return to the American consciousness.

In 1966, he remembered it for an audience at the East Tennessee State University Folk Festival:

> . . . a lot of my tunes and other people's tunes, they faded out. They was in the old tradition, and the modern music pushed them out. Along about '61, this old record was found in the Music Library of Congress, and some of the people were studying the old folksongs. They went to checking up on me to see if I was a-living, and they wanted me to go back to New York and record it once again . . . Well, it's been going around the country.

That captures how old-time musicians fit into the folk revival after they were "rediscovered" in the 1960s, in many cases by urban northeasterners. Unlike Rossie Holcomb, who had never been recorded until John Cohen "discovered" him, these men (and a few women) had recorded commercially, then gone back to their lives. That was the story with Mississippi John Hurt and with the Appalachian musicians Dock Boggs and Buell Kazee, and it was the story with Ashley.

In his case, the return was serendipitous, as recounted by Ambrose Manning and Minnie Miller in a 1981 mini-biography. In April 1960, the folklorist Ralph Rinzler was visiting the Old Time Fiddlers Convention in Union Grove, North Carolina, when he saw Ashley's group tuning up. He got into a conversation with the man identified as "Tom Ashley," after his boyhood nickname, and—noticing he had the same surname as the old-time musician Clarence Ashley whose songs had appeared on Smith's *Anthology*—asked if the two Ashleys knew each other.

Ashley, whether genuinely suspicious or just being contrarian, allowed that he may have heard of the guy. When Rinzler told of trying repeatedly to reach Ashley by mail and telegram and began to rhapsodize about "The Coo Coo Bird," Ashley 'fessed up. Rinzler immediately launched a months-long campaign to persuade Ashley to record again.

It worked. On Labor Day weekend 1960, Ashley and his band convened for a recording session at the home of his daughter, Eva Ashley Moore, in Saltville, Virginia, near the Tennessee line. Rinzler spent a day recording Ashley and his family and neighbors in this quiet neighborhood. It wasn't the sort of place where you'd expect musical history to be made, but there was Ashley, after three decades, recording again at the request of a new generation. Irascible though he was, he had to have been delighted.

When I learned, in 2001, that Eva Ashley Moore was still living in the house where the recordings were made, I had to meet her. I hooked up with Ron Curry, the old-time aficionado whom I had met at Joe Bussard's house during a marathon listening session a few months previous. He wanted to meet her as well.

Eva Moore and her son, Tom, a middle aged computing analyst and devout Christian who had played on those early sessions at the house, were quick to invite us over. It's rare, he says, that folks track his family down to talk about his grandfather's music. He loves it; though he says he doesn't listen to much music, he wants to make sure his grandfather isn't forgotten.

On the Saturday afternoon that she receives me, Eva Ashley Moore is eighty-one and has two more years to live. In the living room, where the recordings took place, her oxygen tank sits in the corner. The sunshine casts a warm light onto a faded wood six-string that her father played for years. She lets me hold it.

Family photographs are everywhere, on tables and in overstuffed albums: Eva and her brother J.D. on a horse next to her father and

mother in the 1920s. Her father in London, traveling around to perform his songs in the 1960s, staring quizzically at a Beefeater outside
Buckingham Palace. Her father in the sixties with Rossie Holcomb,
who has his arm around Ashley as they both smile out from under
porkpie hats. The Ashley family album could be printed and sold, as is,
as a coffee-table book about old-time music.

"It was his whole life, this music was," his daughter says. "It was just
born inside him, I think."

Tom Moore, who resembles his grandfather, points out his younger
self in pictures next to Granddaddy. When Ashley, Watson, and their
friends were recording here in 1960, Moore was everywhere, showing
off the skills that his grandfather had been teaching him. "I'm in the
middle with the washboard," he says, pointing to one snapshot. He
likes to tell the story about how, in college, he met Roy Acuff, who had
toured with Ashley in the old medicine shows. "His face lit up when I
told him I was Tom Ashley's grandson," Moore says.

I ask his mother about "Rising Sun," which, as she knows, is the reason why I came. She can add nothing to her father's memories—that he
got it from his very musical grandparents. Then Eva Ashley Moore looks
straight at me and says, "I remember all the words." She proceeds to
recite the song for me, sometimes speaking, sometimes singing softly.

"I know most of 'em that well," she says.

After the Saltville session in 1960, Ashley went on to record a wealth
of old-time material with his band, which included Ashley neighbor
Clint Howard and a little-known blind guitarist named Arthel "Doc"
Watson, who was destined to become one of the most beloved old-time
singers ever.

Watson is a man of few words. He prefers to let his singing do the
talking. Not only has he been blind since birth, but in 1985 his son and
musical partner, the finger-picking guitarist Merle Watson, was killed in
a tractor accident on the family property. Watson has sung "Rising Sun"
through his career—with Ashley, with Merle, with his grandson Richard,
and alone. He learned it from Ashley originally, though in recent years
he's been performing and recording a hybrid version, with parts taken
from the Ashley version and parts taken from the Animals. "There was
only one Clarence Ashley," Watson said years after his mentor died.
"I've heard people try to imitate him. Oh, they fell way short."

Ashley's ride through the 1960s gave him national exposure and put him on the road again. He played on college campuses and at folk festivals, enthralling audiences with his haunting catalog of yesterday's songs. He crossed paths with Bob Dylan, Alan Lomax, and dozens of the modern musicians who were trolling the annals of old-time music for inspiration.

He was the real deal, after all, a guy whose musical traditions stretched back to mountain balladry he learned from his forebears decades before the first country music record was ever cut. And here he was, still singing, hanging out in New York City, and imparting his skills (and his connection to The Village) to young musicians.

By 1963, Ashley's group had played Carnegie Hall. Not bad for a mountain musician who started his career traveling through the hills to help a "doctor" peddle patent medicine. John Cohen, in an obituary published in *Sing Out!* after Ashley's death in 1967, said this: "He once explained how his life was like a flower that bloomed twice—in the early years in the mountains, and again in his late years with the new city audience."

As someone who adapted folk songs for commercial recordings, Ashley acted as a mediator between traditional music and the twentieth century, between The Village and our world. At the same time, though, he felt protective of the songs he sang. Sometimes he complained that they were being bastardized.

That was the case with our song, which Ashley was still calling "Rising Sun Blues" when he performed it on college campuses in the mid-1960s. He made it clear that he didn't like what was becoming of it in the hands of certain 1960s rockers. Some of the folkies, he said, had done right by it—particularly Joan Baez, whose slow, moody take caught his fancy. Ashley said she was inspired by his recording, though Baez, like most revival artists, appears to be using Alan Lomax's version just as her sometime boyfriend, Bob Dylan, did. "She did take this song off of that record, and she's done well with it, and I'm glad she has," Ashley says at a festival performance shortly before he died. "She can sing it better than I can."

Then he takes aim at the version that changed everything, the one that was only a few years old by the time he was speaking.

"The song is rock and roll now," Ashley all but spits. "They murdered it. They murdered that song. . . . Because it's not that type of song. It wasn't made for that. It wasn't wrote for that."

He was, of course, talking about the Animals.

Newcastle-upon-Tyne is an ancient river town in the north of England, with a history that dates to the Roman emperor Hadrian. But it was mining that eventually put England's northernmost city on the map. In fact, if you're American, you're most likely to have heard of the place in an expression of redundancy: "That's like bringing coals to Newcastle."

By the late 1950s, heavy industry was going into a tailspin in Newcastle. This was before the development of the 1960s and 1970s, and the place was isolated, bleak, and filled with people struggling to get by. In that it was not unlike Middlesboro, Kentucky. For a young man trying to make music and break free from the surroundings life had dealt him, it felt all the more desolate. But from the beginning, Eric Burdon was determined to transcend. As other "Geordies"—boys from Newcastle—pursued more sensible paths, he went to art school. He knew, as he would sing later, that he had to get outta this place.

Burdon, an electrical worker's son, was barely sixteen and, as he recalls, "a spotty-faced teenage animal living on fish and chips and Newcastle Brown Ale" when he began to immerse himself in American blues and folk music. This was before the British Invasion, when British proto-rockers and skiffle bands—small guitar groups that incorporated jazz, blues, and folk—were beginning to plunder the same vast pool of Southern roots music that their American brethren had been exploiting for years. One skiffle artist, Lonnie Donegan, was making a name for himself interpreting American folk songs—particularly "John Henry" and the Lead Belly standard "Rock Island Line." In a few years, British performers such as the Rolling Stones and Eric Clapton would incorporate raw blues into a strikingly modern sound and change rock forever. At the same time, a folk-rock explosion was poised to happen in England, but it hadn't happened just yet.

Burdon especially liked a folk performer in Newcastle named Johnny Handel, who sang of shipwrecks and mining disasters. Handel's music *mattered*, Burdon thought: It was great to listen to, but it also spoke of things that people in Newcastle could recognize.

Handel was also playing "House of the Rising Sun," which was making the rounds of folk musicians in Newcastle, and it was from Handel's mouth and guitar, about 1957, that Burdon first heard the song that would change his life. But as folk artists came in and out of town, Burdon noticed that more and more of them were doing "Rising Sun." He wondered where it came from; he figured it was probably from the American black blues tradition, though Handel used to say the song went back all the way back to Elizabethan England.

Burdon remembers thinking, in those early days, that the song sounded like a bastardized church hymn. "Years later, I thought, 'Well, it certainly isn't a black chord sequence. It's a European chord sequence," Burdon says now. "And it's in a minor key, which makes it stick in your head."

Stick in his head it would—and to some extent already had, because the term "Rising Sun" was not entirely unfamiliar to Burdon. When his father worked for the Northeastern Electricity Board, he'd often have to go into the coal pit to check the equipment. It was, Burdon remembers, called the Rising Sun Colliery.

As Burdon became more aware of the song, he realized it had been recorded by American folksingers whom he admired. This was about the time that *Sing Out!* magazine printed the music and lyrics, and the piece was a hot property in the coffeehouses. Woody Guthrie and Lead Belly had done versions, Burdon learned. Then there was Andy Griffith, who had not yet become everyone's favorite hometown sheriff and who had just starred in a harrowing movie called *A Face in the Crowd*, which Burdon had seen. Burdon realized Griffith, too, had sung "Rising Sun" on a recent album, *Andy Griffith Shouts the Blues and Old Timey Songs*.

(Griffith's drawl-drenched, harmonica-accompanied version of "Rising Sun" is intriguing, particularly given his North Carolina roots. He includes a verse that goes like this:

> *The longest train that I ever saw*
> *Was on that seaboard line*
> *The engine come down at six o'clock*
> *And the cab come down at nine.*

That's a line straight out of, among other songs, "In the Pines," a desolation-filled piece of folklore that, while nothing like "Rising Sun" in subject, traveled alongside it through the Appalachian tradition for many years. Griffith continued to dabble in old-time music, though over the decades he focused his energies on being Andy Taylor and Matlock.)

About a year after Burdon first heard the song, he left home. "I ran away," he says, though he was seventeen at the time. He went to Paris and found streets just like Hollywood movies—full of whores in tight satin skirts. He and his friends would hang out near bordellos, watch the hookers, and time their liaisons. "We'd figure out who was there shorter—the French or the Americans," he says. As he watched, the song—what would come to be known as his song—played in his head.

"I realized that's what this song was all about," Burdon says. "Paris opened my fucking head. England was all little red telephone booths and policemen without guns. Paris was whores driving Jaguars around. When I started singing 'House of the Rising Sun' again, I felt I'd really done my research."

Before long, Burdon returned to England to pursue music. He played with a group called the Pagans until, in 1962, he joined the Alan Price Rhythm and Blues Combo, which had been popular around Newcastle for a couple of years. The group straddled rock and roll, folk and R&B, and would come to include all of the musicians who became the Animals. Price played the organ, Hilton Valentine the guitar, and John Steel the drums. Bryan "Chas" Chandler, who would go on to launch and help manage Jimi Hendrix's career, was on bass. Burdon, who played no instrument, was the front man; he sang with a ragged voice that sounded far older than his two decades. It sounded like the blues.

This was a time when American black music had become "the new secret underground teen language," as Burdon put it: "It seemed to us the best of American culture, and though Americans seemed determined to ignore or discard it, we were happy to pick it up, dust it off, shine it and give it a new twist." It was the same process being used in the folk revival.

As the members of the band that would be renamed the Animals came together, playing at Newcastle spots like the Downbeat and the Club A-Go-Go, they heard others singing "Rising Sun." Josh White's version, available at the local record store, made a deep impression on Burdon. Then Dylan's first album arrived in Newcastle's music shops in

1962. New horizons opened. "I was amazed," Burdon says. "Here was this up-and-coming folksinger, and here were all these words."

Before long, they were calling themselves the Animals and their R&B reputation was spreading. They were traveling to London, playing for American servicemen and black Brits. The Dylan and White renditions kept popping up, and though Burdon doesn't remember exactly, he might have heard blues singer Nina Simone sing it as well; her 1962 version, recorded live at the Village Gate, was deliberate and haunting. It's possible he heard Ramblin' Jack Elliott's 1964 take, too. Elliott was a folkie, a Jewish boy from New York City who changed his name from Elliott Adnopoz and reinvented himself as a cowboy. Like Dylan, he was a Guthrie disciple, but unlike Dylan he never quite grew his music into the distinctiveness that would cross genres. Elliott's twangy version, in the Georgia Turner–style major key, mirrored Guthrie's Almanac Singers version almost to the note.

In spring 1964, when Chuck Berry and Jerry Lee Lewis came to Britain on tour, the Animals wanted in. The tour around England was an incredible opportunity for a young band. The Animals needed something more, though—a distinctive oomph, a signature song that would catapult them to a higher level. This posed a problem; great songs aren't always waiting on the tip of your pen when you need them. Plus, as Burdon points out, "I realized one thing: You can't outrock Chuck Berry."

Two generations later, it's hard to say exactly what happened and who deserves credit for what. Burdon remembers it as his idea, shaped by both the Josh White and Dylan recordings he had heard. "I thought, Why don't we take this song, reorganize it, drop some of Dylan's lyrics and get Alan Price to rearrange it?" he says. John Steel told Animals biographer Sean Egan that the idea came from the Animals' love of that first Dylan album—and from nothing else. "That's where we ripped 'House of the Rising Sun' from, no matter what you hear about Josh White," Steel said. "That was another fairy tale from Eric because we didn't want it to be thought that we were just copying from somebody as 'weakened' as Dylan. It had to come from somebody more obscure than that." And Alan Price said it was a Jacobean folk song about a whorehouse in London's Soho neighborhood that made its way to the southern United States.

As a traditional song, "House of the Rising Sun" was copyright-free and thus royalty-free, and the Animals didn't have to pay to use it. All they needed was a memorable arrangement, one that reflected the tenor of the times and would captivate the audience. Valentine says the Animals simply took the chord sequence from the Dylan version and used arpeggios instead of strumming. That, Egan writes, "gave a hypnotic, winding feel to the arrangement."

Everyone was skeptical about something or other. In rehearsals, Price didn't like Valentine's now-classic guitar chords. Producer Mickie Most didn't really want the song recorded at all. EMI, whose Columbia label had signed the Animals, was concerned about what in 1964 was a preposterous length for a single—nearly four and a half minutes. And of course there were the implications of prostitution.

The night that their "House of the Rising Sun" made its public debut, the Animals had just joined the Berry-Lewis tour. They were scheduled to close the first half of the show and lead into intermission. The band stood on the stage, bathed in darkness except for a single scarlet spotlight shining on Burdon—whether to invoke a red-light district or not, we'll never know. Burdon belted out the song and the lights went down as the final note reverberated over the applause. From that moment, Burdon knew that the song would be part of his life forever.

Recording it was the next step. On May 18, 1964, nine days after they had begun touring, they loaded their equipment onto a train and hurried down from Liverpool to London. There, in ten minutes, for ten dollars, the Animals cut the seminal modern interpretation of the old song. "A spark hit the room, was caught on the magnetic tape," Burdon recalls with his usual flourish. "And the magic began, all reflected through half-empty bottles of Newcastle Brown Ale."

It was like nothing that had come before.

Valentine's seven-note introductory guitar arpeggio, now so familiar, sounds like a laser cutting crystal as it clones itself for twelve seconds, moving inexorably toward the beginning of the vocals. Burdon, sounding like a bluesman on a rough night, is low-key at first, hinting at restraint; then, suddenly, his voice is gloriously untethered and aggressive and insolent. *My MOTHER was a tailor . . .*

Behind Burdon's voice, Price's distinctive organ emerges gradually to take over the repeating seven-note signature from Valentine. Steel's drums are audible, too, subtle but necessary, adding to the orchestral feel. The minor key haunts the whole performance.

A year before the Beatles issued their landmark *Rubber Soul* album, with its strange and wonderful experimentations, this song was introducing the definitive sound of what would become the psychedelic '60s. It was raw, out of control yet controlled, utterly modern, something pure born of technology—all our yesterdays and everything of today. It was the sound of a generation ravenous for experience and claiming its space. It would not take no for an answer. It would not go away.

Despite its noisiness, this "House of the Rising Sun" builds to its crescendo subtly and remains, today, an astonishing piece to listen to. By the time Burdon cuts in after Price's organ solo with his two climax verses—"Oh, mother, tell your children . . ." and the even rawer "Well, I got one foot on the platform, the other foot on the train . . ." the agony of the song has emerged fully. Burdon's vocals and the band's instrumentation have merged. This is no longer a folk song about a whorehouse or a gambling den or a prison or the ruin of a poor boy or girl. This is about pain, plain and simple. Even if you spoke no English whatsoever, that agony would still come through. When the Animals recorded that song, they turned pain—whose pain, exactly, is unclear—into music.

That, of course, is the definition of the blues.

The entire sequence of events—the Animals rearranging the song, introducing it on the tour, and rushing to London to record it—represented one extended musical moment. It was, in the story of "Rising Sun," the narrow part of the song's historical hourglass.

All that had come before flowed into this moment in 1964: Alan Lomax and Georgia Turner in Middlesboro, Woody Guthrie, Josh White, Lead Belly, Dave Van Ronk, and Bob Dylan. English ballad tradition and Appalachian angst and mountain beginnings, the technology of recorded sound and the musical sampling of the folk revival. Dim echoes of an event long ago and a place that may or may not have existed. They all cascaded into that historical pivot point in 1964. And from the narrow part of the hourglass, the sand flowed out again, renewed, refined, filtered by the Animals and their unforgettable performance—and the echo of it that their recording created.

There was now a canonical version, a springboard from which musicians could jump, a song that *Rolling Stone,* in 1988, would rate the seventy-fifth most popular single recording of the quarter century. It didn't mean that future musicians wouldn't improvise—we'll examine some of the joyous ways they did that—but the Animals were the standard. Through three decades and into the twenty-first century, when a group wanted an easy, familiar hit, they would turn to the version conceived by Price, Burdon, Valentine, Chandler, and Steel. Sometimes they would begin with the same riff; sometimes they would enlist the same organ music. Many times, they'd keep the same verses in the same order—a lament sung by a boy, not a girl, led astray by his excesses.

The oral tradition of the nineteenth and early twentieth centuries allowed for infinite variation: As a song moved from porch to porch, from miner to miner or rounder to rounder, it took on new form, new meaning, and new life. You might hear a song from someone, then never see that person again, leaving you to create your own interpretation. Today, musical diversity exists in a different way. Technology and mass media allow us to create endless permutations of a piece of culture; Andy Warhol showed us that. But the previous pieces always remain in existence, pulling us back to standards. No matter how many musicians interpret "Rising Sun," we'll still be able to go to Wal-Mart or iTunes, pick up the version that the Animals recorded that day in 1964 and listen. That changes how music unfolds in a world where everything of the past half century remains available at our cultural buffet table.

If, as Burdon said, the recording session itself was magical, what happened next was firmly grounded in the ugliness of the real, commercial world.

From four decades later, it's hard to sort out the hurt feelings and financial recriminations. Alan Price doesn't talk about it; Eric Burdon still does so, and loudly. According to Burdon, who has been backed up by his bandmates to some extent, Animals manager Mike Jeffery, who had taken over the band's affairs after they rose out of his Club A-Go-Go in Newcastle, told the band their names wouldn't all fit on the single. Jeffery, who went on to manage Jimi Hendrix and face accusations of questionable business conduct, said the Animals should choose one name to appear on the 45 and sort out the details later. Burdon says the name suggested was Alan Price's. Fine, said the band, and the credit on the single went like this: "Trad.: Arr. A. Price."

That decision, and the ripples it caused, would tear the Animals apart long before their creative genius had played out. The other band members, their biographer Egan says, "never saw a penny in publishing royalties."

It galls Burdon to this day. He allows that Price deserved credit, but for other band members to be excluded entirely? For him to be denied any royalties over four decades? Burdon feels betrayed by Price and has accused Jeffery and Price of collusion. "With the stroke of a pen, the rest of the Animals were screwed. Ripped off from the get-go—from inside," Burdon wrote in his autobiography. He wonders why they didn't just decide to have "Arr.: The Animals" on the record. It would have fit just fine, and "the biggest mistake of our lives never would have happened."

After the recording, things unfolded fast. The song was mastered and released in a month. The BBC wasn't playing it at first; it was, after all, an extremely long single with bawdy undertones. But the Animals did the song on *Ready Steady Go!* a popular British musical TV show of the era, and it shot up the charts—first in England, then in the United States.

On September 5, 1964, it displaced the Supremes' "Where Did Our Love Go" as number one on *Billboard*'s American chart. There it would remain for three weeks until it was overtaken by "Oh, Pretty Woman" from Roy Orbison, whose music drew on some of the same musical traditions as "Rising Sun." The Animals found themselves en route to New York and *The Ed Sullivan Show,* where the notoriously prickly host—months after hosting the Beatles in one of the most fabled television appearances ever—told the band that they would perform "Rising Sun" for his audience or would not appear at all.

After "Rising Sun" hit the top, the Animals became one of the British Invasion's top bands—behind the Beatles, the Rolling Stones, and the Kinks, but still a top-shelf force—and recorded such hits as "Don't Let Me Be Misunderstood" and "We Gotta Get Out of This Place." Then, only months later, on April 30, 1965, Alan Price left the band that once bore his name. Five days later he sent word that he had quit, that his fear of flying was making touring unbearable.

Subsequent reports from both the Price and Burdon camps suggested that Price was exhausted, both emotionally and physically, and that there was a clash between the introverted Price and the outgoing—sometimes showboating—Burdon. But the rancor of the "Rising Sun" credit brouhaha had cast a pall, and Price's fellow bandmates have wondered openly if he left because he had enough money to do so. Price hung around with Bob Dylan after leaving the Animals and appears in the background a few times on D. A. Pennebaker's Dylan documentary *Don't Look Back.*

Price hasn't discussed the "Rising Sun" matter in much detail; my efforts to reach him over the years met with no success. In the 1998 book *Behind the Song: The Stories of 100 Great Pop & Rock Classics,* though, he was quoted as claiming ownership. "I based our version on the Bob Dylan record. I took his chord sequence and I rehearsed the band, so it was my arrangement," he said. Today, his official website has only this to say:

> Price's hypnotic arrangement of the band's epic version of "The House of the Rising Sun" was released in June 1964 and went on to become a worldwide smash, topping both the UK and US charts. . . . [T]he record propelled the group to undreamed-of success.

Years later, Price recorded his own version of "House of the Rising Sun," nearly a minute longer than the 1964 version. The newer arrangement is jazzier, reflecting his sensibilities, and contains few of the hallmarks of his Animals' version. Price's voice is far smoother than Burdon's and evokes a nightclub rather than a sweaty roadhouse. It contains only snippets of the organ segment and no trace of Valentine's arpeggio guitar. Most interesting, Price has played with the gender of the piece. He says that the House of the Rising Sun has "been the ruin of many a poor boy," but later asks: "Mother, tell my baby sister not to do what I have done."

Price moved on long ago. His website focuses on his post-Animals accomplishments as a solo performer, particularly on the piano and in stage projects. The section about the Animals says he was "a complex, moody character, prone to prolonged bouts of bleak introversion" who had "always somehow been slightly estranged from his colleagues" even though they came from the same background and shared "a fondness for drink." It seeks to differentiate Price from his bandmates, saying he had more sophisticated musical tastes and, "having achieved a higher level of education, he had interests he couldn't share with the others." In short, while they were out picking up babes, he was sitting on the tour bus reading Kafka.

The original Animals tried to reunite a few times—for a benefit concert in 1968, an album in 1977, and a world tour in 1983—but it never lasted. Musical tastes had changed, members had moved on, and old grudges hadn't faded entirely. In 1994, the group reunited once more to be inducted into the Rock and Roll Hall of Fame. Today, in his midsixties, Burdon is still on the road making music, touring with a band he calls the Animals. He is its only original member. There can never be another true reunion, for Chas Chandler died in 1996.

There is a postscript to this tale. It is the stuff of legend how Bob Dylan famously and notoriously "went electric" at the 1965 Newport Folk Festival, to the chagrin of Pete Seeger, Alan Lomax, and thousands of folk purists. According to John Steel and Eric Burdon, what pushed Dylan to this decision was hearing the Animals' version of "House of the Rising Sun."

Steel, in the band biography *Animal Tracks*, says he heard this from Dylan himself: "He said he was driving along in his car and (the Animals' "Rising Sun") came on the radio and he pulled the car over and stopped and listened to it and he jumped out of the car and he banged on the bonnet. That gave him the connection he could go electric."

Is this true? We may never know. Dylan doesn't say much. But I like the idea that our song's splashiest moment might have inspired a hard right turn by the folk revival's most recognizable icon. It fits the song's travels perfectly—the notion that purists are romantic and necessary but ultimately unrealistic. In music and in culture, what matters is the journey, and purists allow no journey: They are consumed with beginnings, and they are always frozen in the past.

NEW ORLEANS, LOUISIANA

The bungalow is empty. A knock on the front door produces no response, so I walk around to the fence that rings the yard. It is a blistering spring day in the Garden District of New Orleans, a few days after Jazzfest's conclusion and many seasons before the winds and waters of Hurricane Katrina. The humidity—water from the Mississippi a few blocks away, absorbed into the air and then recondensed on my forehead—drips down my brow.

"Hello?" I say, knocking on the fence door. Nothing. Thirty seconds later, a British accent sounds across the lawn inside. "Here! Coming! On my way!"

The fence door pops open to reveal a man in his late fifties. He squints in the midday light, and his face is weathered in a tropical, Jimmy Buffett sort of way, as if wine, sun, and late nights have preserved a modern, vibrant, handsome mummy. His feet are bare. He is wearing a loud, Hawaiian-style shirt. So am I.

"We match," says Eric Burdon. Then he grins, and I am immediately charmed.

I am meeting the performer that a newspaper reporter once called "one of the blackest white men in blues." I have arranged, through a stroke of fortune, to meet him in the city he has sung about for so long. He is staying with a friend he often visits when he goes back to New Orleans. And Eric Burdon always goes back to New Orleans, which he considers a pleasing mix of Paris and his native England. He does wonder, though, what folks here think of him: "They're trying to build up tourism, and here's this Brit singing about a whorehouse."

Despite his good humor, the Animals' lead singer, about to turn fifty-nine, looks as if New Orleans and its bounty have claimed his energy, at least for the moment. On his wrist, he wears a Bob Marley watch—though, he allows, it also occasionally serves as a stand-in for his long-dead friend, Jimi Hendrix: "It turns into Jimi depending on how stoned you are."

We sit in the darkened living room of his friend's house. Burdon lives in California these days—he became an American citizen years ago—but this week he is living out of a suitcase that sits on the floor, open. More loud shirts are visible. As we talk, he grows animated, occasionally turning to air guitar or air piano to make his points.

My agenda this day is, I suppose, unclear. I don't really need to know anything about how the Animals recorded "Rising Sun" and where it went from there. I guess I want to get a feel for this man whose voice was the conduit that gave our song a new identity. So many people think Eric Burdon wrote "House of the Rising Sun," and, while of course he didn't, he placed an indelible stamp on it before sending it on its way.

Burdon is full of stories about "House of the Rising Sun," many of which are probably apocryphal, either through others' inaccuracies or his own much-documented embellishments. Some you simply want to believe, the ones that show how deeply the song resonated among the people of his generation. One night in the 1990s, Burdon was playing in Amagansett, a Long Island beach town, when an aging Vietnam vet approached him after the gig. He told Burdon he was in the Cambodian jungle on a secret operation on Christmas Eve 1968. The GIs had been permitted a guitar, and they chose "Rising Sun" to play and sing. There was an echo in the jungle, the vet told Burdon, and the men could hear their counterparts in the North Vietnamese Army out there, in the darkness, singing along as the insects chirped.

Even Burdon doesn't entirely know the roots of the song that changed his life. His autobiography repeats the common internet boilerplate—that it "has its roots in a seventeenth-century British folk melody, but became what it is today after circulating among Southern American musicians." Quite possibly true, but unproven. Then he repeats the common inaccuracy that "it was first recorded . . . by black bluesman Texas Alexander in 1928." Remember, that Alexander piece, "The Risin' Sun," has nothing to do with our song. Burdon also says he "changed the lyrics to make it the story of a 'poor boy' rather than a 'poor girl,' as it was originally written." Sure, he did change the point of view at that moment in time. But as we've seen, some of the earliest versions are sung from a man's perspective.

The Animals were evolutionaries, not revolutionaries. Their goulash of folk, rock, and R&B was the blending of genres that our song needed at that moment. But they were doing what everyone else had done— taking something memorable and malleable, applying their circumstances and making it their own.

Burdon is something of a walking Trivial Pursuit of rock, coughing up nuggets that relate to the topic at hand only tangentially, then riffing. At one point, he starts to talk about Elvis. He is discussing something or other about the King's music when he shoots me a look. Did I know, he asks, that the horse stable at Graceland was called the House of the Rising Sun? Then he winks at me.

(I have no choice but to follow this up. When I make it to Graceland a year later, I take the very intricate—and not inexpensive—audio tour. After learning that Elvis's father kept a firing range that sometimes doubled as a meat smokehouse, I pop in Tape No. 35, "Horses/to Trophy Building" and learn about Presley's steed. "His own favorite horse was a golden palomino named Rising Sun," the velvet-voiced narrator says. "He nicknamed the barn House of Rising Sun." Alas, I never found any evidence that Elvis immortalized his horse by actually ever *singing* "House of the Rising Sun.")

The conversation keeps turning back to Jimi Hendrix, Burdon's guitar-genius friend who choked to death on his own vomit in 1970. Burdon tells of a poem found by Hendrix's bedside after his death. I can't find any record of it, but Burdon is certain. Jimi, he said, wrote this: "I've seen angels from heaven, flying saucers in the sun, and must make my Easter Sunday in the name of the Rising Sun."

Burdon is going through my stack of CDs, looking at different versions of the song. He leafs through Woody Guthrie, Monsters of Rock, Dolly Parton, Nina Simone. He grins when he comes across *Hot Dog: Don Thompson Plays Ragtime and Blues,* which features a Wurlitzer organ. (Like so many artists, Thompson told me that he was inspired to adapt the song after hearing Burdon sing it. "His version really builds. And I thought it would be a very powerful number.")

As Burdon eyes the assortment of discs, he begins to sing. I'm not even sure he realizes he's doing it, though he's such a performer that he probably takes few steps unconsciously. Still, it is an oddly informal moment: I am accustomed to hearing his voice doing this song backed by electric instruments, delivered iconically. And here's the guy in the loud shirt sitting in a living room, a suitcase in front of him, and the voice that emerges is the iconic one. *Been the ruin of many a poor boy . . .*

He can't help it; he's sung it so many nights on so many stages in so many gin joints that it is second nature. "I'm chained to the song like a tethered slave is to a chain gang," he says. If you hear him performing it, though, you might find that it sounds . . . unfamiliar. We've seen this song move, grow, mutate, adapt. Usually it does that when it is passed from performer to performer; the mutation occurs when a new singer reshapes it. But it seems that Burdon, the man whose voice froze "Rising Sun" in time, likes to play around with it—to make it different as often as possible.

"I change it every night. . . . When I hear those opening chords and step up to the microphone, it's like a new song every time," Burdon says. His face gets serious; he looks straight at me. "How can I sing it all these years and still sing it with conviction? Because I didn't get paid for it."

The conviction still reverberates, even a cappella in the little room with me. Somehow the Animals channeled something. No, that's not exactly it; what I'm talking about is more the reverse. That's what I learn from Eric Burdon: that a song can engulf a man, that it can channel *him*. Because though the song, to much of the world, is owned by the Animals, it is the Animals—and Burdon in particular—who are actually owned by the song. Even Burdon, though he likes to hint at ownership, is the first to acknowledge that it eludes him.

"I don't have the rights to it. Nobody has the rights to it," says the man who turned our song into an emblem of twentieth-century music. "It belongs," Burdon says, "to the world."

A few years back, a middle-aged British guy finds himself in Seattle with some time to kill. He is staying at a place called the Black Angus Motel, and one evening he is walking over to the adjacent bar and grill for dinner. As he passes the bar door, he hears a guy singing a very competent karaoke version of "Are You Lonesome Tonight?" He looks in and sees only the singer and the bartender; the rest of the place is empty. So the man goes in.

Perusing the list of musical choices, the man sees "House of the Rising Sun" on the list and, like many before and after him, can't resist the temptation. Because the lounge is deserted, there is little risk of embarrassment. The man commandeers the microphone, cues up the song and performs it in the classic style of the Animals. After he finishes, he ambles over to the bar, where the barkeeper, who has never seen the stranger before, offers up an enthusiastic greeting.

"Hey, that was pretty good!" the bartender tells Eric Burdon, and gives him a free margarita.

6 Everywhere

I hear America singing,
the varied carols I hear . . .
each singing what belongs to him or her
and to none else.

—WALT WHITMAN, "I HEAR AMERICA SINGING"

Voices from nowhere and voices
from the larger towns . . .

—JOHN MELLENCAMP, "R.O.C.K. IN THE U.S.A."

The Animals' arrangement rippled out into a world of musical genres that had been and were still evolving, blending, and globalizing in ways never before considered. The British Invasion was steaming forward. Delta Blues and Appalachian folk were being cannibalized and reworked into hard rock, soul, rhythm & blues. In Vietnam, GIs fighting the war blasted rock music from radios in the jungle, sending the Doors, Jimi Hendrix, and Creedence Clearwater Revival through the Mekong Delta. The Beatles went to India with the Maharishi, and the sitar, for a micromoment in history, echoed across the rock landscape.

And "House of the Rising Sun"? Artist after artist claimed it and reshaped it. Disco. Country rock. Jazz. Cajun. Elevator music. German tango and harmonica. In South Africa, singer-activist Miriam Makeba sang it as an apartheid-era lament. The hard-rock band Frijid Pink cut a version that a young serviceman named Gillis Turner grew to love while serving in Vietnam, and had no idea it was connected to his Aunt Georgia back in Middlesboro, Kentucky. "I think," he says, "that everybody who's had a bad day can relate to that song."

In the decades since, Billy Joel has sung it in concert. Jerry Garcia, two years before he died, cut a rambling, warbling 1993 version with David Grisman and Tony Rice on a jam CD called *The Pizza Tapes*. Reggae artist Gregory Isaacs brought it into his genre with a "vocal mix," a "wicked dub mix," and a "slightly dubful vocal mix." Musicians from everywhere, with all manner of unusual names and styles, have contributed renditions—from Nixon Grin (Denver, hard alternative rock) to Sex Mob (New York City, jazzy funk) to the Pork Dukes (Witham, England, early punk) to Crazy Otto's Ragtime Band (Germany, oompah).

It has been appropriated into hip-hop, a collage-driven genre that relies upon the reinterpretation of music that came before. When Wyclef Jean used the melody of "House of the Rising Sun" in the background and added Haitian lyrics for the moody 1997 song "Sang Fezi," Georgia Turner's old song was enlisted to explore the themes of police mistreatment and cultural identity in New York City. Wyclef even got Lauryn Hill to sing a couple verses to the tune:

> *Then you should know that one day we are gone*
> *so keep your head to the sky.*
> *See the path we refuse*
> *is the path we should choose.*
> *You can't take the world when you die.*

It's not limited to hip-hop. For more than a generation, we have lived in an age of engulfing collage. More than ever, quotations—printed, visual, aural—help us tell our stories. Something happens in our lives, and someone says, "That's like in *Seinfeld* when George and Elaine . . ." The entire history of human endeavor has become one vast pool of potential citations—items and ideas to be appropriated and reinterpreted, digested and spat out in assorted, sometimes barely recognizable forms. In 2004, Bartlett's—the familiar quotations folks—even came out with an "expanded multimedia edition" that incorporated works of art, music, video, and movie stills as "quotations." Culturally, we are our ingredients, and they keep bubbling up.

So it is that "On Top of Old Smoky," a bitter lover's lament from the

Appalachian tradition, becomes "On Top of Spaghetti," a whimsical children's song ("I lost my poor meatball when somebody sneezed"). Canada's Moxy Fruvous folds a line from the Lead Belly standard "Irene" into one of its own compositions, a lament about drunkenness. "Bonaparte's Retreat," an old Appalachian fiddle tune that Aaron Copland borrowed, evolves again into the theme music for a commercial: "Beef—it's what's for dinner." And the solemn, moving "Battle Hymn of the Republic" is appropriated for a schoolboy's insolent rebellion (one that was sung frequently in my childhood but today would probably result in a call to 911):

> *Mine eyes have seen the glory*
> *of the burning of the school*
> *We have tortured every teacher,*
> *we have broken every rule.*
> *We have raped the secretary,*
> *we have hanged the principal.*
> *Our truth goes marching on.*

The tune "Turkey in the Straw" is as traditional as they come (and once was known as "Old Zip Coon"), but my first exposure to it as a child was in a cleaning-solvent ad: *I've been using Murphy's Oil Soap all through this house of mine / Now the dirt is finished but the finish is fine.* I will spare you the second verse, which remains lodged in one of the deeper recesses of my mind, where it refuses to be purged.

So pervasive are these acts of expropriation that we barely notice them unless they're egregious, like Mercedes using Janis Joplin's countercultural "Mercedes Benz" as an irony-free advertisement for cars. "I wonder why it took them so long, in a way," the song's cowriter, Bob Neuwirth, said in 1995. Even Woody Guthrie's "This Land Is Your Land" was once co-opted for a United Airlines jingle.

In this cultural context, the Animals' version takes on new importance. The argument can be made that "House of the Rising Sun" ceased to be a folk song that day in 1964, when it assumed a kind of formalism and became part of written, not oral tradition. I don't buy that. The traditions we draw upon have changed—an influential recording instead of a grandparent singing—but we're still chewing up and digesting things, albeit at an accelerated pace and with tools our ancestors never contemplated. While The Village has become a city, many of our old habits remain.

Since the Animals, "Rising Sun" has emerged as a canvas for artists in genres so different that juxtaposing them creates a tapestry of the absurd. Yes, the song's legal status as traditional accounts for some of its wide use, but it has also developed a reputation as good album filler: You have your original works, and you fill out the rest with a really good cut of "House of the Rising Sun." You put your mark on it—or sometimes you don't—and voilà! Instant listenability.

And occasionally, from the collage, comes a truly original take. An artist grabs the song, parses it, contemplates it, and reconceives it with new circumstances and new miseries in mind.

A tour is in order. Let's embark upon an amusement park ride through the various versions of "Rising Sun" that have emerged since the 1960s. Separately, they are symptoms of the culture. Together, they illustrate a musical movement in miniature—a funhouse of many mirrors, each singing, each with something to say.

ALAMANCE COUNTY, NORTH CAROLINA

I am driving down State Route 87 in North Carolina, a rural two-lane about a fifty-mile ride from Raleigh. I'm not certain, exactly, what I'm looking for, but I will know it when I find it.

About eight miles south of I-40, there it is: a low-slung roadside building at the edge of a thicket of trailers. It is sad and a bit menacing, its black paint and Play-Doh purple highlights interrupting the Carolina greenery. The frond-festooned plastic sign ("Adult Entertainment at Its Best") and a ratty second sign set up in the gravel parking lot ("Girls Girls Girls: Dancers needed") undermine it further. It is midday, and the place appears closed.

This is the Paradise Club. Joints like this line America's back roads by the hundreds—low-end clubs where girls looking for cash and, sometimes, validation peel off garters and panties to reveal . . . what? Themselves? Hardly. Their bodies, and little more. Such establishments are Whorehouse Lite, where glimpses of the forbidden and twenty-dollar lap dances take the place of penetration. Usually.

The Paradise Club existed in obscurity until, one day, Melissa Swingle came along and wrote a song. It is "House of the Rising Sun" reconceived for twenty-first-century circumstances—rocking hard, with entirely fresh lyrics, but complete with the tune, cadence, and feel of the familiar song.

> *There is a joint out on Old 87*
> *they call the Paradise Club.*
> *It's been the home of many Alamance County girls*
> *when they hit bad luck.*

"It's just like the seediest-looking strip club you've ever seen," Swingle says.

Formerly the lead singer of a band called Trailer Bride, she is now half of the Moaners with Laura King, formerly of Baltimore's Grand National. It's hard to listen to the Moaners' first album, *Dark Snack,* and not be captivated. I arrange to meet them at a dimly lit, members-only bar in Carrboro, just south of Chapel Hill, called the Orange County Social Club.

When Melissa and Laura arrive, they are yin and yang. Melissa Swingle, thirty-five, is tall and intimidating, cool and reserved, a sexy Morticia Addams. Laura King, twenty-eight, is pretty and soft-spoken with an easy smile—very alt-rocky, but sweet, too. You can see how the uniting of these personalities could produce some serious originality. Melissa orders a Jim Beam-rocks; Laura is a Tecate girl.

Their musical histories are just as divergent. King started playing drums at age eleven; she began with a drum set themed to the 1970s shark cartoon *Jabberjaw* and quickly moved up to a Toys "R" Us model. By the time she entered what she calls her "Black Sabbath phase" a couple years later, she was playing in Baltimore clubs with her first band, Pedge. She started touring while still in high school, and quickly had one of the more quintessential band experiences—the tour van caught fire.

Swingle grew up in the Deep South listening to Delta blues before, at age eleven, moving to the Ivory Coast in West Africa with her Baptist-missionary parents. For six years, she absorbed African rhythms and integrated them into her Southern sensibilities. She became a musician in her mid-twenties when, pregnant with her daughter, she had to give up smoking and painting ("I thought I was a painter") but realized that the music she listened to while painting was actually the point.

"I realized, 'I want to make my own,' " she says, so she picked up a guitar. That led to Trailer Bride, an outfit that produced dark Southern music and specialized in tunes about sex, decay, and people gone wrong. One fan, reviewing a Trailer Bride CD on Amazon a couple years ago, quoted her husband as saying it "sounds like the house band for some country graveyard." Perfect environment for a "Rising Sun" interpretation.

Melissa was playing with Trailer Bride and Laura with Grand National when they met at a honky-tonk festival in Chapel Hill in 2001. They hit it off, exchanged numbers, and agreed to jam sometime. "I saw her play drums and I was blown away: 'That's the best drummer I've ever seen and she's pretty, too," Melissa says. Laura returns the compliment. "I said, 'She has nice legs and she rocks'" From that encounter eventually emerged the Moaners, who say they want to blend Appalachian music, blues, and rock into something entirely fresh.

I want to hear how they decided to rework "Rising Sun," and how the Paradise Club became inspiration. They are game and start talking with each other.

Melissa: "I kind of thought Bob Dylan wrote it. I thought the Animals had ripped Bob Dylan off."

Laura: "I thought Eric Burdon wrote it. We just started playing around with it."

Melissa: "She just started a beat up, and I started playing chords to go with it. We said, 'Great, we have a new song. Then, in the twilight, in the morning, I thought, Oh, no—this is 'House of the Rising Sun.' So we went from there."

Laura: "We put it aside for a while. It was like, I really wanted to write an original song here."

As we've seen, though, original can take many forms. For the Moaners, there was something missing—something that would allow them to put their stamp upon the old song. That something came when they started contemplating the Paradise Club.

Melissa knows a girl who once stripped there and a guy who dated a stripper. Every time she drives home to Mississippi, she passes the place.

"That's what fascinated me about it. You're driving, and suddenly there's a strip club," she says. "It gives me kind of a thrill, I don't know why."

We drink some more. She figures out a little bit of why.

"They don't discriminate," Melissa says. One girl had one leg shorter than the other. One had diabetes and wears an insulin patch. "She got a lot of tips. I guess they felt sorry for her."

Pause.

"It's kind of where stripper rejects go."

Laura chimes in with her own detail. "They have trailers out back, and the strippers live there and call the owners Mommy and Daddy. At least, that's what we hear."

A carpenter and local character walks up and greets Melissa and Laura. The women ask him about the Paradise Club. "I've been there once," he says. "Best strip club I've ever been to. What I appreciate about it is that there's no fake tits in the place. They can't afford 'em."

I'm not certain what to say to that, so I buy him a beer. In return, he does my job for me: "How'd you end up making the song about that?" he asks the Moaners.

"I didn't want to do a cover. So late one night I just thought, Let's make it about the Paradise Club," Melissa says. "I put myself in the position of maybe a boyfriend or girlfriend of someone who worked there—like, 'I'll save you from this life.' But I didn't want it to make fun of strippers or be condescending to the strippers."

As happy hour melts into evening, the Orange County Social Club grows crowded and Laura and Melissa grow more animated. We talk about piling into the car and actually heading out to the Paradise Club, but the notion never reaches critical mass. Finally, it grows so noisy that I suggest we find someplace where I can play them the unusual versions socked away in my iPod. Melissa suggests her car. It proves to be a perfect music-listening car—a sky-blue 1964 Chevy Impala. We order another round, gather up our drinks, and make our way out to the parking lot in back.

Swingle takes up position in her driver's seat; King clambers into the back. I take shotgun. This is the kind of car you dream about when you think of kicking back in small-town Southern twilight and developing a nice buzz. The seats are like park benches. The steering wheel is huge and uncushioned, just as it should be. Chrome detailing is everywhere.

The radio is AM, with those large numbers on the dial that have long since been replaced by the far less satisfying digital display.

I plug in my portable speakers and play them Georgia Turner's version. I always get a kick out of watching people hear her long-dead voice singing from 1937. Georgia's twang echoes through the Impala as Melissa Swingle takes a hit from her latest Beam. "That was amazing," Laura says. "I've never heard anything like that. I can't believe that's the same song."

I play them Clarence Ashley's 1933 version, with its Jimmie Rodgers riff at the beginning; the Callahan Brothers' haunting 1934 version; Roscoe Holcomb's otherworldly effort from the 1950s. Then we turn to the weird ones: the Latin-flavored Santa Esmeralda, French pop king Johnny Hallyday, the elevator-music stylings of *Golden Trumpet Favorites*.

"What's *your* favorite?" Swingle asks. I cite EverEve, a hardcore band from the 1990s whose take is the darkest and most energetic I've ever come across. We play that, and both grin at the driving guitar and EverEve's sneering vocals. "That's fucking incredible," Swingle says. "That really rocks."

"You want to hear more?" I ask, tentatively. Here I am, pleasantly buzzed, sitting in an 1964 Impala with two of the coolest women I've met in a long time. The last thing I want be is the music nerd who can't control his enthusiasm. "I recognize that I can get carried away with this," I say, smiling sheepishly.

"No, no. I'm having a great time," Melissa says. Laura nods enthusiastically from the backseat. "Nothing wrong with a little obsession," she says.

They laugh as I play them the honky-tonk-on-speedballs version sung by Steve Power, an American who recorded it in England a few years back. It's cheesy, but it's a contender for my favorite, too. Swingle agrees. "It's totally wrong for the story, but it still captures it perfectly."

Throughout the evening, the women have expressed reservations about "Paradise Club," despite the critical praise it received. They worry about originality and want to ensure the Moaners' contribution to music is unique. But as we talk, they grow more open to the notion that you can transform something by interpreting it your own way. Original thought may not be restricted to eureka-style ideas.

"If you take something familiar and make it unique in some way, and if you really mean what you say, you've done something," Melissa Swingle says.

The folk process in a nutshell, served up in the front seat of a 1964 Impala on a warm spring evening in North Carolina.

Years ago, when my quest was just beginning, I started calling artists to find out why they recorded "Rising Sun." Before long, I had a file of dozens of interviews, from famous musicians to people you've probably never heard of, like Don Thompson, the pipe organist whose version I played for Eric Burdon. All had different stories about how they came across the song, but all came back to the same notion: It contains something universal, something timeless.

Hank Williams Jr., son of the father of country music (does that make him the brother of country music?), did a grumbling, honky-tonk version on *Hank "Live"* in 1987 and tweaked some of the lyrics to make it his own ("It's been the ruination of many street guitar blues boys"). He told me through his publicist that he first heard it during the folk revival and was struck by the poignancy of the lyrics. "It's sad to know that any human is trapped and confined to anyplace that is a mental hell, be it the House of the Rising Sun or maybe even at home," Hank Jr. said.

Country music icon Dolly Parton, raised poor in eastern Tennessee (she has since built a 125-acre theme park nearby, including a reconstruction of the Smoky Mountains cabin where she grew up), reconceived the song for her *9 to 5 and Odd Jobs* album in 1980. Mike Post, best known for his electronic theme songs from TV shows like *Hill Street Blues,* worked with Parton on the arrangement. What emerged was a poppy disco take that rewrote the first two verses entirely, adding details that leave no doubt what the song is about:

> *There is a house in New Orleans*
> *down in the Vieux Carre.*
> *A house they call the Risin' Sun*
> *where love and money are made.*
>
> *My father, he was a gambler*
> *mother died when I was young.*

> *And I've worked since then to pleasure the men*
> *at the House of the Rising Sun.*

Parton learned the song as a girl. "Mama used to sing a version of it from one of the old folk songs," she wrote back to me after I asked her how she came to record it. "It's one of the first songs that I ever learned to play on the guitar." When she was doing *9 to 5*, she and Post were experimenting with different songs about various jobs and what they were like. "I said something like . . . 'and then there's prostitution.' We both looked at each other at exactly the same time and said 'House of the Rising Sun,' " Parton says. Post said to her, "Let's not do just the same old version of it, let's do it different." "So he did an uptempo arrangement. It's always been one of my favorite songs that I've recorded," Parton says.

She's not the only one to tweak the lyrics; many have done so to make the song fit their circumstances (or their stage persona) better. David Allan Coe, for example, beefed up the family's role in the song by blaming the singer's ruin on his father and adding more detail about the mother trying to save her offspring from his vices:

> *My father was a gambler*
> *he lived by the gun.*
> *He swore someday he'd take me to play*
> *at the House of the Risin' Sun.*
>
> *My mother was a lady*
> *she never hurt no one.*
> *She cursed the day I went to play*
> *in the House of the Risin' Sun.*
>
> *She said, You're like your daddy, boy—*
> *livin' on the run.*
> *Someday you'll draw a dead man's hand*
> *in the House of the Risin' Sun.*

Lorie Line, a Minnesota pianist, used to play in a Minneapolis department store called Dayton's. Every time she played "House of the Rising

Sun," shoppers responded. "People said it takes you back in time," she says. "We all grew up with it in one way or another." Her ambient 1994 version features her piano backed by various sounds—including male and female voices moaning—but no words. "I didn't want lyrics," she says. "I opted to have the moaning and the wailing and the humming and the vocal expressionism on the piece. I just felt it needed it."

People still shout out for her to play it. "One hundred years ago, you would perform in front of a few people in a living room, and they might go out into the countryside and talk about it. Now, because of the technology we have, we can take something that's so ancient and so old and put our own stamp on it and communicate it to the world."

I have 119 CDs that contain versions of the song, jammed into a zip case that unsettles some folks when I open it up and show them. These have been gathered from record stores around the world and from Amazon. They have made my American Express bill far beyond what it should have been. *Mothers, tell your children, not to do what I have done.* I have another 260 on my computer from various downloaded digital files, both professional and amateur. I have barely scratched the surface; musicians crank out new ones every month.

To see this wealth of talent (and marginal talent) turning to this song, over and over again, illustrates its winding path. Each version has its merits, even if said merits must occasionally be described using sarcasm. It reminds me, too, that after all this time, "Rising Sun" still sells. "When we play that song, they buy the album," says Jason Coomes, singer for the Laramie, Wyoming, alt-country band Blinddog Smokin'.

In the interest of brevity, then, let's convene a brief awards ceremony to showcase the highlights, lowlights, and weirdlights of the post-Animals' "Rising Sun" canon.

ODDEST: The Timo Kinnunen One-Man Band, a Finnish outfit, if you can call one guy an outfit. Timo's take features no discernable tune, random squeaks in the background and a voice like what you might hear if Stephen Hawking took requests. Midway through, Timo plays what appears to be a kazoo. You will have a headache after listening to this—not because it's bad, but because you'll be trying to figure out exactly what motivated him. (I have another Finnish version that's actually *in*

Finnish and much less weird, but it was sent to me with no credits and I can't find the band that did it.)

This category has a runner-up—a Greek musician named Demis Roussos, who assembled a seven-minute, fifty-four-second version that manages to combine elements of speed metal, background music, Philip Glass, a Led Zeppelin laser show, and the themes from *Chariots of Fire* and *The A-Team*. The result: a Gen-X-friendly goulash that you don't really *want* to hear but simply can't turn off.

MOST HAUNTING: Mark O'Connor and Vassar Clements, two accomplished fiddlers, playing in tandem with a quiet guitar in the background. Slow, deliberate, and mournful, it sounds like the lonely hills from which "Rising Sun" came. It sounds exactly like what this song means—pain and unadulterated regret.

MOST DANCEABLE: A fast-paced, honky-tonk take by an American artist named Steve Power who spent years playing in Great Britain. It's a delightfully cheesy send-up of the Nashville Sound, and I mean that in the best way. Of hundreds of versions, Power's rendition is one of my absolute favorites; as Melissa Swingle of the Moaners put it, it's utterly inappropriate for the subject matter and, at the same time, absolutely perfect.

Power, who counts Bill Monroe and Bruce Springsteen as equal influences, told me his version simply "came from the ether" one night years ago while playing at a rough-and-rowdy seaport bar in Cardiff, Wales. By the end of the night, "all that was left was the hard ladies," he says, and the slow version wasn't cutting it, so he injected a bluegrass beat and sang in a major key instead of a minor one. It works wonderfully.

"I used it for a long time as a closer and to separate the men from the boys in the band," he says. "I always loved real country that rocked." The recorded version, with Ian Lawrence on the pedal steel guitar and banjo, is unlike any other. With this song, that's saying a lot. I've danced with my wife to it. It somehow manages to tell a sad story and leave you happy.

MOST UNLISTENABLE: The New Age stylings of David H. Yakobian on his album *Alpha States with Exotic Recorders* capture this category. His overwrought, instrumental "Rising Sun" features a guy saying, in a reverb-rich stage whisper, "Rise! Rise!" and finishes up with birds chirping gently. Does Yakobian's desire for his "joyously transcendent sound" to be "a call for tranquility and peace" mitigate or aggravate the problem? The jury's out.

MOST COMMUNAL: British singer-songwriter John Otway performed "House of the Rising Sun" for years, and audience participation grew each time. In 2002, at Abbey Road Studios in London, Otway and a thousand of what he calls his "closest fans" gathered to give the musician a celebration for his impending fiftieth birthday. There they recorded a "House of the Rising Sun" like no other—a call-and-response extravaganza that must have been the most audience-participatory studio recording ever made. It was a unique blend of production and folk music—with lots and lots of actual folks.

Here's a bit of it:

Otway: "My mother—she was a tailor."
Hundreds of Otway fans, shouting in unison: "What'd she sew?"
Otway: "She sewed my new blue jeans . . ."
Fans: "What about your father?"
Otway: "Yes, well, my father. He was a gambling man."
Fans: "Where?"
Otway: "Down in New Orleans."

And so it goes, through the entire song. By the end, Otway is singing only sporadically and the crowd is carrying most of the verses. When it was issued, each fan got credit on the release—by name.

MOST TECHNO: This award goes to an outfit from Plano, Texas, called Non Prophet Organization, made up of Justin Guardipee and Phil Mobeus. They recorded computerized tracks in the early 2000s that mixed ambient, trance, and house styles, and they described themselves thusly: "We sound like artists that actually own and play instruments." With a Yamaha keyboard and music software called Cakewalk, they recorded a fast-paced version and a "mellow edit" that's only mellow if you've heard the non-mellow one. Both songs would be at home at a rooftop rave. "People say they either love it or hate it," Guardipee told me. "A lot of them say we've ruined a good traditional song. But I'm just doing my take on it."

They posted it on the old MP3.com download site and, in two years, got nearly three thousand downloads for both versions. Some may have been techno fans, but others were Boomers who wanted to hear a new take on an old favorite. "I have a lot of friends who are DJs. They say, 'This sounds familiar,' " Guardipee says. "When I tell them it's 'House of the Rising Sun,' they say, 'You've gotta burn this to CD, man—my father would love this.' "

When I last spoke with Guardipee, he was lamenting that Mobeus wasn't writing much lately, throwing the future of Non Prophet Organization into question. "He's got a girlfriend now. He's all boring. I've been trying to get him to break up with her."

No word from the pair since.

FREAKIEST ADAPTATION: Both the Blind Boys of Alabama (famously) and the Christian group Unhinged (less famously) recorded compelling spiritual versions of "Amazing Grace" to the "Rising Sun" tune. But they didn't come close to Their Eminence, a forgotten garage band "of complete unknown origin," according to the liner notes of *Seeds Turn to Flowers Turn to Dust: A Collection of Totally Unrelated Garage/Psych Records from the Late 60s*. Their Eminence took the Animals' melody from "Rising Sun" and fashioned a sneering, spitting, metallic song called "Mary" by adding their own lyrics—sort of. They substituted the words from "Mary Had a Little Lamb." Didn't realize they fit, did you? Meter it out:

> *Mary had a little lamb*
> *Its fleece was white as snow*
> *And everywhere that Mary went*
> *The lamb was sure to go.*

"Were they serious? From the sounds of the song, yes," the CD notes say. "But when they end the number, the laughter during the fade proves otherwise." This one's obscure enough that the CD's label includes this exhortation: "If you were in any of these groups, contact us!"

HARDEST ROCKING: The Adolescents, a punk band, steal this award from my favorite version, by EverEve, with a rendition that starts deliberately and menacingly before, upon the beginning of the third verse, becoming an growling, headbanging extravaganza. Not a good choice for putting the young ones to bed.

MOST PSYCHEDELIC: Believe it or not, this award doesn't go to the Animals but to Sedale, an electronic group I found on the internet that cut a computer-redolent version in 1999 on an album called *Pre-Millennial Tension v.2.0.* It lasts just fifty-eight seconds but sounds like the background to the Beatles' "Being for the Benefit of Mr. Kite!" which enlisted the music of British calliope and fairground organs to achieve its unsettling feeling of psychedelia.

BEST IMPOSTOR: I was in West Africa, in a taxi on the streets of Lome, Togo, when a street hawker shoved some CDs into the open window. Among them was *Kenny Rogers: 20 of the Best,* an obvious knockoff that featured an orange-faced Kenny (cheap printer) on the label and, as track 16, the alleged Gambler doing "Rising Sun." This was during a period in my life when Kenny Rogers–related items were turning up inexplicably in every country I visited, from Nigeria to Thailand.

I was skeptical; no discography listed him as singing our song. Then I listened. It was clearly not Kenny Rogers. It was an African man with an African accent. Still, I had to give the knockoff producers credit: At least they delivered me a version of the song they promised. What's more, much of the Togolese population might not know the difference.

YOUNGEST ARTIST ON CD: Nate Leath, a musician from Hickory, North Carolina, came out with a moody, professionally produced mandolin version on his album *Extra Medium* in 2000 when he was just fifteen.

MOST OBLIQUE HOMAGE: A techno-laced song called "Carmen Queasy" by a demonic, kilt-wearing, genre-blending musician called Maxim samples Hilton Valentine's guitar riff to back a song that's entirely unlike "Rising Sun"—and credits the Animals version that it borrowed. ("Sheriff John Brown," by the Coral, also uses a strikingly similar guitar riff in the background.)

BEST VERSION FOR A FORMAL NIGHT ON THE TOWN: Cuban band-leader and Charo spouse Xavier Cugat did a frisky, orchestral "Rising Sun" on an album called *Invitación al Mambo y Cha-Cha-Cha*. Sometimes called by its Spanish name, "Casa del Sol Naciente," it sounds like something you might hear in the background of an early Bond film. I haven't been able to determine exactly when it was recorded. Cugat, while a tireless advocate of Latin music in America, was no enemy of popularization. He was widely quoted as saying that "I would rather play 'Chiquita Banana' and have my swimming pool than play Bach and starve."

FRENCHEST: Aging French pop *chanteur* Johnny Hallyday is an icon in his home country. Whether he should be or not is another question. His public persona is a mix of Eric Burdon–style working-class roots, teen-idol beginnings, and a motorcycle-rebel attitude that evolved through the 1970s and 1980s. His piercing blue eyes and goatee give him an almost Mephistophelian look.

In 1964, during his teen-idol years, Hallyday was just twenty and already France's most famous pop singer when he came out with a version of "Rising Sun" that used Alan Price's arrangement and organ style almost verbatim but reconceived the song, in French, as a prison lament:

> *The doors of the penitentiary*
> *will soon close*
> *and that's where I'll finish my life*
> *as other guys have finished it.*
>
> *. . . The sun is not made for us;*
> *night is our time for trickery.*
> *You who this night have lost everything*
> *Tomorrow you can win.*
>
> *Oh mothers, listen to me:*
> *Don't let your sons alone*
> *to hang out in the streets at night*
> *they'll go straight to prison.*

Hallyday is still singing it today. He is *of* the song, too: a rambler, a self-styled bad man who revels in his reputation and is constantly taking steps to accentuate it. After three dozen albums and a life worthy of the song itself—five marriages (two to one woman), lots of sex and drugs in the 1970s, character roles in assorted movies and, in 2000, the completion of the Paris-Dakar rally on a motorcycle—he has a unique view of how he fits into the global rock music scene. "There's just me and Mick Jagger and Keith Richards left," he told an interviewer in 2003. That same interviewer described Hallyday thusly: "He's so French he's almost a cliché."

And, finally,

BEST OF SHOW: In 2002, a Canadian female trio called the Be Good Tanyas, which blends roots music with a very alt-progressive sound, came out with a soulful, acoustic guitar version of "Rising Sun." It quietly passes all the other horses to take this award. It manages to be at once bouncy yet entirely mournful, ancient, and modern. It changes the pacing and the tune enough to sound innovative but manages to preserve the song's soul: The "Rising Sun" identity shines through.

"We almost didn't put it on the album, because we thought, Damn, this is sure a tired old trad that everyone's done. Maybe we shouldn't bother; maybe we should just leave it as a B-side or something," singer-guitarist Trish Klein told an interviewer. But her bandmate, Frazey Ford, wrote an alternate melody. So, Klein said, "It's sort of like it's kind of rocked out a little, but all the while it's kind of countryish."

So many versions to listen to. In my travels, I have met only one person as obsessed with accumulating different takes on "Rising Sun" as I am (the world can only hold so many of us, I surmised). The late Paul Meskil was a rewrite man at the *New York Daily News* for years. By the time he retired to Florida, he had collected more than one hundred forty records—including a Korean version, which eluded me.

Meskil's interest began in the 1960s when he heard the Animals on the radio, went to work the next day and said to a colleague, "I heard this great song." The colleague lent him Nina Simone's version, and he started asking around. The obsession hatched. "Once you start, it's like acquiring a taste for olives or something," he told me. "You just keep going."

Meskil found his favorite version while on a trip to Indonesia. "I was in Sumatra in a park. And there was a band playing," he said. "It was an

Indonesian rock group, and the leader spoke some English. And I said, Do you know 'House of the Rising Sun'? And he said, 'You sing it and I'll play it.' And I sang it. They knew it right away. And I said, 'From now on, you can call me Frank Sumatra.' "

The group called Snakefarm is a duo of musician Michel Delory and his wife Anna Domino, who grew up listening to family folk songs from the Ozarks and developed a voice that sounds positively unearthly. Their 1999 CD, *Songs from My Funeral,* is a bit of trance, a bit of trip-hop and a lot of traditional—electronified takes on old folk songs. Soaked in minor keys, it is, in fact, one of the most beautiful and haunting things I've ever heard, as if someone took the Appalachian death-ballad tradition and plugged it in, adding echoes, metallic riffs and other bells and whistles (literally, sometimes). "We wanted to give these songs a chance to breathe a little differently," Domino told me when I tracked her down in California, where she and Delory fled to the desert from New York City to mix their CD a few years back.

To listen to their reworkings is to enter a mirror universe of American roots music. The old North Carolina murder ballad "Tom Dooley" adds a chiming clock bell and an accordion to become something more menacing, more eternal; it renders the Kingston Trio's folky 1958 version simplistic. You can feel yourself gliding across the clouds to the hills of Wilkes County, North Carolina, where in 1866 the real Tom Dula dug Laura Foster's grave and "rolled the cold clay over her and left her there to sleep." You can almost see the gallows tree in the lonesome valley where they hanged Dula in 1868. Similarly, Snakefarm's "John Henry" pulsates with a house beat and a minor key that builds to a crescendo of human grunts, as if the legendary steel-driving man is banging away inside the stereo, raging against the machine before he lays down his hammer and dies. By the time they take John Henry to the graveyard and bury him in the sand, he has come to life and fallen again in my mind, as if it actually happened—the mark of a powerful ballad.

Snakefarm's take on "Rising Sun" begins with the ghostly rattle of a tambourine. It rearranges the lyrics to put "One foot is on the platform and one foot is on the train" into spoken words at the beginning, framing the song in a different way by condemning the singer to finality before the story is ever told. It becomes even more eerie that way, and a bass line, contrasting with Domino's buttery voice, ratchets up the desolation.

Like many musicians, Domino says "Rising Sun" was the first song she learned on the guitar. When she and Delory decided to do the album, it began, "like most good ideas, as a joke," she says. They started playing with "Rising Sun" and "Streets of Laredo," an old cowboy lament popularized by Tex Ritter in the 1940s and possibly related, distantly, to "Rising Sun."

"I stayed up all night, and these arrangements just came out of nowhere," Domino told me. "I didn't think these verbose old songs would do so well with a strong drum and bass groove. But every song we tried worked. I guess that's why they're still around—because they lend themselves to this kind of abuse so readily."

Though Domino had grown up all around the world, from Tokyo to Florence, the DNA of traditional music was handed to her by her family. She grew up hearing her Ozark forebears singing "all about dying babies and girls jumping off ridges," as she puts it, "stories that are metaphors for that awful feeling you've got in your gut." Her ancestors, she says, were "out in the woods" until her grandfather's generation. "My grandparents, after a particularly good meal, would sit around and sing all sixty-three verses of whatever song came into their heads," she says. Her grandfather liked "Rising Sun" in particular and sang it from a woman's perspective. "My grandmother wouldn't touch it with a pole," Domino says. "It was his way of saying he enjoyed the meal: He'd just start singing."

Domino is entranced by the story of a lost girl coming to grips with the prison that her life has become. "She doesn't have a chance in the world. She, with all her youth and energy, thought she could be a part of this life and make it work for her. And she realizes she's owned, body and soul, by this thing that's bigger than her, and she can't get away from it."

Critics have tried to pigeonhole Snakefarm's music—"acid country" and "speed folk" are two of the funnier attempts—but Domino emphatically avoids categorization. She loves blending genres and confusing people as she throws them material that is part of the American fabric. She has dismantled these songs into their component parts, reassembled them, and found out something that surprised her: She couldn't break them. "No matter how much we did to them, you could still recognize them," she says. "I think for a song to really last, it has to be open to interpretation. You have to be able to take the song and make it your own, even if it's not your experience."

Some people were angry at her reworked versions, she said, "as if there was some kind of definitive point at which they had been defined, and we shouldn't mess with it."

How could people be upset at a reinterpretation of something that had already been reinterpreted hundreds of times when they first heard it? The answer lies in modern Americans' comfort with the technology of music over the past century. We used to define the song by the singer, and each was different. But now, there are definitive recordings like the Animals' that give songs a home base from which to riff.

And riff they have. "I contain multitudes," Walt Whitman once wrote. Every time I listen to a new version of the song, I think of him.

BOWLING GREEN, OHIO

"I can't drive without music. It's just impossible," Bill Schurk tells me as some 1930s jazz begins to play on his car stereo.

Schurk is driving me to lunch at the Waffle House in Bowling Green, a college town in northwestern Ohio. I have sought him out because he oversees a monument to modern music unparalleled anywhere in the country, including at the Library of Congress: the Bowling Green State University Sound Recordings Archives, home to more than 700,000 recordings (and that's without the 45s and 78s that remain uncataloged), including scores of versions of "House of the Rising Sun." If there is a single place where I can capture a sweeping picture of the song's trajectory in the past forty years, it is here.

To describe Schurk as animated is an understatement. On a scale of one to Joe Bussard, he's about an eight. I have to bob and weave to avoid his hand gestures. Being an archivist of any kind requires obsessiveness, and I can identify, especially when he says things like: "It's so cool to be able to go through and make a tape of, say, an hour and a half of 'I Left My Heart in San Francisco.'"

In the 1980s, the Music Librarians Association invited Schurk to its annual meeting to present whatever he wanted. He chose, as he puts it, "Bill growing up with music." He still had records his mother and father had stored in the bottom of an old Victrola—the music of the first ten years of his life—and he talked about and played those. That was the first part of his talk. The second was an informal history of "House of the Rising Sun." It is, he points out, "one of the few songs that's not about love."

"I wanted to, by using one song, tell the story of American history. Some songs can lend themselves to that," he says. "Who's singing it? Why did they choose it? The lyrics, the music, they all tell a story. Do they think they're making history at the moment they're in the recording studio?"

Schurk has probably listened to more music than my entire circle of friends ever will ("It's just part of my life to hear twenty, thirty versions of a song."), so I hoped he could answer a question for me. I had been wondering why topical songs had vanished from the national vocabulary (I visited Schurk three months before September 11, 2001, and the resulting wave of Toby Keith patriotism music) and why Americans, with such a rich history of songs that tell stories, had become so focused on songs that don't paint pictures at all.

I was wrong, of course. Country music and rap have always specialized in telling stories, and some of that occasionally bleeds into Top 40, like U2's "Sunday, Bloody Sunday" or many of Bruce Springsteen's songs. But in the early twenty-first century, bubblegum songs dominate the tunescape. Radio stations shun topical material, Schurk says, because of potential controversy (witness the shunning of the Dixie Chicks after they criticized George W. Bush) and because the newsier mass media— TV, the web, newspapers—now claim that place in our society.

At Bowling Green, I hoped to see, from the nearly two hundred versions in Schurk's archives, how different artists had interpreted the "Rising Sun" story. This visit would fill in an important gap for me—obscure versions recorded just before and immediately after the Animals'. "It was the thing to do on these budget labels," Schurk says, because the song was in the public domain. "You had these unknown studio groups doing 'Bridge over Troubled Water,' 'Dying Hobo,' 'Mule Skinner Blues,' and 'House of the Rising Sun.' "

As I suspected, the versions that recorded in the years after 1964 share striking similarities—even the ones that don't credit A. Price for the arrangement. "All of a sudden, when the Animals did it, everybody who did it after did it their way," Schurk says. But even within those versions, a vein of originality flows. In each, the traditional and the Animalesque come out, but so does a certain distinctiveness.

"This song produced one of the most varied cross sections of American pop music examples," Schurk says. "There's a lot of songs that wouldn't be played in certain ways. A bluegrass band would not do 'I Left My Heart in San Francisco' or 'Feelings.' But this song lends itself to almost every musical style."

Two things are becoming clear: First, Bill Schurk has a thing for "I Left My Heart in San Francisco"; second, my foray into the Bowling Green archives is going to make for a very interesting afternoon.

Astrological Series, Vol. 1: The Astronomical House of Scorpio has no date but appears to be from the early 1970s. A black woman in a flowing pantsuit stares out from the cover. The liner notes are written by "world-renowned astrologer Carroll Righter," whose picture on the back cover resembles one of the less diabolical Bond villains. I learn later that Righter was reportedly Ronald and Nancy Reagan's astrologer. But here, he has turned his attention to music.

Apparently GWP Astro Records issued theme albums rounding up music that corresponded to each astrological sign. Here is Righter's take on "House of the Rising Sun," which surfaces on the album one track before "Strangers in the Night":

> The "House of the Rising Sun" bears a threat and a warning in its nearly melancholy melody. The repetition of musical phrases suggests there are ultimate experiences just beyond the horizon, and one would be better off not daring to explore. The Scorpio is fully aware of the outcome of passions surrendered and ulterior desires fulfilled. He knows the pain and heartache that lie in wait for the person with uncontrollable desires.

Impressive. I have made this song my business, and even I never thought it suggested "ultimate experiences just beyond the horizon."

Nor had I ever considered that the song was threatening me. I would think that, after all the time I've spent with it, it would have made its dastardly move by now.

I am sitting in a sound booth in the Bowling Green archives. The astrological take on "Rising Sun," credited to an A. Ambrose, brims with flutes and tubas; it sounds like the theme from *The Rockford Files* had it been hosted by Rod Serling. It is one of dozens of albums containing "Rising Sun" that Schurk's assistant has pulled from the stacks for my review.

They're stacked high next to me, and it feels weird to be dealing with vinyl, which I left behind back in the days of an album collection that included REO Speedwagon, Styx and, sadly, the frothy stylings of Jack (Frisco Jones from *General Hospital*) Wagner. One day in the not-too-distant future, I expect a nostalgic revival of digital music that includes some enterprising entrepreneur coming out with a special gadget that plays MP3 files "just like your grandfather used to listen to on his iPod."

I move on. The Supremes, on an album called *A Bit of Liverpool*, capitalize on the Beatles' early success by donning bowlers and singing songs made famous by English rockers. Their version begins with the Animals' guitar licks before easing into Diana Ross singing from a girl's perspective. Back then, she was still including Mary Wilson and Florence Ballard in things, because the song warns mothers to tell their daughters "not to do what *we* have done."

Peter, Paul and Mary, on *Lifelines*, their 1995 album of duets, trios, and quartets, offer a Mary Travers–B.B. King take that features King's famed guitar, Lucille, and was produced by Phil Ramone. "When we got in the studio, Phil said to me, 'Why don't you take it in a whole different direction?' " Travers says in the notes. But Ramone didn't say how, so they improvised a piano-bar version. "I had this image in my mind of a blues singer in a bar, and the dishwasher is washing the dishes and the bar's closed," Travers says. "And it stinks of that horrible stale smoke and beer—and she's singing this song."

It offers a call-and-response between King and Travers that gives the song a different, warmer feel—a sense of collaboration and sympathy.

"If you had listened to what your mama said, you'd be at home today," King sings in his smooth baritone.

"But I was young and foolish, oh, Lord," Travers responds, and King shoots back: "Yeah, yeah, you let a gambler lead you astray."

The versions begin to run together, and after a while only the weirdest stand out. A doe-eyed, amply mascara-ed chanteuse named Lana Cantrell manages to put hers—which sounds like the opening from *That Girl!*—on an album with "On the Good Ship Lollipop" and Disney's "When You Wish upon a Star." Another woman with the unlikely name of June Bugg sings a creditless "House of the Rising Sun Blues" to an acoustic guitar. Billy Strange, who arranged the sax-heavy "House of the Rising Sun Ska," says rather stuffily that he was "trying to present the top tunes with a swinging sound and a beat."

Dave Ray, on *Snaker's Here! Blues and Hollers,* cribs Lead Belly's barrelhouse version masterfully and does not suffer from a small ego. " 'Rising Sun Blues' is so totally overpowering that one has to hear it to believe it, and even then—!" he tells his audience. "Done to extremes by extremists. I shall rise above all with my penetratingly pure and unadorned version." Unadorned? He needs to hear Georgia Turner.

I had heard rumors that the Beatles once sang "House of the Rising Sun." But it's not part of the Beatlean canon. I was sort of taken aback, then, when I came across an obscure Beatles outtake album called *Sweet Apple Trax* that included a barely recognizable offering of our song that lasts for a rather excruciating 2:35.

It's so ragged that you can't tell who's singing—unusual, given how different Paul's voice is from John's. Both are screeching, trying to sound like Burdon and failing horribly. They seem not to know the words, so they slur them, and they all sound drugged, which was quite possible at that hurtling-toward-breakup moment. The bass sounds straight from *Abbey Road*—the background riffs of "I Want You (She's So Heavy)"—and even Ringo chimes in to tell his public "not to do the things I've done."

"God, I know I'm one," someone sings.

"He's one, alright," John Lennon quips.

Then Udo Jurgens's album *Udo Live* arrives at the top of my stack. Udo Jurgens is evidently huge in Germany—enough that he doesn't need a last name on his album, *Udo Live.* His version of "Rising Sun" was recorded on September 10, 1968. In accented English, he sings over an accordion and a tambourine. Of all the "floating verses" I have found dropped into hundreds of versions of "House of the Rising Sun," his addition is my favorite of all. Not for him the mother who was a tailor, who sewed his blue jeans. Instead, there's this:

> *My mother she did raise me*
> *She fed me pork and beans.*

Let's not sugarcoat. Some of these versions were crap. The Beatles' certainly was. The most annoying were those that sounded like all others—that either mimicked the Animals or offered up a dull, indistinctive folky take. It's as if they were saying, "Hey—this song's traditional and royalty-free, so it's easy filler. Let's get it on tape and move on." Which is sort of obnoxious.

Yet I emerge from the sound booth realizing I have enjoyed not only the really bad ones but the mediocre ones. There's something moving about a story that resonates across the decades, inch by recorded inch.

In the 1970s, I played a fill-in-the-blank children's game called Mad Libs in which a story was offered up on a pad with key descriptive words missing. One kid would hold the tablet and ask the other for adjectives, adverbs, nouns, verbs. Depending on what the second kid suggested, the story would change. It could end up funny, ridiculous, dark, sad, bawdy—all depending on what details were salted into the tale. "The (*adjective*) (*noun*) went (*verb ending in "ing"*) (*adverb*) into the (*adjective*) (*noun*)" could become "The furry clown went bouncing happily into the giant sassafras tree" or, conceivably (granted, we never came up with this one), "The forlorn girl went shambling sadly into the dark bordello."

Mad Libs seems an apt metaphor for "House of the Rising Sun" as it spread to hundreds of artists after the Animals. Though the words are usually the same, the song itself functions as a template with just enough detail to whet the imagination. It contains wisps of truth that evoke a long-ago story. But it's always up to the individual musician to fill in the blanks, to breathe life into the golem.

That's what traditional songs do. That's why the "Stagolee" ballad becomes something gentle and melancholy in the hands of Mississippi

John Hurt, raucous when interpreted by the Grateful Dead, and profane and menacing from the mouth of Nick Cave. It's how Lead Belly can sing "Where Did You Sleep Last Night?" and evoke piney woods somewhere in the remote Deep South of a century ago, but Kurt Cobain, with a few sullen guitar licks and insolent lyrics, can turn the same words into a grunge ballad that evokes his native Northwest.

Beginning with my generation, the post-Boomers, many Americans have lost music's sense of continuity. Just as it would be easy, as disconnected as we are from the land where our food originates, to believe that meat begins life under plastic wrap in Styrofoam trays, so, too, can we conclude that music is born the moment it appears on the Virgin Megastore racks or in the search results of the iTunes Store. Tens of millions consume it, but so few produce it anymore.

On the Friday nights in high school when I rode around in Bill Dreyer's beat-up Pinto and listened to Springsteen do "Thunder Road," it never occurred to me that the Boss could not have existed without a lineage that traveled through Roy Orbison and Woody Guthrie to scores of forgotten traditional musicians. When John Cougar Mellencamp preceded his 1985 hit "Small Town" with a brief fragment of a train song, we didn't dream that it was part of a nineteenth-century ballad about a child who had lost its mother. And when Simon and Garfunkel did "Scarborough Fair" at their 1981 reunion concert in Central Park, we would have laughed if you told us that the tune and the words reached back into the Ozark Mountains and beyond that to England and Elizabethan balladry.

"When you delve into it, you realize how pervasive traditional songs are in our culture," Peggy Bulger, the director of the American Folklife Center at the Library of Congress, told me. "They're so much a part of us, but we don't even recognize it."

In undergoing this process, "House of the Rising Sun" has become a standard. How else can you explain its presence on *Golden Trumpet Favorites*, a CD box set that set me back nearly twenty dollars. Crack open the box for software called eMedia Guitar Method ("As Seen on TV, with Peter Frampton") and it's the featured song. Search Google for its chords and come up with forty-three thousand entries. Countless people, from my friend Colleen Long to Jon Bon Jovi, learned it before anything else when they first picked up a guitar. "Once a guitar player knows those chords, it's in their head forever," Eric Burdon says. And Nora Guthrie, Woody's daughter, says that "it's everybody's first folk song. I remember my brother"—Arlo, he of "Alice's Restaurant"—"playing it when he was fifteen."

Colleen, a singer in a college band who has a voice that will knock you backward, was in middle school when she learned it from her father. They'd had a rocky relationship, and music was one of the few things they shared. "He taught me that one specifically because the riff"—Hilton Valentine's seven notes—"was simple and a child could pick it up," she says. "It totally sounds complicated, but it's really easy. So it was like a parlor trick, you know? When you're fourteen and can say, 'Check this out,' and you can play this song, everybody thinks you're really cool."

A few years ago, after a lengthy period of not playing and also not talking to her father much, Colleen turned to both again. He built her a new guitar from the remnants of an old one. "When I picked up the guitar again," she said, "that was pretty much the only thing I remembered how to play."

Bon Jovi was fourteen when he got his first guitar lesson from Al Parinello, who worked in a club band in his native New Jersey. "He asked me, 'Why do you want to learn to play?' 'To get chicks, what else?' " Bon Jovi recalled in *Playboy* in 1987. " 'Good thinkin',' " said Al, and the first song he taught me was 'House of the Rising Sun,' about the New Orleans whorehouse." Even Tony Blair hasn't been immune: In 2005, in an appearance on the television show *Top of the Pops,* the Baby Boomer and British prime minister named "House of the Rising Sun" as his favorite song of all time—largely because it was the first one that he, too, learned to play on the guitar. Critics later accused him of trying to sound cooler than he was.

But it's doubtful many performers came upon it earlier than comedian-musician Adam Sandler. Long before he was singing bizarre turkey songs on *Saturday Night Live,* Sandler's entire career, in a way, was built upon the song, as he told E! Online: "My first public performance was singing 'House of the Rising Sun.' It was in a seventh-grade talent show. I remember my mother driving me home afterward, and she said, 'You kept cracking your voice.' So she thought I didn't nail it. But I thought I did a pretty good job."

That's the thing that's becoming clear with this song: A lot of people think they do a pretty good job with it. YouTube is chockablock with scores of clips uploaded by amateur musicians who want to play their versions of "Rising Sun" for you, set it to their own music videos, or teach you how to do it yourself. "Anybody can learn this song and play it," says BoyLT, a jovial, guitar-wielding Asian American from "somewhere in Texas" who spends four minutes and thirty-seven seconds teaching us his acoustic version. France's Shion2A, meanwhile, offers his own shirtless video performance. Another user, ggin, films an infant watching, stone faced, as he sings fragments of it for forty-seven painful seconds. The most entertaining take comes from go4it340, who posted a homemade cartoon that features a performance by stick figures playing against a van Gogh–like backdrop. Each YouTube user, in his own way, implicitly claims ownership of the song.

One page on the internet, put up by a guy who calls himself Doc Doc, offers a MIDI version of an old arrangement of the song. "House of the Rising Sun: By Everyone," he says.

By everyone. That's it exactly. Each group of musicians made it their own, brought their own set of experiences to the table. "The only difference was they didn't sit down with a grandfather and get it face to face," Peggy Bulger says. "People have been thinking for forever that folklore is going to die. It's living culture, and culture is not dead. It keeps evolving. Mass culture today *is* folk culture."

It keeps on moving, keeps on changing, keeps on finding new outlets for its old story. And as we're about to see, the story is so ornery that it often ceases to be simply a song and becomes something else entirely.

7 Diaspora

Never seen New Orleans,
Oklahoma or Tennessee.
Still I dream of those black hills
that I ain't never seen.

—THE KINKS, "MUSWELL HILLBILLY"

SCOTTSDALE, ARIZONA

The man named Mad Dog hurtles through the cathouse door and into the sunlight—disheveled, enraged, probably trashed out of his mind. His undershirt is stained, his hair wild, his face tomato-red. Spittle cakes on his bushy mustache as he rants. In the dirt street of the nineteenth-century boom town, in front of the nearby jail, saloon and hotel, a crowd has gathered. Bystanders are silent, horrified, wondering how bad the situation can get. Which is pretty bad indeed.

"You give me a girl that doesn't know nothin'?!??" Mad Dog yells.

"Well, what did you expect? You wanted a virgin!" The place's madam, in green dress and matching feathered hat, is shouting, too.

"I want my money!" Mad Dog grabs at a fistful of cash that the madam clutches in her hand.

The door of the bordello grows dark again. Out runs a voluptuous young woman, clad in flowered blue undergarments, obviously fresh from a transaction. Her voice is streaked with pain. In her right hand, she holds a revolver.

"What have you done to me?" she screams at Mad Dog, and raises the weapon. A lawman, his attention drawn, strides down the street toward the commotion. The girl's father, who has sold her into this life, appears. Accusations are traded; angry yells drown each other out.

184

Then it all falls apart.

A series of sharp reports sounds—a fusillade of gunfire. Mad Dog goes down, bloody, his life ebbing. The madam, hit by another bullet, falls to the ground too and is still. The scent of gunpowder fills the air. The whore stands, her hand to her mouth, realizing what she has done. At the door of the bordello, prostitutes watch and shake their heads. Next to them, in a window, is a red-and-yellow sign that gives the establishment's name: "Rising Sun."

From loudspeakers, familiar music swells: *Mothers, tell your daughters, not to do what I have done . . .*

A man named Bob Charnes walks up into the middle of the mess, clad in a black vest, black pants, a black hat, and dark wire-rimmed sunglasses. If Elmore Leonard had directed *High Noon,* this is what Marshal Will Kane would have looked like. Charnes is the ringmaster of this controlled circus. He surveys the consternation in the crowd. Some have put down their camcorders and look a bit fraught. One mother is holding her young son tight to her hip. The gunned-down john and madam rise, nod to the audience and stand to the side right next to the girl gone wrong, who smiles tentatively, too.

It is 2005, and the shells from the guns, though real, are filled with florist's foam where lead would normally be.

"Unfortunately, folks, that happened all too often," Charnes says.

The place is Scottsdale, Arizona, in the desert outside Phoenix. The landscape is a two-dimensional clapboard town designed to be a stand-in for some of the Old West's most enduring stories. The occasion is the Festival of the West, an annual celebration of all things frontier, featuring everything from funnel cakes to live animals to shooting contests to an appearance by child actor turned *NYPD Blue* star Rick Schroder. At the gate of the fairgrounds is a sign: "No live ammunition. No concealed weapons."

This corner of the festival is the purview of Charnes and his wife Dale, who oversee a troupe called the Arizona Gunfighters. Charnes is a former Hollywood stunt man ("Hollyweird," he calls it) whose career evolved into leading elaborate, meticulous performances of historical and pseudo-historical events from the Old West. The Gunfighters' cast includes a sheet metal worker, a guy who works in an auto parts yard, a retired postal worker. Then there's the life insurance salesman. His name is Wyatt Earp, and he is the legendary lawman's great-grandnephew and namesake—and, not incidentally, allergic to gunpowder.

From place to place they travel, across the West, fashioning reenactments of such time-tested tales as those of Wild Bill Hickok, Bat Masterson, and the gunfight between the Earps and the Clantons at the O.K. Corral in Tombstone, Arizona.

And, for the past decade, a six-minute show that tells the story of the House of the Rising Sun.

We know by now how far our song has traveled, how musicians from across the decades and across the planet have applied unique talents and circumstances to make it their own. But here is the Rising Sun story itself, extricated from the song, salted with fresh details, transplanted from New Orleans into the Old West, and brought dramatically into the physical world as a Western tale. Could Georgia Turner have imagined this path?

"We are a little careful about where we do it because of the subject matter," Bob Charnes says backstage between shows. "We've had occasion where when the show's over, we have people with tears streaming down their face." As for the actors, he says, "I've seen them after the show, hugging." Cast members with menacing miens ignite cigars with Bic lighters, sip Diet Cokes, and chat on Motorola cell phones. Wyatt Earp wears wraparound shades. Kevin Hoelzer, a casino-machine builder who plays Mad Dog, is an occasional extra on HBO's *Deadwood* (though apparently a versatile one; he was also an extra in *Miss Congeniality 2*).

Charnes contemplates the "Rising Sun" show for a moment and comes up with this: "At one point in time, New Orleans *was* the West."

Jarae Taylor, who works for an import company, has spent the past seven years playing the girl whose father sold her to the Rising Sun. Since she joined the Gunfighters, she has immersed herself in the part and spent a lot of time reading up on prostitution in the Old West. At times, she has noticed mothers with small children get up during the "Rising Sun" show and leave. "Gunfighters, that's different. Women and violence, it's not something they want their children to associate with," she says. "But it did happen. There's some really dark things that happened. It wasn't all *Little House on the Prairie.* "

Dale Charnes is the den mother of the Gunfighters, a mix of effervescent grandmotherliness and no-nonsense stage management. Long ago, she worked as an in-house secretary to Phyllis Diller, buying the comedienne's undergarments and helping her sign autographs. Before that, in 1961, she was living in New York City and dating a drummer. One night, in a folk club, a grungy, scraggly young man came up to her right before his gig. He looked hungry. "He says, 'Can I have half your sandwich? I'm Bob Dylan,' " Dale recalls. "I said, 'Get your own sandwich.' "

Doing a "Rising Sun" performance was Dale's idea. Before the Gunfighters, Bob Charnes's old performance group did a bit called "Angel of the Morning" about a widow who became a prostitute. Dale had always wanted a show to feature women, who generally were relegated to being saloon girls in Old West dramas. She thought of Bob's earlier show, and "House of the Rising Sun" came to mind. "The song seemed to be the perfect thing for this," she says. "It was in my head."

I walk around the festival a bit to capture the flavor, and I realize it has the feel of a *Star Trek* convention with an Old West backdrop. Many visitors dress the part, sporting bolos and chaps and Bob Wills shirts and flowing skirts and spurs. It's difficult to tell whether they're dressing up or simply wearing their usual weekend outfits.

Affection for the West and for old time living is ubiquitous, even as it mixes with the fusion culture of modern consumer America in the usual odd ways. Two horses in a trailer are named Waylon and Willie. Vendors offer roasted corn and a bungee-cord swing and sarsaparilla and a petting zoo and burro rides and Dead Eye Bill's Shooting Gallery and a kid-friendly saloon and gambling parlor. A man plays "Back in the Saddle Again" on an accordion. Food stalls sell chicken Caesar salad, chow mein combo plates, and Bavarian bratwurst—the culinary equivalent of all those different versions of our song. As I eye a stand called DC's Fried Catfish, a woman walks by. Like the gas station I saw in rural Kentucky, her T-shirt bears a slogan: "Follow the Sun."

Following the Rising Sun out of its standard habitat—by which I mean a popular song, presented by a musician as a standalone composition—produces unexpected results, of which the Arizona Gunfighters' production is but one. The story, in whatever form it pops up, has pushed beyond its original boundaries and been absorbed into the culture everywhere. It has been parsed into its component parts—idea, lyrics, music—and reassembled into everything from books to advertisements to a mainstream (if little noticed) film to several porn movies with vague whorehouse themes who use the title as a synonym for forbidden sex. Several houses have taken on its name, too, including a bed and breakfast in New Orleans. Even Eric Burdon was surprised when he rented a purportedly haunted house overlooking the port in Menorca, Spain, and learned that, long before he arrived, it had been called the House of the Rising Sun.

This universal knowledge of the basic "Rising Sun" story cannot be divorced from the song itself and its popularity. As the music and lyrics crisscrossed the planet from the 1960s into the twenty-first century, from the mouths of countless artists, they planted seeds of cultural familiarity that were ripe for the riffing.

Jimmy Thibodeaux, a Louisiana musician who has traveled the planet with his Gumbo Cajun Band, says audiences from everywhere on Earth—Israel to Pakistan to Japan—ask him if he knows it and then demand it. "There's only a few songs, tourist-wise, that people really know. People from all over the world, that's one of the first songs they'll ask for," says Thibodeaux, who recorded the song in 1992 and sang the first verse in Cajun French.

The late black American choreographer Alvin Ailey, whose modern dance credentials were unparalleled, created a *Blues Suite* that is still performed today, two decades after his death. It contains a choreographed "House of the Rising Sun" set to a bluesy rendition of our song. In it, female dancers in nightgowns flail in precision frustration as they try to escape from their fallen-women fate. It's worth noting, too, that Ailey was a vigorous advocate of black culture; thus has *Blues Suite* helped bring "Rising Sun" squarely into the modern African American artistic tradition.

Casio made the song a standard preset on its electronic keyboards. On my CTK-541 100 Songbank Keyboard, song No. 37, a computerized keyboard version of "Rising Sun," hews closely to the Animals. The company's Japan offices decide what music to include, and a song's public-domain status is crucial. It makes traditional music like "Camptown Races," "Grandfather's Clock," and "Home on the Range" free to use—unlike Elton John's "Crocodile Rock," which cost Casio a great deal more to include.

Casio calibrates the mix of songs on its keyboards with precision. John Pallini, the director of marketing at Casio's entertainment division in Dover, New Jersey, said the company uses market research to generate lists of current hits and standards, then creates a menu that mixes genres to entice younger and older consumers alike. Pallini told me, "When one of these things sits on the shelf in Circuit City or Best Buy and it plays in demonstration mode, it has to strike a chord with a consumer—maybe bring back a memory, at least be recognizable and make them feel, 'Boy, I'd like to be able to learn how to play that.' "

In recent years, as cell phone ringtones became a multimillion-dollar industry and another outlet for the metamorphosis of music into fragmented cultural quotations, "House of the Rising Sun" became available as a ringer for your Motorola, Nokia, or T-Mobile Sidekick. In eight seconds, for $1.50, I downloaded a digitized version of it for my phone and used it for six months until I, too, grew sick of it playing with every incoming call and switched to Elvis Costello's "Veronica" for a while.

In 2005, the sheer intensity of "Rising Sun" vaulted it into another out-of-context location: a nationally televised Gatorade commercial called "Origins 3," the third in a series delving into the product's three-decade history. The sports-drink company was aiming to prove, as its PR people put it, how well Gatorade works.

The spot that enlisted "Rising Sun" opens with a parched runner on a scorching day, collapsing during competition as an extended version of Hilton Valentine's opening guitar riff cuts in. The runner is Chris Legh, an iron-man triathlete whose body including some of his vital organs—simply shut down during a 1997 competition. He was hospitalized, underwent surgery, and only recently began competing again with the help of the Gatorade Sports Science Institute in Illinois, which taught him to hydrate and recalibrate his bodily fluids.

The scene that depicts Legh's collapse, accentuated by the "Rising Sun" riff, sounds ragged and tired, and the warm, dry colors of the footage underscore the moodiness. Gatorade learned in focus groups how much music accentuated the effect of its ads, and its director of communications, Dustin Cohn, realized that few bits of music are more memorable than the opening of "Rising Sun," Animals-style.

Gatorade, helped by the ad firm Element 79 Partners, had used other songs for similar "Origins" spots, and all evoked heat and intensity.

They'd deployed the Lovin' Spoonful ("Hot town, summer in the city, back of my neck gettin' dirty and gritty) and the Zombies ("It's the time of the season when the love runs high"). For "Origins 3," Element 79's team didn't hone in on "Rising Sun" immediately. But when they did, they knew they had hit on something. Danny Schuman, Element 79's group creative director, set his team to deconstructing the song and figuring out what made it tick. The interpretation they returned with—simple, direct—speaks to the core of what "Rising Sun" evokes in people who hear it, though they may not realize it consciously.

"There were two important things about the song that made it so important for the commercial—one is what it feels like and one is what it sounds like," Schuman told me. "It feels like pain, which is how the first half of our 'Gatorade Origins' commercials start. They start with heat, with dehydration, with pain, and Gatorade helps to resolve that." What's more, he says, the song "feels kind of hot. It feels like the South. The name itself has to do with heat beating down on people. The title conjures up painful, hot images. . . . It may be the pace of the notes being played on the guitar. It may be the sad, soulful sound of those notes, the way those notes are played. But to us it just conjured up images of struggle and trying to make your way through something that's very hard."

What it sounds like matters just as much: "What it helps us to do is snap people to attention if they're thinking about changing a channel. They hear those first five, six, seven, eight notes, it stops them."

These examples demonstrate how marketing and technology, mass media and globalization have digested a piece of music. This is the diaspora of "House of the Rising Sun," the assorted paths it has traveled. Some of those paths relate to what the music implies; others focus on the words. Still others condense our song into its most basic themes, or at least the emotions they evoke, and create entirely new ideas and new works of creativity from the basic kernel of origin.

Consider the short story by a California writer named Gene O'Neill called "House of the Rising Sun," which depicts on its cover a black-and-white drawing of menacing-looking mansion with phantasmagoric creatures hovering over it. It follows a sixteen-year-old boy named Adrian, sent to live with his sister after his parents die in a car accident that leaves him temporarily mute. The sister is a prostitute who lives in New Orleans—in the actual House of the Rising Sun. Which, it turns out, is occupied not only by fearsome proprietors but by strange creatures and unearthly goings-on.

O'Neill's story is notable for its specificity. It fleshes out an image of the house as something that's not only the ruin of the whores inside, but also home to a force of evil that transcends vice and sin. The descriptions of its corridors, intended to evoke ghostly unease, also paint a compelling picture of how claustrophobic life must have been for prostitutes in such situations.

> Adrian had never lived in a really large place, and the Rising Sun was no ordinary house, no indeed. It was almost mazelike, full of corridors shooting off at funny angles with sudden dead ends, walls with no doors; and he still didn't know how to find the front entrance. . . . Also it was impossible to determine the time of day, with no windows to look out and no clocks anywhere—it was *always* cool, dark and gloomy in the hallways.

Chuck Hustmyre, a retired special agent with the Bureau of Alcohol, Tobacco and Firearms who lives just outside New Orleans, took a different literary approach in 2004 with his full-length novel of the same name. It is a gritty crime tale set in the modern French Quarter, in an illegal bordello-casino run by a mobster named Vinnie Marcella on behalf of his brother, Carlos (a thinly veiled riff on the real-life New Orleans mobster Carlos Marcello, whom the Warren Commission investigated in connection with the Kennedy assassination). Hustmyre uses different verses of the song to introduce several chapters and, at one point, describes "the House" itself.

> The Rising Sun, the place everyone called the House, was in an old four-story hotel, right in the middle of the French Quarter. Owned by the mob, it had been renovated and had become part strip club, part illegal casino, and part high-class whorehouse. Every girl in the club, the strippers, the waitresses, and the table dealers, could be had for a price.

Hustmyre's tale, which focuses on an ex-con and ex-cop named Ray Shane who works in the house, is all about intrigue and violence and, of course, sex. Through it, the lawman-turned-author frequently throws in his own takes on the song's warning verses and points up how working at a place like the Rising Sun can reduce a person to a product awaiting a transaction.

> As Jenny finished drying off, she wrapped the towel around her head and stepped to the vanity. The naked reflection staring back at her from the mirror above the sink made her want to cry. On the outside she looked the same as she had before, before Ray went away, before her mother died: five-foot-seven, a slender waist and soft curves. She had the kind of body that men wanted—and would pay well for—but she could see past the roundness of her hips and the swell of her breasts, she could see the hollowness inside, she could see the degradation she'd done to her soul.

Hustmyre turned his book into a screenplay, which is slated to become a movie. The director, Ron Judkins, says the story will focus on "moral choices" made by the characters. "The grit and texture of old-world New Orleans," he says, "will inhabit every frame."

In recent years, the Rising Sun theme has popped up frequently on television and in movies as well. The inexplicably iconic TV show *Knight Rider*, about David Hasselhoff and a talking car named KITT, debuted on September 26, 1982, with a pilot episode in which a bar called House of the Rising Sun, in the fictional town of Millston, California, figured prominently (it was right across the street from the tech company where much of the action took place). This Rising Sun, which one character called a hangout for "amoral" truckers, is a honky-tonk saloon with leopard prints on the wall that gets wrecked in a bar fight. The pilot features covers of several popular songs, including the Eagles' "Take It Easy" and Fleetwood Mac's "Don't Stop (Thinkin' About Tomorrow)," but our song never makes an appearance.

And in the popular ABC-TV drama *Lost*, one of the key plane crash survivors is a Korean woman named Sun Kwon, played by Yoon-jin Kim. A 2004 episode that focused on Sun was called, in a play on her name, "House of the Rising Sun." It had nothing to do with our song but brought its name to a wide audience that, producers surmised, would understand the reference immediately and the appreciate the pun.

A little-known 1987 film called *House of the Rising Sun* opens with a shot of a sun rising, though the music that accompanies it is Tina Turner singing "What's Love Got to Do with It?" Set the Hollywood Hills and peppered with Bryan Ferry music, it is solidly of its era, filled with pinks and light blues and freeze frames reminiscent of early MTV. In this movie, the Rising Sun has become emblematic of prostitution; the name itself is enough to evoke vice.

The film tells the story of Janet, a newspaper reporter, and Corey, a hooker who lives in a well-heeled LA bordello, and how their lives unfold as Janet tries to get a scoop about the criminals who run the house and finds herself in mortal danger. "Can posing as a call girl be too high a price for a front-page story?" the video box asks. The film is trying desperately to be neo-noir but is as forgettable as the *Miami Vice* episodes it emulates. What makes it worth watching is a most unusual version of our song that appears only when the closing credits roll. Performed by a band called Denise Mitchell and Friends, it starts out a cappella but grows into a full gospel rendition unlike any other.

In 2004, a director with the stage name Vin Crease did a horror movie designed to fool audiences into believing it was an early-1970s exploitation slasher picture. He went so far as to scuff and age the film stock itself. *Slaughterhouse of the Rising Sun* told the tale of an evil California desert house where bad things happen to bad hippies. Though it addressed no aspect of the "Rising Sun" legend, the end credits roll over a haunting remix of our song that tells of "a house at the edge of town" and adds a verse. Strangely, though the new stanza is supposed to play off the film, it would be right at home in a ruined girl's lament:

> *Well, it's one foot on the staircase*
> *the other in the grave*
> *The time has come to sell my soul*
> *there's nothing left to save.*

Then there's porn.

Narrative details aren't generally the main attraction of skin flicks, and the two adult movies available today under the *House of the Rising Sun* title don't exactly flesh out the old tale. The first, made in 1993, appears to have nothing to do with prostitution or New Orleans, making its title inexplicable. Like much porn, it takes place in LA. The "plot" revolves around Jack Picard, a fugitive fleeing a cop-killing rap who has sex with every girl he encounters and says, "Ciao, baby" a lot. All the women are Asian, and the DVD box shows one of the stars, Isis Nile, posing with Asian lions under a decidedly Eastern font, so perhaps the title is intended to be a play on Japan as the land of the Rising Sun.

The second, a 1999 production, at least tries to riff off our song. The opening credits (top-billed starlets include Syren and Cherry Mirage) are a quiet acoustic guitar piece that evokes the beginning of the Animals' song without being the same tune. The movie tells the story of a brothel called the House of the Rising Sun that resembles a small bar and casino, complete with craps tables and girls in feather boas. The proprietor, a pasty, unpleasant pimp who mistreats his employees, is the schemer whose economic and sexual escapades keep the film moving. "The owner of the House of the Rising Sun is giving it away through his own twisted lottery," the cover art says. "His six close friends and one missing hooker named Mandhy are out to get it all! They'll do absolutely anything to crack the secret code."

At least three other porn movies have riffed off "Rising Sun," though two—*Rope of the Rising Sun* and *Bondage of the Rising Sun*—are merely Japanese-style ropes-and-whips porn that invoke the song's title, not its subject. The only movie that appears promising in extending the tale is an out-of-print 1985 flick called *Bordello: House of the Rising Sun*. Here's how one adult video site describes it:

> In this scintillating sexvid, we meet the gals of the Rising Sun, a naughty New Orleans bordello where the women are always eager to please.

But the house's owner dies, according to the synopsis; a corporation takes over and modernizes, only to find that "the place has lost its charm—and its profits." Naturally, the company's chairman visits and finds that sometimes "good old-fashioned romance and passon" trumps slickness.

Couple these movies with the immense amount of sex-saturated websites that a Google search for "House of the Rising Sun" returns, and it's clear that the term has become synonymous with sex. This harks back to the unusual verses collected from an Ozarker in 1950 that characterized the house as a place that, "when you want your pecker spoilt, that's where you get it done."

I can't help but be put off by this particular riff. So much pain and darkness are associated with the "Rising Sun" theme and the life it depicts that to make it a flashpoint for pleasure seems cruel. Somehow the incorporation of this particular story into narratives designed to satisfy a viewer's urges, while understandable, strikes me as quite sad.

The most effective transference of "House of the Rising Sun" into cinema is neither sexually explicit nor titular. *Casino,* Martin Scorsese's 1995 epic about the wages of sin in mob-saturated Las Vegas during the 1970s, enlists the entire song—the Animals' arrangement—as the soundtrack for its bloody climax. What's more, when you look a bit deeper, you see that the film's story line is very much an updated, neon-drenched take on the story that our song tells.

The opening credits evoke Las Vegas and sin itself, showing someone falling into a pit of fire and the city as a bright, almost Gomorral beacon in the darkness of the desert. "Guys like me, Las Vegas washes away your sins. It does for us what Lourdes does for humpbacks and cripples," says the sort-of-hero, Sam "Ace" Rothstein (Robert De Niro). Ace runs the Tangiers, collaborates and tangles with his enforcer Nicky (Joe Pesci) and romances Ginger (Sharon Stone), a high-priced prostitute who is the poor girl put up for ruin in this story ("Once a fucking hooker, always a hooker," Ace says, and I can't help but think of Hally Wood's voice in her haunting "Rising Sun" version of a girl lost). This sounds a lot like how New Orleans functioned in the post–Civil War nineteenth century—a haven for countless would-be impresarios of vice dreaming of a more sordid brand of success. "Back home, they would have put me in jail for what I'm doing," Ace says. "Out here, they're giving me awards."

The use of popular music in *Casino* is striking; it shoves the story along in magnificent fits and starts, and grounds it firmly in 1970s Vegas. The musical barrage is continuous, with songs from all eras used as quotations, from Dean Martin to the Moody Blues to Fleetwood Mac to the Rolling Stones' "Gimme Shelter." But with all the period songs he drafted for his storytelling, Scorsese saves the darkness of "House of the Rising Sun" for the gripping montage that is his climax.

The mob is falling in Vegas, the 1970s are ending and prosecutors are encircling Ace's house of cards. You hear the famous opening chords, and suddenly, inevitably, it all collapses for Ace and the gangsters who propped him up. The mob bosses, old men, go on trial as Burdon sings about "the ruin of many a poor boy." One character is shot—silently, in the head, from behind—and falls dead in the snow as Scorsese unfurls an orgy of bloodletting. The guilty are punished.

"Mothers, tell your children, not to do what I have done," Eric Burdon spits over the carnage, and the soundtrack's volume rises as he warns them not to "spend your lives in sin and misery." As he sings about "going back to New Orleans, to wear that ball and chain," Ginger—the ruined girl, the expensive whore—dies of a drug overdose, collapsing on the cheap carpet of a motel hallway, penniless and stoned out of her mind. The song crests as Nicky, who thinks he has prevailed, is driven out into the desert, and it ends as he is forced to watch his brother beaten with a baseball bat and buried alive before he, too, is set upon and battered into an unrecognizable pulp.

If "House of the Rising Sun" is indeed a bare-bones template awaiting a story, *Casino* acts as a dead-on infusion of details and characters. Despite the neon and glitz and loud suits, the tale is pure Appalachian Gothic: People who come from the East—"back home," as they keep putting it—arrive in a place where consequences are few and temptations are many. They lose their souls gradually, until they are almost unrecognizable. And of course they can never go home and return to the fold again, because they have become products of their new environment. Sure, they might appear to be classy and high-living (one foot on the platform) but they're consumed by their transgressions (the other one on the train). They're screwed, and there's no going back.

When the thugs buried Nicky in a shallow desert grave, my mind echoed with songs of murdered girls in old songs like "Pretty Polly," "Banks of the Ohio," and particularly "Tom Dooley": "I dug the grave four feet long, I dug it three feet deep. I rolled the cold clay over her, and I left her there to sleep." Even Ace, who survives to finish his voice-over narration, is shown at the conclusion as a caricature of himself, shambling into the 1980s as the same small-time crook he was when he began the whole mess. And Ginger is dead and forgotten. The wages of sin: It's been the ruin of many a poor boy and girl. The details change, but the story is ever the same.

Drafting songs for purposes that their composers never intended is nothing new. When he conceived "Ride of the Valkyries," Richard Wagner couldn't have fathomed that it would be performed by two cartoon characters—a rabbit in drag with a Brooklyn accent and a lisping, bald hunter (see "What's Opera, Doc?" Warner Bros., 1957). Still, globalization has served up all manner of weird, unintentional or context-free cameos for our most familiar songs.

The Ukrainian Embassy in Beijing, when it puts you on hold, plays "Love Me Tender." When I was on assignment in Pakistan, one of my colleagues' cell phones rang, and I recognized a digital version of Scott Joplin's "The Entertainer," which my father played on the piano throughout my childhood. Do you know that song? I asked Munir. No, he said, it just sounded better than the ring that came with the phone.

"House of the Rising Sun" has appeared on David Harp's 1989 album *How to Whistle Like a Pro* and in the fall 2002 repertoire of the Farragut High School Marching Band in Knoxville, Tennessee. In 1969, the Commodores—not Lionel Richie's 1970s band but a U.S. Navy musical outfit—played a swing version under director Larry Kreitner (the band said it was accomplishing nothing less than "helping to keep American music from becoming a dead item in a museum"). In 1996, it provided the soundtrack for figure skaters Renee Roca and Gorsha Sur, who used a recording by the London Philharmonic to skate to a silver medal at the U.S. Figure Skating Championships. In 1998, a group called Apocalypse Hoboken issued a CD called *House of the Rising Son of a Bitch*. In 2001, a fourteen-year-old dancer named Autumn Sicking of Havelock, Nebraska, bested 243 other solo acts at the Premier 2000 dance competition in Florida with an interpretation of "House of the Rising Sun." In 2005, at the Big East Finals in Madison Square Garden in New York City, scantily clad Syracuse University cheerleaders danced come-hither routines as their band played it. Attila Weinberger, the Romanian-born "Transylvania Guitar Man," plays his own take of it in Vegas. It's even been quoted in another song: Charlie Daniels, in "The Devil Went Down to Georgia," offered this line:

Fire on the mountain, run boys run
The devil's in the House of the Rising Sun

Religion, too, has appropriated the ballad. In San Antonio, Texas, in 1997, an elementary school music teacher named Melissa Durham took the song several verses further, singing about what happened to the young man after he left the house that ruined him—"finding Jesus, repenting of his misdeeds and asking forgiveness," according to the *San Antonio Express-News*. And a few years ago, one Christian website set to repurposing a raft of popular songs to make them more holy—with some pretty silly results. It's fine that Robert Palmer's "Addicted to Love" becomes "Addicted to God," and it's not a preposterous stretch to turn Billy Joel's "Only the Good Die Young" into "Only the Pure Get Blessed." And yes, "House of the Risen Son" is an easy riff. But when "(Sittin' On) the Dock at the Bay" becomes "Sittin' at the End of the Pew" and "Hey! Hey! We're the Monkees" devolves into the anti-Darwinist "Hey! Hey! We're Not Monkeys," a divine intervention of some alacrity is needed.

Would-be composers have found it ripe, too, for parody, and their efforts number in the hundreds. When Newt Gingrich was serving in the House of Representatives, he found himself skewered with this six-verse take:

> *There in the House in Washington*
> *he's called the White-Haired One*
> *and he's been the ruin of many poor folks*
> *and he's not even done.*
>
> *Oh, Mother! Tell your children*
> *of the bad things that he's done*
> *He gave our lives such utter misery*
> *from the House of the White-Haired One.*

For political fairness, an internet parodist and George W. Bush supporter who calls himself Bubba postulated the "House" as the White House and the "Rising Son" as Bush—as in son of George Herbert Walker Bush. In his parody, he took aim at Bill Clinton for the Lincoln Bedroom campaign scandal.

Oh mother tell your children
not to do what Clinton done
Sell off nights to sleep in history
in the House of the Rising Son.

Tom Smith, a musical parodist who did a "Rising Sun" offshoot that poked fun at the annoying and much-maligned character of Wesley Crusher on *Star Trek: The Next Generation,* considers the song a perfect starting point for parody. In doing so, he isolates the song's basic structure and its potential to become universal:

> One of the secrets of Instant Parody is to know a bunch of songs that can be quickly adapted to just about anything. "The House of the Rising Sun" is one of the best, because (a) everybody knows it, (b) it starts out "There is . . . ," which can lead to anything you like, and (c) it's structured to set up a story, tell the story, and deliver the moral (or the punch line).

That potential transcends language as well. In addition to the popular interpretations in French (Johnny Hallyday) and Spanish (Sandro), versions appear all over the internet in the languages of Bosnia, Russia, South Korea, Germany, Finland, Vietnam. In Portuguese, it begins, *"Há uma casa, em Nova Orleans que eles chamam de a casa do sol nascente, e ela tem sido a ruína de muitos pobres rapazes, e Deus, eu sei, fui um deles."* And in Czech, *"Snad znáš ten dům za New Orleans, ve štítu znak slunce má . . ."* A young Hungarian woman, Agnes Risko, wrote on her website a few years ago that she plays the guitar—"mostly Hungarian songs but my favourite song is The House of the Rising Sun from Animals." Virgis Stakenas, a popular Lithuanian singer who expropriates American pop melodies and inserts lyrics from his homeland's traditional poets, carried the "Rising Sun" tune into a more epic realm. He inserted words from a nineteenth-century Lithuanian poet named Maironis, telling a tale of castles and knights and princes.

When I moved to China for three years in 2001, I was determined to find every appearance of "House of the Rising Sun" in the Middle Kingdom. That was less difficult than I expected, because China was—and remains—a Wild West of intellectual property violations. Despite the best efforts of customs agents, economic enforcers and thought police, the streets of China's cities remain a riot of glimpses into global popular culture. We're talking fake Hershey bars, fake North Face jackets, fake Reeboks, even fake Crest and Colgate toothpaste.

The granddaddy of all counterfeiting operations, though, is the vast nationwide juggernaut of fake music and movies. On every street corner in Beijing, you could find someone rushing toward you on foot or, more alarming, on a bike, carrying a shoulder satchel and stage-whispering, "CD? DVD?" Often, police were standing right there and just smiled and looked off into the distance. The purveyors would pull from their bags vast fistfuls of American movies in plastic sleeves; some hadn't even reached theaters in the United States yet.

Many of the credits on the back were scanned with character-recognition software from an old copy of *Patton,* so there were an inordinate amount of new American movies starring George C. Scott and Karl Malden. I ignored this until I came across a copy of *Henry and June* starring George C. Scott and Karl Malden, a visual no one wants to contemplate. Once, I purchased for about ninety cents a DVD that was billed as *Spider-Man.* When I got it home, it turned out to be a cheap film called *Earth vs. the Spider* starring a weathered-looking Dan Aykroyd. Think about this: China's DVD pirates didn't just rip me off with a blank disc; they *took the time to find another human spider movie to substitute.* You can't help but appreciate a petty criminal truly committed to good customer service.

Music was the same story. Every hole-in-the-wall CD shack, as well as many major bookstores, carried Chinese compilation albums that were obvious knockoffs of American CDs with some riotous differences.

Exploring these permutations of American music, and how the Chinese framed it for their own audiences, offers a glimpse into how culture moves around and how it breaks the bonds of its original context. I wanted to explore that notion and how it related to "Rising Sun," so I went to Harbin, the frigid capital of China's northeasternmost province, and spent two days in music and book shops assessing the cultural diaspora—and looking for our song.

The streets and shops of Harbin, like those in so many Chinese cities in the early twenty-first century, are a grab bag of contextless cultural snippets—a compelling mélange of American commercial culture, Japanese products, and emerging Chineseness. This is the kind of place where globalization is playing out for many Chinese, and I cannot imagine what they make of this dizzying stew. Perhaps it is less strange to them because they lack the American cultural reference points to notice the strangeness.

In one department store, "Oh, Susannah" blares over the PA system, set to some Chinese lyrics that I can't discern beyond being certain it has nothing to do with Alabama and banjos and knees. Up the road, the proprietors of a music shop play a CD of some Australian singing "Scarborough Fair." It is looped and plays a half dozen times while I am there.

In Harbin's Central Bookstore are three discs featuring Da Bizi Xiansheng—"Mister Big Nose," the Chinese translation of Mr. Magoo (some Chinese call foreigners "big noses," a vaguely derisive term). And in the book department of Central Shopping City, a literary series with impressive bindings and elaborate script on the volumes' spines features, translated into Chinese, works by A. Camus (*The Stranger*), E. Brontë (*Wuthering Heights*) . . . and S. Sheldon (*Rage of Angels*). Nearby, displayed prominently, is a Chinese self-improvement book called *The Leadership Secrets of Colin Powell*.

The music sections are even odder. Over two days, I see:

- A four-CD series titled *Infatuated in Coffee, Coffee in Love, The Joyful Coffee,* and *The Leisure Coffee.*

- *Shafa Hao Yinyue,* which translates as "Good Music for the Sofa." That's weird enough, though at least it implies romance and seduction. Yet its producers translate it into English as "White Collar Officer's Heart."

- *Scathland Bagpipes,* which features a picture of a Scottish bagpiper beside the decidedly un-Scottish Stonehenge.

- From the Hobnob with Children's Music series comes *Mozart Makes Your Baby More Lovely* (with a baby with fake wings on bright pink cover) and its companion CD *Mozart Makes Baby More Clever,* with two infant hands reaching skyward toward a celestial copse of trees. Unrelated, but nearby, is *Mozart: The Most Shining Trumpet in History.* Who knew?

The Chinese music cognoscenti are familiar with "House of the Rising Sun." I know this because of a very Serious-Looking Text that I purchased upon my arrival in China called *An Anthology of English Songs.* With an elaborate cover and a staid typeface in both Chinese and English, it resembles *The Norton Anthology of English Literature* that many American college students use. This anthology, however, contains among its thousand songs the work of the Pet Shop Boys ("It's a Sin"), Poison ("Souls on Fire"), Richard Marx ("Endless Summer Nights"), and Irene Cara ("Flashdance . . . What a Feeling").

And on page 63, there is *xuri luguan,* or "Rising Sun Hotel," with lyrics in both English (largely the Alan Lomax composite version) and Chinese. The historical detail is surprising. In Chinese, a brief biography of the song tells of *luomakesi,* or Lomax, collecting the song from a mine worker's daughter in *midesiboluo,* or Middlesboro, Kentucky. It also offers some helpful glossary items for would-be Chinese singers, explaining the definitions of "gambler," "astray," and "shun," among other terms.

Now I need only to find it on a CD. On the fourth floor of the City of Harbin No. 1 Hundred Goods Store, next to the air conditioners, I hit pay dirt—two discs containing "House of the Rising Sun." The first is a 2002 two-CD set called *Elite of the Folk Song,* whose cover depicts a black American in a suit, sitting at a bar, inhaling a cigarette, and looking generally bluesy. A six-string guitar is also featured prominently. The folk-song elite include such implausible candidates as "Luka" by Suzanne Vega, "Wonder" by Natalie Merchant, and "Losing My Religion" by REM. These, however, seem to fit the mold more so than many of the songs chosen to populate Chinese CDs, and Dylan and Baez are also represented. Track 12 on disc one is listed as "(The Animals) The House of Rising Sun" (in Chinese, *risheng zhiwu,* or "sun rising house").

The second, *American Country: Special Hit,* features a horse grazing on grass in a meadow and a superimposed cowboy type with a guitar leaning against the horse's neck as he sings. Songs feature "The Sounds of Silence" and "Five Hundred Miles" as well as "Blowin' in the Wind" and "Take Me Home, Country Roads" (John Denver is, alarmingly, about as ubiquitous here as the Kennys, Rogers and G). "House of the Rising Sun" is track 16, with the same Chinese name, no artist listed.

The young clerk overseeing the CD counter says she's not familiar with the song. She allows, though, that like other Western songs, she might well know it if she heard it. I briefly contemplate an impromptu performance but decide against it.

The following day, on the fourth floor of the Golden Sun Sofia shopping city, just below the *Background Music for Restaurant* CD and next to *Lennon Leegend* (I bought that for the post-Beatle classics "Nind Games," "Gold Turkey," and "Give Peace a Change") was "Rising Sun" again—on an album called *Best Country Ballads* that features New Mexico–style mesas and what appears to be the amply antlered head of a caribou. Orthographically challenged songs include "Fallow Me," "Blawintn the Wind," "Gome the Rainbow," "Tie a Yellow Ribbon Round the De Cak Tree" . . . and "The House of the Rising" (this time, *renai de jia,* or "warm and dim house").

Meanwhile, Dawei, a small music store just off Central Boulevard, features *The Best Country in Town,* with a cover showing what appears to be tourists in leisure dress on a simulated Conestoga wagon steered by a cowboy in a button-down Oxford shirt. When you live in China, every day brings these kinds of encounters. Included is Joan Baez performing "Rising Sun." I purchase some of the more entertaining discs because I can't bear to walk away and because most are less than $3:

- *Perfect Music of Car,* which includes Wham!'s "Careless Whisper," perhaps the most undriving pop song ever recorded.

- The two-CD set *First Love Music from Occident* and its sequel *Deep Love Music from Occident,* which feature pictures of attractive but generic young men and women that might have been lifted from Kmart perfume ads around the time Michael Dukakis was seeking the presidency. This time around, the scanning software gives us "Unchained me lady" (I approve, in a British Isles kind of way) and the always popular "With You I'm Boron Again."

- Two discs of a five-CD series called *Country Club: Western Train* and *Country Club: Cowboy Songs.* Aside from missing the entire connotation of the term "country club," these CDs offer broad-brush marketing of iconic American notions but—like so many of the others—don't follow through. Hence *Western Train,* which could have drawn from hundreds of great American train songs, instead wrangles together "Yesterday," "Greensleeves," "Bye Bye Love," and that old hobo-riding-the-rails standard "Don't Cry for Me, Argentina." Meanwhile, *Cowboy Songs* includes "It Never Rains in Southern California" (another infuriatingly omnipresent fixture on Chinese compilations of American hits), "Hey Jude," and the rugged Manifest Destiny ballad that the cowhands liked to call "Edelweiss."

My personal favorite has to be one of the many Kenny G. albums I've been less than fortunate to spot. Originally it must have been something like *Kenny G. At Home* or *Kenny G. Returns to His Roots.* But the Chinese name of the album is *huijia*—which, translated back into English literally, produces this supremely appropriate title:
Kenny Go Home.

BEIJING, CHINA

Room 329 of PartyWorld Cash Box Karaoke in Beijing, opposite the towering Foreign Ministry, is chilly. There are two microphones, a computer, a monitor, and speakers. The introduction video shows us how to apply a grappling hook and rappel down the face of the building in case of a fire and how to apply a full-head cellophane oxygen mask to breathe. The instructions are accompanied by a disco soundtrack.

Cash Box is representative of how karaoke has evolved in China. It is a four-floor warren of rooms that resemble miniature recording studios—which they essentially are, except nothing is preserved for posterity. This is merciful. Each booth has a round window in it, like a door that leads to a restaurant kitchen, so the rooms can't be used as fronts for prostitution.

I have been to Cash Box three times, and it is always teeming with would-be performers—though from the yowling and growling emanating from many of the rooms, it's probably best that they are essentially locked up. The place is bedecked like a slick modern hotel, with glittery corridors, gaudy chandeliers, an ample supply of "service attendants" and a free buffet.

We are here, on one of our final nights after three years living in China, to sing bad English songs. On our playlist, accessible by a key-pad on the computer, are such standards as "How Deep Is Your Love?," "All by Myself," "Don't Go Breakin' My Heart" (whatever happened to Kiki Dee, anyway?), and the inescapable "Hotel California." The micro-phone echoes like the voices in radio monster-truck ads ("Let's Go . . . RACING!"), lending a pleasing resonance to my attempts to duplicate George Michael's sensitive-boy whine on "Careless Whisper" and Kenny Rogers's Southern-man mumble on "The Gambler." The atten-dant comes in, carefully puts fresh sanitized foam covers on our mikes so we won't pick up previous patrons' germs, then blows into them for a sound check, leaving traces of his spittle behind.

Most of the videos on the big screen in front of us seem frozen in time. That time is the 1980s. People wander through these videos doing things that bear no relation to the songs at hand—Eurotrash folks with feathered hair and loafers without socks looking extremely intense against sun-drenched urban backdrops, filmed by auteur wannabes who may or may not have graduated to directing lesser Phil Collins videos. Some of the visuals are inexplicable. Barry Manilow's "I Write the Songs" (which, to my endless entertainment, Barry Manilow didn't write) appears to document a bike race and accompanying street fair on a rainy day somewhere in New England. Dylan's "Like a Rolling Stone" shows various random road scenes and walks through woods. It's all vaguely entertaining to an American, yet I can't help but lament that these are the stories an entire generation of Chinese will attach to these songs and imprint upon their memories. Thirty years from now, if a Chinese person born in the 1980s hears "Tears in Heaven," Eric Clapton's eulogy for his son, Conor, who fell out of a skyscraper win-dow, odds are he or she will visualize what appears to be an equestrian meet in Tidewater Virginia.

In the three-ring binder of polyethylene-encased sheets that serves as the song menu, our tune comes up twice. No. 82067 is "House of the Rising Sun." And, in inimitable Chinese style, under the "T"s is No. 82883—"The House of the Rising Sun." This is the best I'm going to do in China because, alas, in three years of living here I have failed to turn up a Chinese-language version.

The karaoke version served up on this night—the one without the

"The" in the official title—chronicles the journey of a Filipino woman in a halter top walking through what slightly resembles New Orleans, albeit a very generic and clean Big Easy. No prostitution, no misery, no gamblers, no drunks. A pan flute can be heard at the beginning under the title and the credit—"words and music by Traditional," as if Traditional were an Alan Smithee of music lost to the ages. I sing the words without looking at them on the screen, and improvise a bit to add Clarence Ashley's verse—"Boys, don't believe what a girl tells you"—into the mix. Later, when we view it for a second time, I realize that the woman is actually two separate women. Also, it's not really New Orleans but, apparently, somewhere in Europe. One scene appears to be London, but others are clearly southeast Asia, and temples and coconuts are visible.

This bothers me at first—no specifics—but then it occurs to me that this is precisely what makes our song so universal. The women—walking around the city alone—could be any women in any big city. Bangkok in particular would be an appropriate setting for a whore's lament. Some things, sadly, are everywhere.

I have done the Asian karaoke thing once before with "Rising Sun," four years previously at a place called the BMG Karaoke Box in Bangkok. It was equally weird in an entirely different way. That "House of the Rising Sun" karaoke video featured footage of young black men on the streets of New York City playing basketball and climbing into cars. (The joint also offered, amid its repertoire, the opportunity to perform the jingle "Always Coca-Cola" in front of a Thai crowd, which is the kind of thing that helps me understand why some people really dislike America.) The BMG Karaoke Box's most unusual feature was a screen that allowed the proprietors to rate singers as they sang and offer commentary. When I was doing "Rising Sun," belting out my Eric Burdon best across the octaves, the best I could muster was "A WIDE-RANGING VOICE." Thai patrons, including several young women who appeared to be workers at their own local House of the Rising Sun, watched impassively as I sweated to the oldie.

Karaoke occupies a unique space in music. For many of us in the modern world, it is the only way we can take the music we consume and make it our own. True, we are riffing from packaged, produced videos, and parroting musical superstars. True, it can often be just plain silly. But karaoke is a faint echo of front-porch music, integrated with technology. We may not be able to sing "Rising Sun" on an Appalachian front porch and share hand-fashioned music with our neighbors, but we can go into a karaoke bar anywhere in the world, punch a few buttons and throw ourselves into the songs that we love. "It is said that since the popularization of records, radio, and TV, people have become passive receivers of entertainment," says the online magazine *Karaoke Scene*. "The advent of karaoke might help correct this phenomenon and make a great contribution to the history of musical entertainment."

Cheesy? Certainly. But behind the machinery, karaoke is unmistakably an art form that belongs to the people. And no matter how far it strays from its roots, no matter how unrecognizable it becomes, that's what folk music is all about.

8 Family

The past is never dead. It's not even past.

—WILLIAM FAULKNER

From the hills of Kentucky to the soundtrack of a Las Vegas mobster film. From a 1937 Library of Congress field recording to a Chinese department store and a Thai karaoke bar. From front porch obscurity to the high-velocity global monoculture in a single lifetime. Our song has filled its passport with countless exotic stamps. But what of the woman who started it on its journey? What of the sixteen-year-old Appalachian girl who sang into Alan Lomax's primitive recorder in Middlesboro so many years ago? As I chased "Rising Sun" into the twenty-first century, I couldn't shake the shadow of Georgia Turner.

Was she still alive? She'd be an old woman if she was. For me, she represented something fascinating: events that unfold quietly in their moments yet cause ripples far away and long afterward. Because of what she sang for Lomax one September day, I was pursuing a single song around the world. Because of it, Eric Burdon's life had changed immeasurably and people of every musical stripe, in dozens of nations, knew this tune and these words.

I wanted to ask her what her life had been like, why she sang this song, where she learned it. Maybe she just liked it. Maybe it was complicated: Music historian Bill C. Malone has speculated that, in rural America, songs with "tales of sexual intrigue and murder provided catharsis for many women whose lives were blighted by deprivation and pain." But in trying to find Georgia, I had little to go on. Almost certainly she would have married and taken a different name. She might have moved elsewhere. If she was still alive, though, I could play for her all the versions that hers begat. That was enough to get me searching.

At the Woody Guthrie Archives in New York City, where I found a typewritten copy of the song in Guthrie's notebooks, archivist Amy Danielian referred me to the Lomax archives, also in Manhattan. I called Matt Barton there, who told me he had little on "Rising Sun Blues" other than a card listing Georgia Turner as the originator. But when I talked to Barton again, he told me he had found something else: a letter from Lomax to the former Georgia Turner in 1963—in response to a letter from her. "And," Barton said, "it has her married name."

The next morning, I hurried over to the archives, in a towering brick building in western Manhattan near the Hudson River. There, Barton produced copies of two letters for me. The one from Lomax was dated 1963. The one that prompted it was written in Georgia's hand, in flowery script, from her home on East First Street in Monroe, Michigan:

Alan Lomax

Dear Sir I am writing you at the request of Pauline Inman who told me you was trying to locate me over a record of which I rember very vaugley which I sang at Tilman Cadles House at Noetown Middlesboro Ky So maney years as it Seem almost like a dream These thangs that have been brought to my meomrey if I could talk to some of the People that was there at the time I could tell you So much I am Georgia Turner my Mother Name was Mary Mast ever one Called her Mary Gill My father was Gelles Turner and I have Married Twece since this Has Happened I have no Birth record of which to Prove this My marrage Lecins My Name Now is Georgia Connolly And I Live at 1258 East first Street in Monroe Michigan you can find me Home most of the time I have a Postoffice Box Which you Could Write if you (illegible) the Box is 214 Monroe

 I hope you Can read This And if so Will help me I'm Very Grateful indeed

Georgia Connolly

I immediately started searching for Connollys in Monroe, Michigan. Nothing. I did a reverse directory lookup, found the person now living at that East First Street address and called. She'd never heard of Georgia Connolly. I began scouring records—not easy, since searches for "Georgia" and "Turner" produced thousands of documents about Atlanta-based CNN and its founder. I printed out a list of Turners in Middlesboro, Kentucky, and began cold-calling them based on how old-school the first names sounded. Homer Turner and Clarence Turner were two of my first calls.

None had heard of Georgia. A few knew of Gillis Turner, as they spelled it. "He's my people, but I don't know just how," one told me. At A. E. Turner's house, a woman suggested someone named Mabel Munger might know something. Mabel was charming but knew nothing; she was born, she said, in 1937, the year Georgia Turner sang the song. She gave me the number of an Ed Hunter, who used to play music in the area years ago.

Hunter seemed to recognize the name Georgia Turner. "I'm not sure, but I think she's dead," he said. I was disheartened, but I had found no death record, no obituary. So I wasn't convinced. He was busy and told me to call back. Three days later, I raised Hunter and we talked for a while. He said he knew Georgia and lived near the Turners when he was a boy. All of the Turner kids he knew were dead, he thought, except maybe the youngest. Beyond that, nothing.

After I talked to Hunter, something occurred to me. As someone who's researched my family history since I was fourteen, I knew how to look for dead people. I'd been to the genealogy databases online and found no leads on my Georgia Turner (I had come to think of her as "mine"). But what about her father? Was somebody looking for him?

And there it was: someone inquiring about Gillis Turner.

The poster was a woman named Jana Bruce with a University of Michigan email address. I wrote her, then got her number from the Michigan website and planned to call her from work first thing the following morning. Which I wouldn't do. Because the minute I walked in the door, the phone rang. The voice sounded excited, expectant. "This is Jana Bruce. Georgia Turner was my great-aunt."

I had been hoping for a *Lost Horizon*–like moment, when Conway learns the high lama is actually Father Perrault and all the eternal connections fall into place. I wanted someone to pick up the phone and tell me, "I am Georgia Turner. I sang that song. Let me tell you about it." I wanted to hear about that day so long ago in another world that was part of The Village.

Instead, Jana Bruce, twenty-eight years old, said this: "Aunt Georgie's dead. She died before I was born."

MONROE, MICHIGAN

When the phonograph made its debut in 1877, cementing Thomas Edison's reputation as the Wizard of Menlo Park, some of the earliest supporters of the invention that captured sound from the air had a specific hope for it. They surmised—not unexpectedly, given the era—that the contraption would have an uplifting cultural effect by bringing good music to the masses. They meant highbrow music, of course. "Instead, it brought the music of the lower economic strata to the rest of us," says David Morton, author of *Off the Record: The Technology and Culture of Sound Recording in America.* The ability to capture voices and instruments, he says, "gives you not only the song and the words and the ideas, but the performers who were there. And what they added to it is also carried through time."

Without a device to record sound, who beyond the confines of Middlesboro's Noetown neighborhood would have heard Georgia Turner sing? How would her performance have rippled out to other places? How could there have been a chance that, years after her death in 1969, her children could hear her voice as a teenager? Because of that invention, they were about to have the chance.

By contacting Jana Bruce, I had opened a door. After I told her about my quest to find her great-aunt, she called Georgia's kids. Some, she said, were near tears when they heard what I had called about.

With Jana's help, I arranged to travel to Monroe and meet with five of Georgia Turner's children to play the tape of their mother's voice for them. But when the day arrived, Jana Bruce paged me with a problem. One of the siblings had just undergone surgery to unblock an artery, so they had to postpone. Then she paged again, in short order: It was on again. But wait—yet another page: Reno Taylor, the eldest child, had called, and it was off again. I agreed to meet Jana at the Monroe Diner the following afternoon, a Sunday. I wanted to see Monroe, at least, and Jana said there was a silver lining: Her grandmother, who had known Georgia, would accompany her.

Monroe, a pugnacious Lake Erie town just over the Ohio state line into Michigan, is known these days for being the global headquarters of La-Z-Boy and the site of an enormous paper mill, the River Raisin Paper Co. A sign at the edge of town bills it as home to both General George Armstrong Custer and Bronco McKart, junior middleweight world boxing champion.

Monroe is in the heart of what was, for decades, one of the nation's powerhouse manufacturing belts—a swath of Michigan linked closely with the Big Three automakers thirty-five miles north in Detroit. It sits along U.S. Highway 24 and also contains part of the old Dixie Highway, upon which many thousands of poor Appalachian men and women traveled north looking for work during the Depression and the ensuing world war. This mass migration, caused by hard economic times in Appalachia from World Wars I through II, changed the face of Ohio and Michigan in particular; during one decade, the population of Akron, Ohio, increased by almost 150,000 people, many from Appalachia.

Naturally, they brought their culture with them. Ypsilanti, a Michigan town not far from Monroe, is still often (and sometimes derisively) called "Ypsitucky" because of its Appalachian heritage. I saw signs of this when I rolled into Monroe—places like the Little Dixie Restaurant & Lounge that evoke the Old Country to many who came here. Even today, decades later, accents redolent of the Kentucky and Tennessee hills can be heard everywhere in and around Monroe and are ubiquitous in blue-collar satellite towns across the Detroit–Ann Arbor–Ypsilanti region.

When I enter the Monroe Diner, Sunday churchgoers have filled the place and Jana Bruce and her grandmother are already there. June Turner, whose late husband was Georgia's brother, is an elegant woman with an accent that hints at her British heritage. She tells me how jarring it was for her, a middle-class girl from across the Atlantic, to come home with her army husband to Middlesboro and its Appalachian poverty. "It was like being on the moon to me. They never really understood me, and I never really understood them," she says. "I didn't start to understand them until I was old. I wish I could be around them now."

We are commiserating about the meeting with Georgia's son Reno not happening when Jana suggests a last resort: She thinks I should call Reno myself. Perhaps, she thinks, I can persuade him. I go to the diner's pay phone and call his number but get an answering machine. I hang up without leaving a message, but then rethink. As I dial a second time and wait for the machine, a human being answers, catching me off guard.

"Is Reno Taylor there, please?" I say.

"This is he." I hear the familiar strains of an Appalachian drawl.

I identify myself and tell him that I just wanted to check in. He apologizes profusely and says some of his siblings didn't feel up to the meeting. I let him know that I am in the diner with Jana. "You're in Monroe?" he says. "I'll be there in ten minutes."

And suddenly there he is, Georgia Turner's firstborn son. He is fifty-eight years old, a retired construction worker, congenial and dry, with a brush cut and a sharp sense of humor that June Turner says reminds her of his mother. That seems to please him. "All my life I've loved music," he says. "That's on account of my mom. She let me listen to the radio and I would put my ear right up to it."

He is very open about the poverty and alcoholism in the family, and how he stopped drinking and found God. He is open, too, about how his mother and her people coped back in Middlesboro, where he was born. "That's what they did. They sang and they drank," he says. "I don't know how they made it. But when they got a chance, they moved out." It was 1942, just after the United States entered World War II, when Roy and Georgia (Turner) Taylor and their baby boy, Reno, arrived in Monroe from Middlesboro, chasing work at River Raisin Paper.

Reno never knew about the connection his mother shared with "Rising Sun" until much later in his life; he was in the service in the early 1960s when she learned that some royalties might be coming her way. The children never dreamed, though, that a recording existed of the day that Tillman Cadle had Georgia and her mother over to sing into the Presto reproducer that Lomax had carted in over the hills. "We was all stunned," Reno says. "There was a recorder at this guy's house?"

Taylor wishes his mother had at least received enough royalties to afford better medical treatment when she was dying of emphysema in

1969. "It would be so nice if she did get some recognition for something she did good."

I try to put myself in Reno Taylor's position. Your mother dies at age forty-eight after a grueling life. Then, three decades later, some guy you've never heard of calls you up out of nowhere and says, "Hey—I've got a recording of your mom singing a song, and she's the reason the song became famous. Can I come over to your town and show you?" I would probably have kept my distance and suspected the man on the phone was either an Amway salesman or a con artist.

Yet there is something appropriately circular about what is happening. Georgia Turner sang this song to one person, and through him it became something larger in a way that she, given the circumstances of her life, never could. And now, because of the song's trajectory, the culture has coughed up me—the courier who gives her contribution back to the people who will appreciate it most.

"So," I say to Reno Taylor. "You want to hear your mother sing?"

"That's what I came for," he says.

I pull out my Sony Pressman tape recorder, already cued to Library of Congress recording 1404A1. Reno sits at the end of the table as his mother's voice begins singing from the little mechanical box that's a fraction of the size of the Presto Reproducer:

There is a house in New Orleans they call the Rising Sun . . .

I watch him intently. He realizes this, and he tries to remain impassive. His effort is valiant. But this is, after all, his mother, dead thirty-one years, and here he is, not just hearing her voice again but hearing it at sixteen, when he did not yet exist and her life—the marriages, the move north to Michigan, the drinking, the poverty, the emphysema, the early death—was ahead of her. Here he is, listening to her sing the blues before life had dealt her so many reasons to do so.

My mother she's a tailor, she sew those new blue jeans . . .

His eyes betray nothing. He sits ramrod straight, his hand stroking his cheek in contemplation.

The only thing that a drunkard needs is a suitcase or a trunk . . .

Then his cheek muscles began to twitch. He resists, but he can't hide it. As his mother's voice penetrates his mind, as all the associations it unearths begin triggering synapses, the smile just can't stay buried.

One foot is on the platform, and the other one on the train . . .

For one brief moment, Reno Taylor has his Ma back. Sure, she is buried a mile away out in Woodland Cemetery, but for a fleeting instant she is right here in the Monroe Diner, where Reno has shared so many meals of broasted chicken with his daughter under the pink flamingo painting just across the room. On magnetic tape, all the way from 1937, Georgia Turner is serenading her son.

. . . I'm going back to New Orleans to wear that ball and chain.

The song ends. No one at the table speaks. Forks clink against diner plates in the background. Reno looks drained. Gingerly, I open my CD portfolio and show him all the versions I have accumulated—punk, reggae, disco, hip-hop. He is astounded—and more than a bit bitter that she never saw all the royalties he believes she deserved.

"I wish she could have benefited more from all this," Reno says quietly.

He tells us as much as he can about his mother, but it's hard to summarize something so complex. "What do you say about your ma?" he says. "She's just your ma." She was tall with red-tinted auburn hair. She sang. She loved. She married and remarried. She smoked Pall Mall reds. She drank, then she stopped. She died sober. She had eleven children; one was stillborn and another died of spinal meningitis at three months old. She told off-color jokes to her kids and taught them to sing. Now and then, she took them back down to Middlesboro to see the place they had come from and the cautionary tales it offered. And Reno never, ever heard her sing "House of the Rising Sun."

"The talk was around town," he says. "I heard of the song, naturally, and I heard my mom did it. But I never thought that much about it. . . . She never did say anything to me about it."

Reno's a restrained guy, but I can tell he is still processing the voice on the tape. He grows more animated as the conversation continues. He talks more to his aunt, June, whom he hasn't seen in more than a decade, and to Jana Bruce, whom he has never met. He picks up my copy of *Our Singing Country*, the 1941 Lomax book that credits his mother for "Rising Sun," and pokes at it with his forefinger. For him, it's proof. Finally. His voice drips with scorn as he remembers the people who didn't believe his mother could have had anything to do with something so big. "There's probably been a lot of laughter and ridicule about this," he says. "Well, here it is."

A feeling washes over me that I have done something useful. This quixotic quest has not only brought Reno Taylor his mother's voice again, but brought to him relatives that had drifted away. When we wind things up and they vow to stay in touch, Jana is teary-eyed. "You're a friend now," Reno says. I realize that my incessant poking around has put them at the same table again, all these descendants of Gillis Turner, the mine worker from Middlesboro so many miles south and so many years away.

Five months later, Reno Taylor assembles his brothers and sisters at a niece's house in Monroe so I can talk to them. I am a bit intimidated. I was humbled enough in the presence of one of Georgia Turner's children, but all of them? To dredge up memories of long ago, some of them quite difficult? I feel like an interloper, a scavenger. And yet, I keep telling myself, this woman's story deserves to be told.

They welcome me warmly. Seven of Georgia Turner's eight surviving children are there, as is Marilyn "Mert" Baker, a "surrogate sister" who was a fixture in their home as they grew up and knew their mother well. Reno has already played the Library of Congress recording for them, allowing each to hear their mother's voice just as he did. I want to know what they thought.

Barbara Wilson: "I couldn't say anything. I was crying. . . . I could see her right away. I could see her bending over, doing laundry."

Brenda Stowell, who was six when her mother died: "I thought, So that's what my mom sounds like."

Joyce Proskie: "I felt so connected to her again."

Reno Taylor, on his late brother who was a musician and songwriter: "Richard would have enjoyed this more than any of us."

Ron "Tootie" Taylor: "We're now able to share with our kids part of our heritage. . . . Yeah, she sang it, and yeah, it got famous, but she didn't act like it was all that much."

Roy "Whitey" Taylor: "It'll be around long after we're dead and gone."

Joyce: "No matter how poor we was, we always had the latest 45s. We'd take the welfare check and go get them. . . . When my aunts would come over, that's the first thing they would talk about—the newest records."

Barbara: "She'd send you up there with a dollar fifty and say, 'Get that record.' And she'd be waiting on the porch when you came back."

Marilyn "Mert" Baker: "That's why I liked being over there. There was always singing."

Wanda "Faye" Stromberger: "My mother had child after child. And it seemed like the only way she could survive was singing."

Joyce: "She sang when nobody should have been singing. . . . The refrigerator could be broken, but not the stereo."

A thought from Bob Dylan occurs to me: "Folks who are soft and helpless sometimes make the most noise."

More details about Georgia's life emerge as the conversation progresses. She wrote poems. She wept when John F. Kennedy was assassinated. When she heard sad songs, she cried along with the tune. She did a stunning rendition of "Amazing Grace." Before emphysema conquered her, she sang a song called "Smoke Your Cigarette." She gave nicknames to everyone she knew—monikers like Garbage Gut, Smiley, Duck Walk. She battled unremitting sadness with unremitting humor. She had sayings like, "Don't try to sell what you can't give away." And "He looked like he had one eye fishing and the other eye squirrel hunting." And "Her face looks like it wore out a half-dozen bodies." And this one, for her kids: "Anyone, anywhere can survive if they have one person that cares about them. And that's me." And when she died, her funeral was packed.

Because Reno Taylor was away during part of the 1960s—in the military and charting his own path—he didn't hear much about the royalties. But Georgia's other children did. Tootie Taylor remembers bragging for days after the Animals version came out in 1964, though he allows that he didn't much like their electrified take.

Royalties began reaching Georgia Turner only after an old friend from Middlesboro, Pauline Inman, contacted her at Lomax's request in 1963. Inman, the niece of Depression-era activist-folksingers Aunt Molly Jackson and Jim Garland, still lived in rural Kentucky when Lomax wrote her looking for Georgia. Inman knew that the family had moved to Monroe and passed along Lomax's address. Sometime later, Inman told me, Georgia wrote to her. "She said, 'Thank you very, very much, because I needed the money. I am having a really hard time. And I have gotten three real nice royalty checks.' . . . She said, 'I just can't believe it's so.' "

A September 1, 1959, contract between Ludlow Music Inc. (Woody Guthrie's longtime publisher) and John A. Lomax, Alan Lomax, and Georgia Turner, credits the trio (the elder Lomax had been dead eleven years by then) for a song called "The Rising Sun Blues (New Orleans)." It was, the contract said, "collected, adapted and arr. With new words and new music" by the three, and promised the following royalties to be split 50–50 between Alan Lomax and Georgia Turner: three cents for each printed copy sold by Ludlow in the United States or Canada; half of all net money received by Ludlow for use of the song in recordings or movies; and half of all net royalties and fees for use outside of the two countries.

The contract was apparently drawn up and signed by Alan Lomax before he located Georgia, then updated with her signature four years later. That speaks well of him; though he didn't know where she was, he included her in the agreement to seal her involvement in case she ever turned up. That doesn't mean Lomax was optimistic about money, though; by the 1960s, he informed Georgia, the song had already been "pirated." And many in the folk revival were adamantly against the copyrighting of traditional songs they believed should be available to all. Peter Goldsmith, in his biography of Folkways Records founder Moe Asch, *Making People's Music*, examines this conundrum.

> . . . there was the question of whether the collector was entitled to profit from material that he had, in fact, learned from someone else. But at the same time there were legitimate arguments on the other side. If a folk song became the source of a hit record, *someone* would be entitled to the publishing royalties—perhaps the collector might as justifiably be the recipient as anyone else. Certainly Lomax was more entitled to royalties than the [latest recording artist], who had simply helped himself to the song from Lomax's published collection. The Lomaxes often published a version of a song that was a distillation of several versions they had collected, and this in itself could be regarded as a creative process. And without the collectors, who would ever have heard the songs in the first place?

Checks did trickle through to Georgia's family here and there during coming years. Mert Baker remembers when a $500 one arrived. "It was like a millionaire knocking," Joyce Proskie says. "Every time they came, with all those kids, it was great—we'd go out and buy groceries," Faye Stromberger says. And Whitey Taylor remembers the time royalties arrived just before Independence Day. "We had a birthday party for America," he says.

Today, Faye has only a single receipt from 1968 that shows a total of $117.50 in royalties paid from Ludlow. Whitey wonders what finally came of it all. "You see twenty, thirty records," he says, looking at my stash of CDs. "Do you ever see her name on it?"

That's a tough one. Surely Georgia Turner, the primary font of this song ("other stanzas" by Bert Martin notwithstanding), deserved better than she got. More money, or at least recognition for her unparalleled contribution to the song's journey and eventual global success. Yet she didn't write "Rising Sun." It was kicking around long before she was born. She plucked it from yesterday and, unbeknownst to her, launched it into the modern world. This is the kind of conundrum that the inter-breeding of mass culture and the folk tradition produces: Give credit where credit is due, yes. But how, exactly, do we determine where credit is due?

If Georgia instilled anything in her children, it was that love of music that they demonstrate daily. But perhaps even love is too weak a word. Singing helped her endure, and there is something of that in her offspring. To them, music is not mere entertainment. Each has stacks upon stacks of CDs ("I got records," Tootie chimes in). Sometimes they gather for cookouts and sing songs dating to the beginning of the twen-tieth century—and cry while doing so. The other day, Faye was cleaning her house and caught herself singing the ancient ballad "Barbara Allen"—all twelve verses. Tootie often sings "In the Pines," which his ma sang to him.

"Why is music important? Survival," Faye says.

"It takes you away from where you are," Joyce says.

"And if you're a beer drinker," says Barbara, "it takes away the blues."

Faye remembers how, when the first snow of winter fell, her mother would gather the kids together to sing a song called "Here Comes Susie Snowflake." Before she finishes the thought, Joyce cuts in and begins to sing. Suddenly all seven siblings are singing in unison.

Here comes Susie Snowflake
dressed in her snow-white gown
tap-tap-tapping on your windowsill
to tell you she's in town.

Here comes Susie Snowflake
soon you will hear her sing:
"Come, everyone, play with me
before I melt away."

They finish, and they applaud each other. Hugs and tears all around. Georgia Turner Taylor Connolly's children are singing a chorus, and they are dedicating it to their mother.

Later, Faye Stromberger turns to me and looks me square in the eye. She has a request, she says. "Paint a rosy picture of that coal miner's daughter who drank too much and smoked too much and had too many kids," she says. "Basically, she was a good person. She really was."

9 Going Back to New Orleans

New Orleans is as much about death as it is about life. It's the spirit-world walking amongst us.

—ERIC BURDON

Well, I hate to see that rising sun go down.

—"GRAVEYARD BLUES," TRADITIONAL

NEW ORLEANS, LOUISIANA

On January 27, 1821, on page two of a New Orleans newspaper called the *Louisiana Gazette,* a small ad appeared. It ran on and off for the next thirteen days in the paper's English- and French-language editions, occasionally moving to the front page.

RISING SUN HOTEL, CONTI STREET, NEARLY OPPOSITE THE STATE BANK.

The undersigned inform their friends and the public that they have bought out the interest of JOHN HULL & CO. in the above establishment. No pains or expence will be spared by the new proprietors to give general satisfaction, and maintain the character of giving the best entertainment, which this house has enjoyed for twenty years past.

Gentlemen may here rely upon finding attentive
Servants. The bar will be supplied with genuine good
Liquors ; and at the Table, the fare will be of the best
the market or the season will afford.

The business will be carried on under the firm of

L.S. HOTCHKISS & CO.

Jan. 27

Barely a year later, On February 28, 1822, the same paper ran a news item about the destruction of the establishment in a lethal early-morning fire that sent neighbors scrambling to preserve their homes.

About two o'clock, yesterday morning, a FIRE broke out in the Rising Sun Hotel, Conti-street. The whole of that extensive building was entirely consumed, and the kitchens and other back buildings of adjacent houses much injured. It is said that two persons lost their lives in the Tavern, owing to the rapidity of the flames where the premises were of dry wood. The loss of property on this occasion is considerable, and the destruction would have been more extensive had the wind been violent.

These articles, culled from the minutiae of New Orleans life nearly two centuries ago, are part of a mystery we now must address.

During our journey from The Village into the modern world, we have concerned ourselves with a song and its travels. We have tracked a story and seen how a piece of culture moves around. We have seen how the twentieth century—its mass culture, its technological advances, its globalism—could take something local and make it universal.

Beyond the song, though, unanswered questions linger. What *was* the Rising Sun? And was it ever a real place?

When I first began chasing the Rising Sun, I came to this city to find the past in a place absorbed by it. Like most people, I assumed that because our song was *about* New Orleans, it was *of* New Orleans and had crawled out of the primordial jazz and proto blues that once defined the city's French Quarter. I was quickly dissuaded of that notion. After all, the lyrics say as much: ". . . *down* in New Orleans"; "going *back* to New Orleans." They view the city as an outsider would. Still, maybe the Rising Sun was once a real cathouse.

For two centuries, the Quarter—known as the Vieux Carre, or Old Square—has produced some of America's most compelling imagery. Here, French and Spanish, English and African and West Indian melted together into a Creole culture—and a reputation for the vice that accompanied it. New Orleans was the melting pot embodied, and the Vieux Carre was its storefront. You can chart a direct path from its early traditions and loosely enforced laws to today's theme-parkified offerings of everything from gospel breakfasts to "gentlemen's clubs" to bars with blenders built into the walls that churn out frozen drinks in all of Crayola's colors.

In 1936, Herbert Asbury, author of *The Gangs of New York,* published a lurid, sometimes apocryphal volume called *The French Quarter.* Asbury spends 338 vice-saturated pages chronicling how New Orleans earned its reputation as a place where a man went to forget some of his troubles and accumulate others. He tells of dance-hall girls serving up cheap beer, creosote-laced liquor, and themselves, of boat pilots navigating the Mississippi and pouring into the warren of narrow alleys around Canal Street, looking for things they'd never find upriver. "Every flatboat man possessed two major ambitions," Asbury wrote: to become a river champion and "to visit New Orleans for a spree of wholehearted wallowing in the fleshpots, for which exercise the town offered infinitely more facilities than any other city west of the Allegheny mountains." And, of course, railroad men and rounders came from the Southern Highlands to the end of the line with little to lose. Al Rose describes the scene in his book *Storyville, New Orleans:*

> The visitor to New Orleans who arrived by train at the Southern Depot could see the mansions of Basin Street from his window as the train pulled into the station. He would see elaborately bedecked females posing in the windows of these notorious houses, and some of the women would wave to him or make lascivious gestures calculated to excite his interest.

As the twentieth century dawned, a photographer named E. J. Bellocq began shooting moody, haunting portraits of Storyville's prostitutes in their habitats. In doing so, he created a rare record of their lives. To see some of these young women—and aging ones as well—is to gaze into our song's soul by facing its real-life details. They seem like ghosts themselves, eyes empty, some surrounded by elaborate accoutrements, others naked in both fact and spirit. In Louis Malle's 1978 film *Pretty Baby*, which depicted Storyville's prostitutes through Bellocq's eyes, they call their bordello simply "the House." The movie's first sound is the whistle of a train arriving in the darkness.

In recent decades, though New Orleans's reputation for partying remained—at least until Hurricane Katrina interrupted it in 2005—the city made great strides in cleaning up areas that outsiders frequented. Prostitution was outlawed for good with Storyville's shuttering in 1917. The city even renamed some of its streets to purge itself of their tawdry associations. What remains retains a mystique accentuated by ornate old architecture shouts of past dalliances and indiscretions. "New Orleans, unlike a lot of those places you go back to and that don't have the magic anymore, still has got it," Bob Dylan wrote. "Night can swallow you up, yet none of it touches you."

As "House of the Rising Sun" suggests, New Orleans has long embraced sin and shunned its wages. Unlike Appalachia's restraint, nothing feels forbidden here. This is more proof that the song must have originated elsewhere; it took an outsider to see the town this way. Even in the blues here, there's a ripeness that early "Rising Sun" renditions lack. You hear nothing sensuous from the mouths of Clarence Ashley, Homer Callahan, Georgia Turner. Only regret.

Vice remains pivotal to the city's historical fabric. On one occasion when I am in town, the Louisiana State Museum in the old U.S. Mint building features an exhibit on New Orleans drinks, with displays like "Prohibition: The Great Mistake," "The Bartender: Artist and Craftsman" and "The Street: Drinking on the Go." My favorite display, "Rum and the Hurricane: The War Years," recounts how rum became popular when World War II was unkind enough to claim distillery resources for tires and gunpowder. The exhibit is sponsored by the Southern Food and Beverage Museum and such entities as Southern Comfort—which would account for information-card captions like this: "Whether it's the drive-thru daiquiri or the yard dog on Bourbon Street or the football full of beer, each of these containers enables New Orleanians and our guests to enjoy all the beauty our city offers, both inside the bar and out."

In spring 2005, five months before Katrina, very little in the French Quarter feels real. On Bourbon Street, the Cajun Cabin offers wood-paneled cabinets with strategic crookedness and knottiness to evoke a backwoods home. Daiquiri bars sell frozen drinks with funny names and funnier colors, theming the experience of getting drunk. State-sponsored video poker machines beckon from one end of the room. In the neighborhood where once you could die from drink or syphilis or a blade slipped between the ribs, the Acme Oyster House has a sign over its bar: "There may be a risk associated with consuming raw shellfish." Much of the music seems frozen in time, a carefully calibrated representation of the melting pot that created it. Even the sex is slickly packaged: Strippers with artificially inflated breasts and music video names like Tawny and Shalimar seem like Disney characters, and the Hustler Barely Legal Bar is air-conditioned and lacking entirely in seediness. We've divorced the vice from its trappings and made it as wholesome as a cartoon. An adult-DVD store employee wears a T-shirt: "Relax—It's Just Sex."

Yet amid all the plasticization, the ghosts are real. Lives were ruined. Girls—and boys—were lost. There really were places where intimacy was sold, bought, and sometimes forced. Could one of them have been the Rising Sun?

Amateur folklorists, and some professionals, have long debated whether, as the Lomaxes suggested in *Our Singing Country* in 1941, that the term "Rising Sun" was used frequently in England as a euphemism for prostitution. Vance Randolph and G. Legman, in their collection of "unprintable" Ozark folk songs, offered this information as background to the "Rising Sun" versions they had collected:

> The sign itself of the "Rising Sun," probably refers to some gilt or yellow-painted version of the large sculptured or gilt wooden chrysanthemum-style circular decoration often placed as a sun-ray mirror indoors, or over the outside door of fine houses in France, and derivatively in French New Orleans (Nouvelle Orleans until the Louisiana Purchase from Napoleon in 1803), during and after the reign to 1715 of Louis XIV, "le Roi Soleil" or Sun-King, whose royal insignia it was.

Dave Van Ronk, the Greenwich Village folk musician whose version of the song Bob Dylan used, died thinking the Rising Sun was a jail. "I had always assumed that the 'house' was a brothel," Van Ronk wrote in his memoir. Then, while he and his wife were in New Orleans having drinks with the folk-blues singer Odetta (who also sang the song) and a man approached with a handful of turn-of-the-century photos. One of them depicted "a forbidding stone doorway" bearing a carving of a rising sun. "I asked him, 'What's that building?' " Van Ronk wrote. "It was the Orleans Parish women's prison. So, as it turned out, I had gotten the whole business wrong from the get-go." This "proves" nothing except that Van Ronk saw a photograph of a building. But the song, in its primary incarnation, *could* have been about a prison as much as a whorehouse or a gambling den.

The Rising Sun is absent from New Orleans history books, and many doubt the legend was ever reality. "I've never seen it substantiated," Bruce Raeburn, the curator of the Hogan Jazz Archives at Tulane University, tells me. (Raeburn, a former Laguna Beach surfer, says our song "set the tone for an entire summer" before his senior year of high school in 1964.)

Despite the historical dubiousness, sundry French Quarter buildings—many of them commercial establishments, go figure—trade off the legend. One bed and breakfast, the Villa Convento, operates out of a red-brick building with wrought-iron balconies on Ursulines Street. It bills itself as "rumored to be the legendary House of the Rising Sun" and sells T-shirts to that effect. When I stop in, I ask the desk clerk if that is so. "The buggy drivers say it is," he says, "and we don't argue with them." Five minutes later, a tourist cart passes by and the driver proves his point.

A three-story white house on St. Louis Street is also purported to be the Rising Sun and, legend has it, was operated in the mid-1800s by a madam named Marianne Le Soleil Levant—which, translated from French, means "the sun rising." City directories from that time show no such person. Though that's not definitive—bordellos might not be listed in directories—Ms. Soleil Levant is similarly absent from other records.

In fact, New Orleans city directories show no Rising Sun at all, in any incarnation, between 1850 and 1880. Directories between 1890 and 1897 list a Rising Sun Hall in the city's Seventh District, four miles from the French Quarter—an area that did have houses of prostitution but was by no means the epicenter of vice. There is also a 1900 entry for a Rising Sun Society Hall, but it, too, is miles from the Quarter. These listings are intriguing; Rising Sun Hall is only one word away from Rising Sun Dance Hall, the first printed mention of our song with all its implications of low-end prostitution. But the entries would be much more compelling if Clarence "Tom" Ashley, who made the first commercial "Rising Sun" recording, hadn't learned it from his grandparents in the first decade of the 1900s and suggested it predated even them.

New Orleans reference librarian Pamela Arceneaux, who has researched the city's history of prostitution, wrote in 2003 that she came away with no clear answer about whether a House of the Rising Sun existed—and found no mention of it in property records or other documents relating to nineteenth-century prostitution in New Orleans. What's more, she found no mention of the rising sun as a symbol for prostitution. "To paraphrase Freud," Arceneaux wrote, "sometimes lyrics are just lyrics."

Eric Burdon thinks otherwise. He is convinced that, when he went to the St. Louis Street address, he visited the real House. Ever since 1964, when the song defined him and he it, Burdon had been pursuing the real thing. "I'd go to women's prisons, coke dealers' houses, insane asylums, men's prisons, private parties," he told me. "They just wanted to get me there." A few years back, a friend in New Orleans took him to the house, which she believed was the original. It was a restored French Quarter place that featured a mural supposedly depicting voodoo gods. During the house's restoration, Burdon says, a ceiling mural was uncovered—"a golden sun on the rise, surrounded by three cherubs." The host, whom he doesn't identify, prevailed upon him to sing an extended version a capella. "I sang for all I was worth," Burdon wrote. Still, no hard proof links that place with our song.

There really is a house in New Orleans that they call the Rising Sun. It is in Algiers Point, across the Mississippi River from the Vieux Carre, and it is a bed and breakfast run by a couple named Kevin and Wendy Herridge, from Britain and Louisiana respectively (their tagline is "Cajun and Cockney Hospitality"). I stay there for a night. Alone.

The Herridges, who owned seven thousand albums and five thousand 45s at the time of my visit, have collected dozens of versions of the song. The legend is their stock in trade. Their hostel features ample brothelabilia. One old sign advises that "Street girls bringing in sailors must pay for room in advance." Admonishes another: "Ladies—kindly do your soliciting discreetly." An entire bedroom is adorned in Asian-style décor as if it were a classy prostitute's office. Herridge, a jazz historian, pulls out a guidebook to "Offbeat New Orleans," which asserts that the St. Louis Street address was the real Rising Sun between 1862 and 1874. "Pack of lies," he scoffs.

Which brings us back to those 1820s newspaper articles about the Rising Sun Hotel on Conti Street and its eventual consumption by fire.

In early 2005, a bit of serendipity unfolded at 535–537 Conti Street in the French Quarter. The Historic New Orleans Commission owned the property, adjacent to its research center, which had been a parking garage for years. When they decided to level it, they figured—since they were a historical outfit, and this was the French Quarter—that a professional should investigate. That turned out to be Shannon Dawdy, a University of Chicago archaeologist who fell in love with New Orleans a decade ago.

The tract was aggressively nondescript, rare for the Vieux Carre. It is three blocks down from Bourbon Street and two blocks up from the Mississippi River, a one-story building of red bricks and scuffed white paint just around the corner from Paul Prudhomme's famous K-Paul's Louisiana Kitchen. Except for some pallets and piles of debris, the interior was empty. On an exterior wall, someone had pasted a sticker that says, "I (heart) hand grenades"—the cocktail, not the bomb.

Five months before Katrina, Dawdy, two assistants, and a New Orleans archaeology firm cut through the concrete flooring and excavated the site with dustpans, trowels, and mallets. Down they went, through the decades, back to the early 1800s. At that level, they uncovered some compelling artifacts. They found numerous liquor bottles—enough to suggest that the place could have been an establishment that sold alcohol. They also dug up, at the level of the 1810s and 1820s, numerous fragments of wide-mouthed rouge pots—many more than would have been normal in a private home. Other sites in New Orleans have belched forth two to three pots each, Dawdy said, and "to find this much more is extraordinary."

After the artifacts turned up, Dawdy researched old newspapers and land surveys and came up with the *Louisiana Gazette* ad about the Rising Sun Hotel and the news item about the fire that destroyed it. Here was a hotel committed to "giving the best entertainment" to its patrons. Here were "gentlemen" who can be sure to find "attentive servants." Pretty strong terminology for the early nineteenth century, no? Dawdy found the ad's language "very suggestive," though antebellum prostitution in New Orleans is largely undocumented. "It's nothing that people want to leave a record of," she said. Additionally, Dawdy noted, the newspaper ad states no specific address on Conti Street, though the archaeological dig has produced pretty clear evidence of a "burn level" right around the decade that the Rising Sun Hotel supposedly went up in flames. That, coupled with her own discoveries, was—even to a trained eye—intriguing.

"It is true that French and Continental women were using more makeup. A little bit later on, heavy makeup is associated with loose women," Dawdy told me. "In the antebellum era, I don't know. I can't presume continuity of attitude."

Though the Historic New Orleans Collection was more excited about Dawdy's other discovery on the site—early Native American artifacts— the possibility of a Rising Sun find drew global attention. That may be why Dawdy's early comments—that the place was "looking impressively like a bordello"—were stronger than her subsequent assessment. When I visited her at the dig, a couple weeks later, she was using words like "suggestive" and "fascinating but inconclusive."

"People read it the way they want to. So they read it as, 'We've found the brothel that created the House of the Rising Sun,' " she said. "It's very ambiguous." All the attention didn't exactly please her. "There's a pathology about New Orleans," she says, "that everything's marketable."

You can't help but ask, though: What happened inside the wooden building that once stood here? Were painted ladies available for the asking? Were French and English used to negotiate for flesh before corsets and dresses fell to the floor? Was a song of sin and misery born?

Let's say the Rising Sun Hotel was indeed a place where pleasures could be secured for a price. Let's say someone from Appalachia—from our originating mountains, a visitor from The Village—either worked there or patronized the place, then went home. A ruined girl, maybe a man with syphilis or gonorrhea, returned to Appalachia and talked of the Rising Sun, down in New Orleans, where the possibility of ruin was everywhere. Eventually, a balladeer singing the dark warning songs of the Appalachians incorporated the image into a lament. Was it in 1840? 1860? 1880?

Or: Let's say the place was a legitimate hostel, a place for lodging and meals. The old Harry Cox song about Lowestoft, England, included a Rising Sun verse, remember. Maybe it all had nothing to do with New Orleans until some long-ago singer simply united the two ideas and thought they'd work well together.

In August 2005, Katrina hit New Orleans and reshuffled priorities. Thousands lost their homes and began wandering across the land. A PowerPoint slide show of Katrina-related news photos made its way across the internet, set to the Animals doing "Rising Sun," and the ragged electric blues fit the mood perfectly. Dawdy ended up embedded with the Federal Emergency Management Agency, trying to make sure that the rebuilding of the city didn't run roughshod over its rich history. I saw a profile of her post-Katrina work in which she said, of the Rising Sun site, "I love the ambiguity of it all."

And that's it. Shannon Dawdy is not just a scientist but a wise woman. To find the actual House of the Rising Sun, to solve the mystery, would undermine our song's potency. To know for sure what the lyrics were about would make them less universal, less adaptable, less applicable to the blues as any given artist feels them.

After a winding journey of discovery, it turns out that we are richer for not knowing.

Four years after our first visit, my wife Melissa and I return to Nashville with our two-year-old son to see the Country Music Hall of Fame. Of course we stay with Mixt Company—Virginia Lee and David Blood and Virginia's daughter, Letitia. They insist. Virginia—Monkey—cooks up a country meal of meat loaf, mashed potatoes, beans with fatty pork, and biscuits. After dinner, by starlight, we sit on their porch, smoke cheap cigars and talk—about our lives, their lives, tough times, good times. I feel like an impostor, coming out of the suburbs to seek the "authentic" and finding people of substance.

For a half decade, I've talked to the musicians this song led me to, and pondered how different they are from me—how their existence is somehow a purer version of life than the kind I have lived. I have kept my distance, telling myself that I am only the observer. But these people are the exception. They have cooked for me, held my son, become my friends. Monkey is a storyteller, and the tales she spins about her childhood in Beehive Holler are at once unimaginably sad and, I tell her, hopeful. She admonishes me.

"There was no hope," she says. "No hope of getting out."

I think of Georgia Turner growing up in Middlesboro. I think of Rossie Holcomb, Virginia's cousin, whose music carried him to places he never could have imagined—and back again. And I think of the singers who were never discovered by an Alan Lomax or a John Cohen, who sang to dilute pain and never expected anyone to listen—and certainly never thought they had access to a life other than the one into which they were born. Letitia puts it this way about her cousins who never left Kentucky: "The world was too big for them."

But Virginia Lee captured hope of the kind that eluded Georgia Turner. Today Virginia lives in a red-brick home outside of Nashville, not far from where Mother Maybelle Carter spent her final years. She has a good job, a family that loves her, and running water every day. And the days begin with music. Just past dawn, the radio is on, and barely a half hour later David is singing along.

It's past 10 p.m. when Letitia carts up her bass from downstairs. Virginia and David break out the guitar and the mandolin and they start to play. At first, I am uncomfortable. I am accustomed to *receiving* music as a consumer, and it is hard to purge from my mind the notion that they are performing for us. They sing a haunting old song, "Said the Snake," then do a couple of their own compositions. They sing of God and mountains, hope and memories. As David strums the mandolin, Monkey says, "This is why I married him." Then she turns to me. "We're going to do 'Rising Sun' now."

Turns out they've been singing it live for a few years while we've been living abroad. Monkey starts with the guitar and begins with an unusual verse—the warning. "My mother always told me, 'Don't do what I have done . . .' " Then David and Letitia cut in, and the music fills their neighborhood in Nashville's northern suburbs. I can see the city lights in the distance, but otherwise I could be in the hills. I realize that my quest is coming to . . . not an end, but a stopping point. I didn't find the deepest roots of "Rising Sun" as I intended. But I am wiser. The origin eluded me, but the journey was the point.

When we reflect upon the lives of important people, how much time do we spend on their births? Isn't it the life, the path charted through the world, that matters? After a chase across mountains, decades and continents, here I am on a porch again, hearing it with no amplification and no machinery. It's not the front porch of a cabin in some dark holler in The Village, but it shouldn't be. It is attached to a landscaped house full of modern conveniences like a big-screen TV and a treadmill and a microwave. This is exactly where the song should be. It has been amplified and transmitted and duplicated and adapted. And here, in 2005, Mixt Company is singing it—not performing it, but *singing* it—on their own porch, not for an audience but because they love to make music. Because, for them, the echo is just as important as the action.

My uncle Maurice, an insurance man who held a passionate belief in his profession's ability to help people, had promotional coins minted for clients. He gave several to his sister, my mother, and they were always turning up around our house when I was little. On the front, it asks, "Stumbling block or stepping stone?" The back says, "Building today for eternity."

I assumed they were marketing platitudes. Then, years after he died, I saw a video of a training session that he, as a long-retired executive at Prudential, presented. In it, he read a poem by a man named R. Lee Sharpe that, I realized, had inspired his medallions.

Isn't it strange that princes and kings
and clowns that caper in sawdust rings
and common people like you and like me
are the builders for eternity?

Each is given a bag of tools,
a shapeless mass and a book of rules.
and each must make 'ere life is flown,
a stumbling block or a stepping stone.

We move through our lives, buffeted by the shrieks of the twenty-four-hour news channels and the violence done in the name of God and the celebrities and celebrity whores with all their glossy sound and cartoonish fury signifying nothing. But if we take the time to sweep all of that away and examine the texture of American lives, it becomes obvious. Our tools are family and love, experience and excitement, misery and deceit, music and death and, above all else, the road, which is forever giving us the chance to change our story. "When a woman gets the blues, she hangs her head and cries," an old blues sung by Jimmie Rodgers goes. "But when a man gets the blues, he grabs a train and rides."

What was "House of the Rising Sun" but a shapeless mass to those who sculpted it using the only tools they had? For some, it changed their lives. For others, it was a splinter of themselves to pass on, a scaffolding used to amplify misery and loss. How could they ever dream that, thanks to fate and coincidence, it could make a difference? Eternity is, after all, built brick by brick. We can align ourselves with traditional history, in which the loudest and the richest commandeer our stories, or we can decide that the quieter things are what really matter. "Civilization," the historian Will Durant wrote, "is a stream with banks."

> The stream is sometimes filled with blood from people killing, stealing, shouting, and doing the things historians usually record; while on the banks, unnoticed, people build homes, make love, raise children, sing songs, write poetry, and even whittle statues. The story of civilization is the story of what happened on the banks.

Is it so odd that a piece of music—the expression of emotion distilled into spare wording and sound—can become, for so many people in such diverse places, a touchstone? The subject—ruin—is a stumbling block, but the song has become a stepping stone.

Our world today is changing too quickly to keep track. Music is faster than people. We drive and fly, but songs can soar; their wings are airwaves and Virgin Megastores and 99-cent digital files downloaded from iTunes. The very innovations that once threatened to eradicate the traditional and the local—the technologies that Alan Lomax condemned even as, fortunately, he used them—have carried those songs to the planet's farthest reaches, to unexpected ears. And what goes into new ears eventually comes out of new mouths in innovative, thrilling ways. In a collage culture, the old can always become new again. "Everybody might be just one big soul; it looks that way to me," Woody Guthrie once sang.

Why this particular song? Who knows. But it took wing. Doc Doc's credit on the internet—"By everyone"—captures it exactly. Each time a song moves from experienced mouth to fresh ear, it carries its past on its back.

And the songs shout at us. The map sings. If you listen just right, you can hear the chorus that came before. Clarence Ashley and Roy Acuff and the Callahan Brothers are singing; so are Woody Guthrie and Josh White and Lead Belly, each long gone. The Weavers are harmonizing. Eric Burdon is belting out his best. Bob Dylan—plugged and unplugged—is warbling. The Moaners, down in North Carolina, are telling people about the Paradise Club. Mixt Company is playing a set at the Bluegrass Inn, and you can hear cousin Roscoe Holcomb's voice, too. The microphone masters at the BMG Karaoke Box on Silom Road in Bangkok are crooning to Thai girlfriends sipping overpriced pink drinks. Harrison Burnett is singing in that high nasal voice as he strides methodically through the darkness on his night-watchman rounds at the University of Arkansas. Steve Power and Hally Wood and EverEve. Frijid Pink and Santa Esmeralda and David H. Yakobian with his flute. All the teenage garage bands of the eighties and seventies, all the folkies of the sixties and fifties and forties, all the front-porch Appalachian singers of the thirties and twenties and teens and even deeper into the past whose voices were never captured by anyone's Presto reproducer. They're all there, too, singing of the ruined girl or boy, of the whorehouse or prison or gambling den in New Orleans or Lowestoft or Baxter Springs or yondos town or the strip club out on Old 87. If there's a rock and roll heaven, you know they have a hell of a band.

And you can hear, too, the pretty, yellow-headed miner's daughter from Kentucky who never asked for much and never got much in return. Georgia Turner, dead and silent four decades, is still singing the blues away.

They all undertook journeys, though some never left home. And their travels, each of them, are now part of the larger world—a world where tiny connections, and the astonishing things they produce, are the true tales of our age.

An underground river that starts here and flows—right under the pasture! And then . . . well, who knows?

Not far from the center of Monroe, Michigan, sits Woodland Cemetery, a warren of hills and plateaus in a quiet neighborhood. I follow Reno Taylor, Georgia Turner's son, through its gates in my rental car and tail him until he stops. He gets out and strides toward a gray granite stone. First he notices other graves nearby—friends of his family. Treadways. Berrys. He points to one plot. "He was a railroad man. He was my father's buddy." Then he stands in front of the stone he has been walking toward and looks down at the final resting place of his stepfather and his mother.

CONNOLLY

Georgia B.	Edward F.
1921–1969	1918–1974

Married
Sept. 12, 1962

We are silent for a few moments. Reno looks at me. "There's my ma," he says. He reiterates what he said when I first met him, but it seems more imperative here. "The whole idea," he says, "is that my ma gets credit."

Reno falls silent, and I don't want to interrupt. Finally, we shake hands and he walks toward his car. I get into mine and watch him drive off. But I don't leave. I pop in a CD, and the Library of Congress recording comes on. I contemplate the few pictures I've seen of Reno's ma: curly hair, a toothy smile and glasses, a 1960s housewife surrounded by children. Did she dwell on the path her life had taken? Or did she just cope, put her head down, and plug on in the only way she could? I think of what her sister-in-law, June Turner, told me: "If she'd been born at a later time and into different circumstances, who knows what she could have done?"

From the rental car's speakers comes Georgia Turner's teenage voice, low and throaty, singing about the Rising Sun. I look toward her headstone a few feet away. A sixteen-year-old girl sent something on its way. It traveled to places she never imagined. But it left her behind, and this is where she ended up.

I roll down the passenger window and turn up the volume.

Afterword: My Race
Is Almost Run . . .

This story has no moral.
This story has no end.

—"FRANKIE AND JOHNNY," TRADITIONAL

I now stand on the scaffold,
My name it will not be long,
You may forget the singer,
Pray don't forget the song.

—"TANEY COUNTY," ARKANSAS FOLK SONG

After spending more than $10,000 on CDs, I am fortunate. Though I've accumulated a lot of recorded music, my ears can hear far more.

I hear my father singing to me in the darkness of a split-level house north of Pittsburgh in the early 1970s, his reassuring voice passing along wisdom through songs from long ago: *Hi, ho. Anybody home? Meat nor drink nor money have I none. Still will I be merry.* I can almost hear his father singing to him, and fathers upon Anthony fathers reaching back across the centuries. And I can hear my voice singing, to my three-year-old son, those same songs that comforted me.

In a world of confusing, deafening static, I feel hopeful. I feel American. Can one sad song and its journeys really do all that? I would never have believed it.

A few years ago, the musician and radio host Oscar Brand, friend to most of the 1940s performers who sang "House of the Rising Sun," urged me to follow my obsession. "I didn't know Woody was going to be a monument. I didn't know Lead Belly was a giant. I just knew that I liked them. They were my friends," he told me. "And now they're on postage stamps." He sounded kind of sad. "We just liked the music. We never had the slightest idea what would happen, where it would go."

His voice grew quiet.

"Write a book," he said. "Put them in it . . . put Miss Turner in it. And you can tell the story of the kind of people for whom these songs were their daily life."

Not long ago, I was browsing the folk section in Borders when I came upon a CD I didn't recognize. The title was *Alan Lomax: Popular Songbook,* and it promised that it "brings together for the first time the best-known songs collected by folklorists John and Alan Lomax."

Lead Belly was there, singing "The Midnight Special." Memphis Slim and Big Bill Broonzy, too. "Sonny Boy" Williamson doing "Stagolee." My eyes moved down the list and stopped at track 21. "The House of the Rising Sun (Rising Sun Blues), Georgia Turner, 1937." It was her Library of Congress recording—there, on a professionally produced compact disc in a big-time bookstore. She finally made it.

And me? In the end, I remain a pretender—a Blue American with a loud shirt and a camera, touring Red America. Yes, I have felt the music, thrilled as it coursed through me. But The Village never let me in.

Nor should it.

I am neither native nor, like Dylan, "musical expeditionist." I'm not even a musician. I'm a pampered guy from the suburbs who suspected that something small might mean something big. I have no right to sing the blues. I have choices that the Georgia Turners of the world could never have imagined. For me, journeys are not about sadness or desperation or the chance to feed my family; they are about possibility. The forces that have hurled "House of the Rising Sun" around the planet are carrying me, too, and I am a member of a generation that can sample American life—and American lives—like none before.

Like those who built the folk revival, I set out to define my Americanness through authenticity. Instead, I have found that I am defined by the very hodgepodge that created me—the packaged, marketed, mongrel age that was the late twentieth century. I can look back upon yesterdays, but only so much. I can crave mountains and hand-fashioned music and two-lane roads to the horizon, but the mall and the interstate exit and the World Wide Web are my homes. Because of who I am—when and how I was born—I can view the folkways, but only at a distance. Only from the highway.

Yet when it comes to "House of the Rising Sun," none of that matters. This song is mine anyway. Like those who played and sang it far better than I did, I claim it as my own for a brief moment. I reach into the past as far as I am able. I pick it up. And I carry it—and carry them—into the future.

I hope they're watching.

Ted Anthony
Montclair, New Jersey
September 2006

Notes

PROLOGUE: THE MOMENT

To reconstruct the moment in 1937 when Alan Lomax visited Middlesboro, Kentucky, and recorded Georgia Turner singing "The Rising Sun Blues," the author used the following sources for background and documentation: Alan and John Lomax, *Our Singing Country;* Alan Lomax, *Folk Songs of North America;* Ronald D. Cohen, editor, *Alan Lomax: Selected Writings 1934–1997;* Nolan Porterfield, *The Last Cavalier: The Life and Times of John A. Lomax;* Tom N. Shattuck, *A Cumberland Gap Area Guidebook;* Irwin Stambler and Grelun Landon, *The Encyclopedia of Folk, Country & Western Music;* Harry M. Caudill, *Night Comes to the Cumberlands;* Scott Weidensaul, *Mountains of the Heart: A Natural History of the Appalachians;* editions of the *Middlesboro Daily News* from September 1937; performances by Georgia Turner, Edward Hunter, and Mary Mast Turner collected in 1937 by Alan Lomax and deposited in the Library of Congress; correspondence and notes files from the Library of Congress's American Folklife Center, formerly the Archive of Folk Song, documenting Alan Lomax's 1937 trip to Kentucky; interviews with Edward Hunter, who sang on the original Alan Lomax field sessions in 1937; Georgia Turner's children, nephew and great-niece in Monroe, Mich.; Jennifer Cutting of the Library of Congress; and Tom N. Shattuck, a community historian in Middlesboro, Ky.

5 *She is blond:* Alan Lomax, *The Folk Songs of North America* (Garden City, NY: Doubleday, 1960), 280.

5 *Sometimes, when the songs are sad:* Author interview with Roy Taylor, Monroe, Mich., 2/17/01.

5 *The girl has a strong, beautiful voice:* Author interview with Edward Hunter, telephone and Middlesboro, Ky., 7/17/00 and 7/23/00.

6 *Everyone in the neighborhood:* Ibid.

6 *One day, a stranger:* Correspondence and notes from Alan Lomax's 1937 Kentucky trip (Library of Congress American Folklife Center).

6 *"Here the mountains":* Letter from Alan Lomax to Harold Spivacke, 8/14/37 (Library of Congress American Folklife Center).

6 *he hears fascinating things:* Letters from Alan Lomax to Harold Spivacke, Library of Congress American Folklife Center.

7 *He has written ahead:* Lomax correspondence and notes, 1937.

7 *Among them is Mary Mast Turner:* Edward Hunter, 7/17/00 and 7/23/00; author interview with Georgia Turner's children, 2/17/01.

7 *Lomax unloads his Presto:* Lomax correspondence and notes, 1937.

7 *The girl and her mother arrive:* Edward Hunter, 7/17/00 and 7/23/00.

CHAPTER 1: THE WAY-BACK MACHINE

The following sources were useful for background and documentation: Greil Marcus, *Invisible Republic: Bob Dylan's Basement Tapes* (also known as *The Old, Weird America*); Bob Dylan, *Chronicles: Volume One;* Sherwood Anderson, *Winesburg, Ohio;* Edward L. Ayers, *Southern Crossing: A History of the American South, 1877–1906;* Cary Franklin Poole, *A History of Railroading in Western North Carolina;* Carl Sandburg, *The American Songbag;* W. C. Handy, *Father of the Blues: An Autobiography;* Ambrose N. Manning and Minnie M. Miller, "Tom Ashley," from *Tom Ashley, Sam McGee, Bukka White: Tennessee Traditional Singers;* Samuel Charters, *The Country Blues;* Ann Anderson, *Snake Oil, Hustlers and Hambones: The American Medicine Show;* John Parris, *Roaming the Mountains with John A. Parris; American Folklore: An Encyclopedia,* edited by Jan Harold Brunvand; Jan Harold Brunvand, *The Study of American Folklore;* Robert V. Remini, *The Battle of New Orleans;* the correspondence of Robert Winslow Gordon, in the Library of Congress American Folklife Center; Mellinger Edward Henry, *Folk-Songs from the Southern Highlands;* Nathaniel Thompson Allison, *History of Cherokee County, Kansas, and Representative Citizens;* William G. Cutler, *History of the State of Kansas;* Ian G. Robb, *A Century of Lowestoft: Events, People and Places over the Last 100 Years;* Marty McGee, *Traditional Musicians of the Central Blue Ridge;* Sharyn McCrumb, *The Songcatcher;* Roderick Peattie, editor, *The Great Smokies and the Blue Ridge: The Story of the Southern Appalachians;* Martin Crawford, *Ashe County's Civil War;* Mari-Lynn Evans, Robert Santelli, and Holly George-Warren, editors, *The Appalachians: America's First and Last Frontier;* Samuel Charters, *The Country Blues;* Eric Sackheim, *The Blues Line: A Collection of Blues Lyrics from Leadbelly to Muddy Waters;* Cecil Brown, *Stagolee Shot Billy;* Ted Ownby, *Subduing Satan: Religion, Recreation, and Manhood in the Rural South, 1865–1920;* Mark Zwonitzer with Charles Hirshberg, *Will You Miss Me When I'm Gone?: The Carter Family and Their Legacy in American Music;* W. H. Auden, Chester Kallman and Noah Greenberg, editors, *An Elizabethan Song Book;* John Foster West, *Lift Up Your Head, Tom Dooley: The True Story of the Appalachian Murder That Inspired One of America's Most Popular Ballads;* Jean Ritchie, *Folk Songs of the Southern Appalachians;* interviews with record collectors Joe Bussard Jr.

and Paul Mawhinney; Clarence Ashley's daughter, Eva Ashley Moore, and grandson, Tom Moore; and architect Steven Izenour; various internet postings on folk music and the history of "House of the Rising Sun," both accurate and inaccurate. The author also made repeated visits to the areas of western North Carolina, eastern Tennessee, and eastern Kentucky where much of the chapter's action is focused, in addition to visiting Baxter Springs, Kan., Lowestoft, England, and Keene, N.H.

Various early recordings and their liner notes were also invaluable, including Harry Smith's liner notes for *The Anthology of American Folk Music;* Robert Shelton's liner notes for *The Folk Box; Ivy Smith & Cow Cow Davenport: Complete Recorded Works in Chronological Order, 1927–1930; Peetie Wheatstraw: Complete Recorded Works in Chronological Order, Vol. 2, 25 March 1934 to 17 July 1935; Ruckus Juice & Chittlins: The Great Jug Bands; Darby & Tarlton: Complete Recordings;* Peter Kennedy's notes for *Harry Cox: What Will Become of England?;* Ralph and Richard Rinzler's notes for *Old-Time Music at Clarence Ashley's;* reel-to-reel tape of Alan Lomax and Harry Cox in England, 12/1/1953, courtesy of the Alan Lomax Archives; *Greenback Dollar: The Music of Clarence "Tom" Ashley;* tapes of Clarence Ashley in concert in the 1960s, from the Thomas G. Burton–Ambrose N. Manning Collection at the Archives of Appalachia, East Tennessee State University; Ashley & Foster, "The Rising Sun Blues," from the collection of Joe Bussard; *You Ain't Talkin' to Me: Charlie Poole and the Roots of Country Music; Before the Blues: The Early American Black Music Scene,* vols. 1–3; *WPAQ: The Voice of the Blue Ridge Mountains; Classic Mountain Songs from Smithsonian Folkways;* Dock Boggs, *Country Blues: Complete Early Recordings, 1927–29;* Dock Boggs, *His Folkways Years: 1963–1968;* Eck Robertson, *Vintage Recordings, 1922–1929;* John Dilleshaw (Seven Foot Dilly), *Complete Recorded Works in Chronological Order, 1929–1930;* The Skillet-Lickers, *Complete Recorded Works in Chronological Order, Volume 1, 1926–1927; Down in the Basement: Joe Bussard's Treasure Trove of Vintage 78s, 1926–1937; The Rose Grew Round the Briar: Early American Rural Love Songs, Vol. 2; Music from the Lost Provinces: Old-Time Stringbands from Ashe County, North Carolina, & Vicinity, 1927–1931.* Smith's *Anthology* and its many songs were also indispensable in helping to set a scene, tone and characterization of the time and place from which "House of the Rising Sun" initially emerged.

11 *"For the first time":* Greil Marcus, *Invisible Republic: Bob Dylan's Basement Tapes* (New York, Henry Holt, 1997), 120.

12 *It's great fun to read:* Harry Smith, *The Anthology of American Folk Music* (Smithsonian Folkways Recordings SFW40090, 1952/1997), liner notes.

12 *"I had already landed":* Bob Dylan, *Chronicles: Volume One* (New York: Simon & Schuster, 2004), 235–36.

12 *A good portion of the* Anthology's *artists:* Marcus, *Invisible Republic,* 94.

13 *"The coming of industrialism":* Sherwood Anderson, *Winesburg, Ohio* (New York: Signet Classics, 2005), 56–57.

17 *In the decades after the Civil War:* Edward L. Ayers, *Southern Crossing: A History of the American South, 1877–1906* (Oxford: Oxford University Press, 1995), 7.

18 *"Any given year":* Ibid., 5.

18 *The Southern Railroad advertised:* Cary Franklin Poole, *A History of Railroading in Western North Carolina* (Johnson City, Tenn.: The Overmountain Press, 1995), 70.

19 *"Girls with a wild streak":* Carl Sandburg, *The American Songbag* (New York, Harcourt Brace, 1927), 312.

19 *New Orleans had lurked in Appalachia's consciousness:* Robert V. Remini, *The Battle of New Orleans* (New York: Penguin Books, 1999), 24, 42.

20 *"O daughter, O dear daughter":* Carl Sandburg, *The American Songbag,* 313.

20 *"I don't like no railroad man":* Ibid., 326.

20 *Greil Marcus says many songs:* Greil Marcus, *Invisible Republic,* 116.

21 *"The song is based on a 16th-century British ballad":* internet posting by user "The Flying Dutchman" at www.xmission.com/pub/lists/exotica/archive/v02.n612, 10/22/99.

22 *"I understand that the song was written by Alan Price":* Usenet posting by user "APARS" to newsgroup rec.music.country.old-time, 11/11/99.

22 *" 'House of the Rising Sun' is an old blues tune":* Usenet posting by user "Ryant" to newsgroup rec.music.makers.guitar.tablature, 4/17/00.

22 *"Prior to Eric Burdon":* internet posting by user "Neil E" at www.xmission.com/pub/lists/exotica/archive/exotica.200002, 10/23/99.

22 *"I read a serious-looking text":* internet posting by user "Moritz R" at www.xmission.com/pub/lists/exotica/archive/v02.n613, 2/2/00.

22 *" 'The House of the Rising Sun' is about a parrish [sic] prison":* internet posting by user "What Do You Know" at www.xmission.com/pub/lists/exotica/archive/v02.n612, 10/22/99.

22 *Yes, Alger "Texas" Alexander did indeed record a song:* "The Red Hot Jazz Archive: A History of Jazz Before 1930," from website Red Hot Jazz, www.redhotjazz.com/talexander.html, accessed 09/06.

23 *Ivy Smith and "Cow Cow" Davenport's:* "Rising Sun Blues," *Ivy Smith & Cow Cow Davenport: Complete Recorded Works in Chronological Order, 1927–1930* (Document Records BDCD-6039), track 1.

23 *"I get up with the rising sun":* "Rising Sun Blues," *Peetie Wheatstraw: Complete Recorded Works in Chronological Order, Vol. 2, 25 March 1934 to 17 July 1935* (Document Records DOCD-5242), track 16.

23 *And "Rising Sun Blues" from King David's Jug Band":* "Rising Sun Blues,"

Ruckus Juice & Chittlins: The Great Jug Bands (Yazoo Records 2033), track 6.

23 *Another "Rising Sun Blues":* "Rising Sun Blues," *Darby & Tarlton: Complete Recordings* (Bear Family Records BCD15764 CI), disc 3, track 5.

24 *"When the country blues":* Robert Shelton, *The Folk Box* (Elektra EKL-9001, 1964), liner notes, side 6.

24 *You could argue that:* W. C. Handy, *Father of the Blues: An Autobiography* (New York: Da Capo, 1941/1969), 74.

25 *Its melody:* Lomax, *The Folk Songs of North America*, 280.

25 *In 1953, in Norfolk:* Peter Kennedy, *Harry Cox: What Will Become of England?* (Rounder 11661-1839-2, Alan Lomax Collection: Portraits Series, 1999), liner notes.

25 *One day, Lomax made:* Reel-to-reel tape of Alan Lomax and Harry Cox, England, 12/1/53, courtesy of Alan Lomax Archive.

26 *"I'd go anywhere":* Peter Kennedy, "Harry Cox: What Will Become of England?" liner notes.

26 *Lomax, in his 1960 book:* Lomax, *The Folk Songs of North America*, 280.

27 *Ashley was born:* Ralph and Richard Rinzler, *Old-Time Music at Clarence Ashley's* (Folkways FA2355, 1961), liner notes.

27 *Ashley's decision in 1911:* Ambrose N. Manning and Minnie M. Miller, "Tom Ashley," from *Tom Ashley, Sam McGee, Bukka White: Tennessee Traditional Singers* (Knoxville: University of Tennessee Press, 1981), 26.

27 *Ashley's daughter, Eva:* Author interview with Eva Ashley Moore, Saltville, Va., 2/25/01.

28 *"The entertainers sang loud":* Samuel B. Charters, *The Country Blues* (New York: Da Capo, 1959/1975), 101.

28 *"Until movies and radio were available":* Ann Anderson, *Snake Oil, Hustlers and Hambones: The American Medicine Show* (Jefferson, N.C.: McFarland & Company, 2000), 90.

28 *In the mid-1920s:* Ralph and Richard Rinzler, "Old-Time Music at Clarence Ashley's," liner notes.

29 *While he put his stamp: Greenback Dollar: The Music of Clarence "Tom" Ashley* (County Records CO-CD-3520, 2001).

29 *"I got it off":* Manning and Miller, "Tom Ashley," 42–43.

29 *One, William F. Burroughs:* Robert Winslow Gordon papers, Library of Congress American Folklife Center, letter no. 925 from William F. Burroughs to Gordon and attached response.

30 *Then Burroughs wrote down:* Ibid.

30 *Gordon was thrilled:* Ibid.

31 *In August 1929:* Mellinger Edward Henry, *Folk-Songs from the Southern Highlands* (New York: J.J. Augustin, 1938), song no. 125.

32 *"It was known, far and wide":* Nathaniel Thompson Allison, *History of Cherokee County, Kansas, and Representative Citizens* (Nathaniel Thompson Allison, 1904), chapter 13, "History of Baxter Springs."

32 *Even earlier, in 1883:* William G. Cutler, *History of the State of Kansas* (Chicago: A. T. Andreas, 1883), part 9.

32 *"This was a popular old song":* Tape of Clarence Ashley concert in 1960s, exact date unknown (Thomas G. Burton–Ambrose N. Manning Collection, Archives of Appalachia, East Tennessee State University), tape no. BM53A, side B.

33 *He sits in his cellar:* Author interview with Joe Bussard, Frederick, Md., 2/3/01.

37 *"I have all the Nimoys":* Author interview with Paul Mawhinney, Pittsburgh, Pa., 1991.

39 *It starts with:* Ashley and Foster, "The Rising Sun Blues" (Vocalion 02576-B), 1933.

39 *Ashley offers a verse:* Ibid.

42 *Some of his songs: You Ain't Talkin' to Me: Charlie Poole and the Roots of Country Music* (Columbia/Legacy C3K92780, 2005).

42 *The late architect:* Author interview with Steven Izenour, Wildwood, N.J., 1998.

CHAPTER 2: BUBBLING UP

Sources that informed and documented this chapter include: Alan Lomax, *The Land Where the Blues Began;* William Ferris, *Blues from the Delta;* Bill C. Malone, *Country Music, U.S.A;* John Philip Sousa, "The Menace of Mechanical Music," from *Appleton's* magazine in 1906; John A. and Alan Lomax, *Our Singing Country;* Alan Lomax, *Folk Songs of North America;* Ronald D. Cohen, editor, *Alan Lomax: Selected Writings, 1934–1997;* Nolan Porterfield, *The Last Cavalier: The Life and Times of John A. Lomax;* Tom N. Shattuck, *A Cumberland Gap Area Guidebook;* Irwin Stambler and Grelun Landon, *The Encyclopedia of Folk, Country and Western Music;* Harry M. Caudill, *Night Comes to the Cumberlands;* Scott Weidensaul, *Mountains of the Heart: A Natural History of the Appalachians;* editions of the *Middlesboro Daily News* from September 1937; Shirley Collins, *America over the Water: An Emotional Journey into the Cultural Roots of Traditional American Music with Legendary Archivist Alan Lomax;* Jack E. Weller, *Yesterday's People: Life in Contemporary Appalachia;* correspondence and notes files from the Library of Congress's American Folklife Center, formerly the Archive of Folk Song, documenting Alan Lomax's 1937 trip to Kentucky; notes from the Mary Elizabeth Barnicle/Tillman Cadle Collection at the Archives of Appalachia, East Tennessee State University; interviews with old-time musician Homer "Bill" Callahan; musician and scholar Bess Lomax Hawes and Anna Lomax Wood; Edward Hunter, who sang on the original Alan Lomax field sessions in 1937; Georgia Turner's children, nephew and great-niece in Monroe, Mich.; Pauline Inman, Georgia Turner's childhood friend from Kentucky; Joe Hickerson, Jennifer Cutting, and Peggy Bulger of the Library of Congress American Folklife Center; and Tom N. Shattuck, a community historian in Middlesboro, Ky.; and Eva Ashley Moore, Clarence Ashley's daughter.

Relevant recordings and accompanying materials include *The Callahan Brothers;* performances by Georgia Turner, Edward Hunter, Mary Mast Turner, Bert Martin, and Daw Henson collected in 1937 by Alan Lomax and deposited in the Library of Congress; and the songs and Charles K. Wolfe's liner notes for the series *Kentucky Mountain Music; Hard Times in the Country: Down and Out in the Rural South, Songs & Tunes from 1927 to 1938; White Country Blues, 1926–1938: A Whiter Shade of Pale.*

44 *"I was country-raised":* Author interview with Homer "Bill" Callahan, Dallas, Texas, 12/2/00.

45 *My spider sense kicks in:* "Rounder's Luck," *The Callahan Brothers* (Old Homestead Records OHCD-4031, 2000), track 18.

46 *Calling the song:* Ibid.

46 *Sung by Homer:* Ibid.

47 *"If my father and I":* Alan Lomax, *The Land Where the Blues Began* (New York: New Press, 2002), 379.

47 *It could conceivably be:* William Ferris, *Blues from the Delta* (New York: Da Capo, 1984), 68.

48 *The brothers were:* Bill C. Malone, *Country Music, U.S.A* (Austin: University of Texas Press/American Folklore Society, 1968), 124.

49 *John Philip Sousa:* John Philip Sousa, "The Menace of Mechanical Music," *Appleton's* magazine, September 1906, 278.

50 The Folk Songs of North America: Lomax, *The Folk Songs of North America,* 280.

51 *In his trip proposal:* Letter from Alan Lomax to Harold Spivacke, acting chief of Library of Congress Music Division, 8/14/37.

51 *So in early September 1937:* Letter from Lomax to Spivacke, Hazard, Ky., late 09/37.

51 *Even though Lomax had made:* Letter from Lomax to Spivacke, Hyden, Ky., 9/30/1937.

51 *In Hazard:* Letter from Lomax to Spivacke, Hazard, Ky., late 9/37.

51 *One sixty-year-old man:* Ibid.

51 *Bulky battery cells:* Ibid.

51 *The Presto's parts failed:* Letter from Lomax to Spivacke, Harlan, Ky., received 9/24/37.

51 *Lomax kept running out:* Letter from Lomax to Spivacke, Hyden, Ky., 9/30/37.

51 *He caught the flu:* Letter from Lomax to Spivacke, Hazard, Ky., late 9/37.

51 *On September 28:* Telegram from Lomax to Spivacke, 9/28/37, on file in Library of Congress American Folklife Center.

51 *The trip's first burst:* Letter from Lomax to Spivacke, Harlan, Ky., received 9/20/37.

52 *By the time Lomax visited:* Tom N. Shattuck, *A Cumberland Gap Area Guidebook* (Middlesboro, Ky.: Three States Printing Co., 1999), 33.

52 *"It was wide open":* Author interview with Tom Shattuck, Middlesboro, Ky., 07/00.

52 *But in 1937:* Edward Hunter, 7/17/00 and 7/23/00.

52 *In one house:* Ibid.

53 *Gillis Turner:* Author interview with Georgia Turner's children, Monroe, Mich., 2/17/01.

53 *She was shy and attractive:* Lomax, *The Folk Songs of North America,* 280.

53 *Both mother and daughter:* Edward Hunter, 7/17/00 and 7/23/00.

53 *Folks in Noetown:* Ibid.

53 *Neighbors would hear her:* Ibid.

53 *Hunter's uncle:* Ibid.

53 *Through his friend:* Administrative notes, Mary Elizabeth Barnicle/Tillman Cadle Collection, Archives of Appalachia, East Tennessee State University.

53 *He was scornful:* Letter from Lomax to Spivacke, Harlan, Ky., received 9/24/37.

54 *He was hoping for:* Letter from Lomax to Spivacke, 8/14/37; Edward Hunter, 7/17/00 and 7/23/00.

54 *On September 15, 1937:* Edward Hunter, 7/17/00 and 7/23/00; audiotapes, Library of Congress American Folklife Center, batch 4872, tape no. 103, tracks AFS1398-A1 through AFS1411-B3.

54 *Both Georgia Turner and her mother:* Author interview, Pauline Inman, telephone, 7/00.

54 *"Every time":* Lomax, *The Land Where the Blues Began,* xi.

54 *First, with Hunter:* Audiotapes, Library of Congress American Folklife Center, batch 4872, track AFS-1403-B2.

54 *Jennifer Cutting, a folklife specialist:* Author interview with Jennifer Cutting, Library of Congress, Washington, D.C., 7/20/00.

55 *The voice of:* Audiotape, Library of Congress American Folklife Center, batch 4872, track AFS-1404-A1.

56 *Jennifer Cutting is more:* Jennifer Cutting, 7/20/00.

56 *After the stop in Middlesboro:* Letter from Lomax to Spivacke, Hyden, Ky., 10/6/37.

56 *He recorded several dozen:* Audiotape, Library of Congress American Folklife Center, batch 4872, track AFS-1496.

56 *occasionally misspelled his name:* John A. and Alan Lomax, *Our Singing Country* (Mineola, N.Y.: Dover Publications, 1941), 368.

57 *Here is Martin:* Library of Congress, track AFS-1496.

58 *In later years:* Pauline Inman, 7/00.

58 *On the occasions:* Lomax and Lomax, *Our Singing Country,* 368.

58 *Four days after:* Audiotape, Library of Congress American Folklife Center, batch 4872, track AFS-1508-B2.

58 *Details on Henson are scarce:* Charles K. Wolfe, *Kentucky Mountain Music* (Yazoo 2200), liner notes, 16.

59 *In one of the Lomax recordings:* "Swafford Branch Stills," *Kentucky Mountain Music* (Yazoo 2200), disc 5, track 12.

59 *in another song:* "Wallins Creek Girls," *Kentucky Mountain Music* (Yazoo 2200), disc 4, track 18.

59 *When Henson turned to:* Library of Congress, tracks AFS-1508-B1 and B2.

59 *"There is a house":* Ibid.

60 *Over In Noetown:* Hunter, 7/17/00 and 7/23/00.

61 *Clarence Ashley's daughter:* Eva Ashley Moore, Saltville, Va., 2/25/01.

62 *"The collector with pen":* Alan Lomax, *The Land Where the Blues Began* (New York: New Press, 2002), xi.

63 *All Ed Hunter knows:* Hunter, 7/17/00 and 7/23/00.

CHAPTER 3: FROM THE FOLKWAYS . . .

These sources helped assemble a portrait of the song's journey through the 1940s: "Archive of American Folk Song: A History 1928–1939," on file at Library of Congress American Folklife Center; Lomax and Lomax, *Our Singing Country;* John A. and Alan Lomax, *American Ballads and Folk Songs;* Elizabeth Schlappi, *Roy Acuff: The Smoky Mountain Boy;* Irwin Stambler and Grelun Landon, *The Encyclopedia of Folk, Country and Western Music, 2d ed.;* Don McLean, "Josh White: A Farewell," *Sing Out! The Folk Song Magazine,* winter 1969/70; 1943 songbook, *Roy Acuff and His Smoky Mountain Songs;* Nolan Porterfield, *Last Cavalier: The Life and Times of John A. Lomax;* Benjamin Filene, *Romancing the Folk: Public Memory and American Roots Music;* Robert Cantwell, *When We Were Good: The Folk Revival;* Stephen Bishop, *Songs in the Rough: Rock's Greatest Songs in Rough-Draft Form;* Joe Klein, *Woody Guthrie: A Life;* Ed Cray, *Ramblin' Man: The Life and Times of Woody Guthrie;* "Leadbelly," Encyclopædia Britannica; William Rose Benet, "Ballad of a Ballad-Singer," *The New Yorker;* Elijah Wald, *Josh White: Society Blues;* The Weavers, *The Weavers' Song Book;* Pete Seeger and Jo Metcalf Schwartz,

The Incompleat Folksinger; Alan Lomax, Woody Guthrie, and Pete Seeger, *Hard Hitting Songs for Hard-Hit People;* Elizabeth Partridge, *The Life and Songs of Woody Guthrie;* Charles K. Wolfe and Kip Lornell, *The Life and Legend of Leadbelly;* Burl Ives, *The Burl Ives Song Book;* Eric Sackheim, *The Blues Line: A Collection of Blues Lyrics;* interviews with Douglas Yeager, who manages Josh White's estate; Ted Lawrence of Lawrence Record Store in Nashville; Matt Barton of the Lomax archives; folksinger and activist Pete Seeger; folksinger and radio host Oscar Brand; and Josh White Jr.

Audio works consulted include *Roy Acuff: Greatest Hits, Vol. 2; The Almanac Singers: Their Complete General Recordings;* Jeff Place's liner notes of *Where Did You Sleep Last Night: Lead Belly Legacy, Vol. 1;* Sean Killeen's liner notes of the CD reissue of *Leadbelly's Last Sessions; Josh White in Chronological Order, Volume 6, 1944–1945; Vol. 1—The Josh White Stories; The Weavers Greatest Hits; The Legendary Libby Holman: The Torch Songs/The Ballads and Blues;* Esco Hankins, *Rising Sun,* and Kevin Coffee's liner notes; Roy Acuff and His Smoky Mountain Boys, "The Rising Sun," 1938 recording; *Roy Acuff and His Smoky Mountain Boys: The King of Country Music, 25 Tracks, 1936–1947; The Essential Roy Acuff, 1936–1949;* Lead Belly, *Shout On;* Pete Seeger, *American Industrial Ballads;* Pete Seeger and Friends, *Seeds: The Songs of Pete Seeger, Vol. 3;* Pete Seeger, *American Favorite Ballads, Vol. 2;* Lead Belly and Woody Guthrie, *Folkways: The Original Vision;* Woody Guthrie, *This Land Is Your Land: The Asch Recordings, Vol. 1;* Woody Guthrie, *Muleskinner Blues: The Asch Recordings, Vol. 2.*

64 *Alan and Elizabeth Lomax:* "Archive of American Folk Song: A History 1928–1939," typewritten copy on file at Library of Congress American Folklife Center.

64 *He enlisted:* Ruth Crawford Seeger, music preface, *Our Singing Country,* xxix–xxxvi.

64 *While the father-son team's:* John A. and Alan Lomax, *American Ballads and Folk Songs* (New York: MacMillan/Dover Publications, 1934/1994).

64 *"These are the people":* Lomax and Lomax, *Our Singing Country,* xxi.

65 *"New songs grew up":* Ibid., xxii.

65 *Roy Acuff:* Elizabeth Schlappi, *Roy Acuff: The Smoky Mountain Boy* (Gretna, La.: Pelican, 1978/1993), 5.

65 *the Acuff household: Roy Acuff and His Smoky Mountain Songs* (Nashville: Acuff-Rose Publications, 1943), 1.

65 *Acuff was a hell-raiser:* Schlappi, *Roy Acuff: The Smoky Mountain Boy,* 12–16.

65 *he became a professional musician:* Ibid., 17–19.

65 *For much of 1932:* Ibid., 20–21.

65 *The medicine show:* Ibid.

66 *Acuff went to South Carolina:* Ibid., 30.

66 *The session was convened:* Ibid., 34.

66 *Acuff's version opens:* Roy Acuff and His Smoky Mountain Boys, "The Rising Sun" (Vocalion 04909, side B, 1938).

67 *Acuff would record:* Roy Acuff, "The Rising Sun," *Roy Acuff: Greatest Hits, Vol. 2* (Elektra 9E-303, 1979), side 1, track 2.

67 *The Lomaxes sent:* Nolan Porterfield, *Last Cavalier: The Life and Times of John A. Lomax, 1867–1948* (Urbana: University of Illinois Press, 1996), 430.

68 *"We have in certain cases":* Lomax and Lomax, *Our Singing Country,* xxviii.

68 *John Lomax had been doing it:* Nolan Porterfield, *Last Cavalier,* 153–155.

68 *"Their collecting methods":* Benjamin Filene, *Romancing the Folk: Public Memory and American Roots Music* (Chapel Hill: University of North Carolina Press, 2000), 50.

68 *"A lot of people":* Author interview with Matt Barton, Lomax Archives, New York, N.Y., 6/00.

68 *Her verses:* Lomax and Lomax, *Our Singing Country,* 368–369.

69 *But Lomax also included:* Ibid.

70 *"The fact that":* Ibid.

70 *Without being able to ask:* Polly Anderson, "Alan Lomax, musicologist who helped preserve America's and the world's heritage, dead at 87" (Associated Press, 7/19/02).

71 *"He purposely tried":* Author interview with Pete Seeger, telephone, 8/22/00.

72 *Robert Cantwell:* Robert Cantwell, *When We Were Good: The Folk Revival* (Cambridge, Harvard University Press, 1996), 63.

73 *the year after he scribbled:* Stephen Bishop, *Songs in the Rough: From Heartbreak Hotel to Higher Love* (New York: St. Martin's Press, 1996), 2.

73 *Guthrie was traveling in and out of New York City:* Joe Klein, *Woody Guthrie: A Life* (New York: Delta/Dell, 1999), 195–225.

74 *At a series:* Mary Katherine Aldin, *The Almanac Singers: Their Complete General Recordings* (MCAD-11499, 1996), liner notes, 6–7.

74 *Also, the year before:* Ed Cray, *Ramblin' Man: The Life and Times of Woody Guthrie* (New York: Norton, 2004), 174.

74 *From these sessions:* Almanac Singers, "House of the Rising Sun," *The Almanac Singers: Their Complete General Recordings* (MCAD-11499, 1996), track 4.

75 *He remembers:* Pete Seeger, 8/22/00.

75 *"Lawyers rearrange":* Ibid.

75 *Lead Belly, born:* "Leadbelly," *Encyclopædia Britannica,* 2006. Encyclopædia Britannica Online, 9/14/06.

75 *He was an itinerant laborer:* Nolan Porterfield, *Last Cavalier,* 329–34.

75 *In that brief moment:* William Rose Benet, "Ballad of a Ballad-Singer," *The New Yorker,* 1/19/35, 40.

76 *Lead Belly's friends:* Author interview with Oscar Brand, 8/16/00.

76 *It was there:* Oscar Brand, 8/16/00; Pete Seeger, 8/22/00.

76 *The earliest recording:* Bill Dahl, "Leadbelly: Absolutely the Best" (Fuel 2000 Records, 2000), liner notes.

76 *But in a subsequent version:* Jeff Place, *Where Did You Sleep Last Night: Lead Belly Legacy, Vol. 1* (SF CD-40044, 1996/from Smithsonian Acetate 259, date unknown), liner notes, 12.

76 *It follows:* Ibid.

77 *The final existing:* Sean Killeen, *Leadbelly's Last Sessions* (Smithsonian Folkways SF CD-40068/71, 1994), liner notes, 17–19.

77 *As Anthony Seeger:* Ibid.

77 *When Ramsey wrote:* Ibid., 7.

78 *Not only did:* Josh White, "House of the Rising Sun," *Josh White in Chronological Order, Vol. 6, 1944–1945* (Document DOCD-5572), track 4.

79 *Josh White (1914–1969) was in his late twenties:* Author interview with Douglas Yeager, 7/19/00.

79 *White, from Greenville:* Elijah Wald, *Josh White: Society Blues* (Amherst: University of Massachusetts Press, 2000), 1.

79 *his father was sent away:* Ibid., 7.

79 *He spent his late adolescence:* Ibid., 11–21.

80 *When you listen:* "House of the Rising Sun," *Josh White in Chronological Order, Vol. 6, 1944–1945,* track 3.

80 *The deliberate:* Ibid., track 4.

80 *he introduces it:* Josh White, *Vol. 1—The Josh White Stories* (ABC-Paramount ABC124).

80 *"He would say":* Author interview with Josh White Jr., 8/25/00.

81 *White's 1944 rendition: Josh White in Chronological Order, Vol. 6, 1944–1945,* track 4.

81 *White maintains he came by:* Walter Raim, Robert Shelton, and Josh White, *The Josh White Song Book* (New York: Quadrangle Books, 1963), 126–27.

81 *And White's own biographer:* Elijah Wald, *Society Blues,* 105.

81 *"You take a song":* Ibid., 106.

81 *Oscar Brand, a musician:* Oscar Brand, 8/16/00.

82 *In one White rendition:* "House of the Rising Sun," *Josh White in Chronological Order, Vol. 6, 1944–1945,* track 4.

82 *Obviously, White cared:* Josh White Jr., 8/25/00.

82 *Just after White died:* Oscar Brand, 8/16/00.

83 *"Our name meant":* The Weavers, *The Weavers' Song Book* (New York: Harper & Brothers, 1960), vii.

83 *"My own biggest thing":* Pete Seeger, 8/22/00.

83 *In their songbook:* The Weavers, *The Weavers' Song Book,* 138–39.

83 *She tackles it:* The Weavers, "House of the Rising Sun," *The Weavers Greatest Hits* (Vanguard VCD-15/16, 1971/1986), track 17.

83 *"You bounce a song":* Pete Seeger, 8/22/00.

84 *A well-known torch singer:* Elijah Wald, *Society Blues,* 94–95.

84 *It's three minutes:* Libby Holman, *The Legendary Libby Holman: The Torch Songs/The Ballads and Blues* (Monmouth MRS-6501), liner notes.

84 *Esco Hankins's 1947:* Esco Hankins, "Rising Sun," *Rising Sun* (British Archive of Country Music, BACM-058, 2004), track 3.

84 *This is in keeping:* Kevin Coffee, *Rising Sun* (British Archive of Country Music, BACM-058, 2004), liner notes.

85 *Kevin Coffee writes:* Ibid.

85 *according to biographer:* Elizabeth Schlappi, *Roy Acuff: The Smoky Mountain Boy,* 36.

85 *But according to Coffee's sources:* Kevin Coffee, *Rising Sun* liner notes.

85 *Schlappi credits:* Elizabeth Schlappi, *Roy Acuff: The Smoky Mountain Boy,* 124.

86 *Lawrence's is exclusively:* Interview with Ted Lawrence, Nashville, Tenn., 4/28/01.

87 *Ted is still jabbering:* Ibid.

87 *"Found it, huh?":* Ibid.

CHAPTER 4: . . . TO THE HIGHWAYS

To trace the song's path through the 1950s and the Ozark Mountains, the following sources were consulted for documentation and background: *Sing Out!,* April 1957; J. W. Williamson, *Hillbillyland: What the Movies Did to the Mountains and What the Mountains Did to the Movies;* Brooks Blevins, *Hill Folks: A History of Arkansas Ozarkers and Their Image;* Vance Randolph, *Ozark Folksongs;* Vance Randolph and G. Legman, *Roll Me in Your Arms: "Unprintable" Ozark Folksongs and Folklore, Vol. 1* and *Blow the Candle Out: "Unprintable" Ozark Folksongs and Folklore, Vol. 2;* the personal papers of folk song collector Max Hunter, on file at the Springfield-Greene County Library, Springfield, Mo.; various local newspaper files in southwestern Missouri and northwestern Arkansas, including those at the Fayetteville, Ark., public library and the University of Arkansas libraries; the collected papers of folklorists Vance Randolph and Mary Celestia Parler at the University of Arkansas; other audio recordings in the University of Arkansas Library's Special Collections; Doyle Fulmer, *Folklore Project of Summer 1958* (also at the University of Arkansas); Ed Cray, *The Erotic Muse: American Bawdy Songs;* unpublished local genealogical records and cemetery records at the Heritage Center Museum, Berryville, Ark.; various promotional publications from Silver Dollar City, Branson, Mo.; Oscar Brand, *The Ballad Mongers: Rise of the Modern Folk Song;* Dave Van Ronk with Elijah Wald, *The Mayor of Mac-Dougal Street: A Memoir;* Jean Ritchie, *Singing Family of the Cumberlands;* interviews with filmmaker, song collector and musician John Cohen; Roscoe Holcomb extended family, including Virginia Lee, David Blood, Fess Halcomb, Kermit Asher; Harrison Burnett's daughter Dortha Bradley; Jim Comstock, West Virginia editor; and Berryville, Ark., resident Lucy Kell.

Audio and video works consulted include: Ronnie Gilbert, *Come and Go with Me; The High Lonesome Sound: Roscoe Holcomb,* and John Cohen's accompanying liner notes; *The High Lonesome Sound* and *End of an Old Song,* films by John Cohen; *The Music of Roscoe Holcomb of Daisy, Kentucky and Wade Ward of Independence, Virginia;* Dillard Chandler, *End of an Old Song;* the collected recordings of ballad collector Max Hunter, Springfield-Greene County Library, Springfield, Mo.; Harrison Burnett recording of "Rising Sun" by Sandy Paton; *Nina Simone at the Village Gate; Close to Home: Old-Time Music from Mike Seeger's Collection; Echoes of the Ozarks,* vols. 1 and 2; *Alan Lomax's Southern Journey: Ozark Frontier; Ozark Folksongs; Old Regular Baptists: Lined-Out Hymnody from Southeastern Kentucky; Mountain Music of Kentucky; The Music of Kentucky: Early American Rural Classics, 1927–37.*

89 *Sometimes they called it:* Ronnie Gilbert, *Come and Go with Me* (Vanguard VRS-9052).

89 *The liner notes:* Ibid.

89 *A pivotal event: Sing Out!,* April 1957, 3.

91 *In 1959:* Author interview with John Cohen, Putnam Valley, N.Y., 5/16/05.

91 *One Saturday night:* Ibid.

92 *Still, in a landscape:* John Cohen, *The High Lonesome Sound: Roscoe Holcomb* (Smithsonian Folkways, SFW40104, 1998), liner notes, 6.

92 *"untamed sense of control":* Ibid., 2.

92 *Cohen would visit Rossie:* John Cohen, 5/16/05.

93 *Rossie knew more than four hundred:* John Cohen, director, *The High Lonesome Sound* (1962, reissued as part of DVD *That High Lonesome Sound: Films of American Rural Life and Music by John Cohen,* Shanachie 1404, 2002).

93 *"I say it is a gift":* Ibid.

93 *He once told Cohen:* Ibid.

93 *Shortly after meeting Rossie:* John Cohen, 5/16/05.

93 *This was called:* Roscoe Holcomb and Wade Ward, *The Music of Roscoe Holcomb of Daisy, Kentucky and Wade Ward of Independence, Virginia* (Folkways FA2363, 1962), liner notes, 5.

93 *Cohen already knew:* John Cohen, 5/16/05.

94 *"Ah, way on down":* Roscoe Holcomb, "House in New Orleans," *The High Lonesome Sound: Roscoe Holcomb* (Smithsonian Folkways, SFW40104, 1998), track 4.

94 *"Sometimes, you know":* The High Lonesome Sound, John Cohen, director.

94 *Once, in his early sessions:* John Cohen, *The Music of Roscoe Holcomb of Daisy, Kentucky and Wade Ward of Independence, Virginia* (Folkways FA2363, 1962), liner notes, 2.

94 *At the end:* Roscoe Holcomb, "House of the Rising Sun," *The High Lonesome Sound: Roscoe Holcomb,* track 4.

95 *In 1962: The High Lonesome Sound,* John Cohen, director.

95 *"Life is hard here":* Ibid.

96 *Cohen's film is chockablock:* Ibid.

97 *Identical themes surface: The End of an Old Song,* John Cohen, director (1969, reissued as part of DVD *That High Lonesome Sound: Films of American Rural Life and Music by John Cohen,* Shanachie 1404, 2002).

97 *"I feel sometimes":* Ibid.

98 *It contained an unaccompanied ballad:* Dillard Chandler, "Sport in New Orleans," *End of an Old Song* (Folkways F-2418, 1975), track 10.

98 *He picked up his repertoire: The End of an Old Song,* John Cohen, director.

98 *The lyrics use:* Dillard Chandler, "Sport in New Orleans," *End of an Old Song,* track 10.

98 *The earlier movie: The High Lonesome Sound,* John Cohen, director.

99 *"Here's the disquieting thing":* John Cohen, 5/16/05.

100 *"Did I hear you":* Author interview, Virginia Lee, Nashville, Tenn., 4/28/01.

100 *"I hate the word":* Author interview, Virginia Lee, Slemp, Ky., 7/7/01.

101 *We pull into:* Author interview with Virginia Lee and members of Halcomb and Asher families, Slemp, Ky., 7/1/01.

102 *Various family members:* Ibid.

103 *"The distance between":* J. W. Williamson, *Hillbillyland: What the Movies Did to the Mountains and What the Mountains Did to the Movies* (Chapel Hill: University of North Carolina Press, 1995), 35.

103 *Comstock, famed for his tall tales:* Author interview with Jim Comstock, Richwood, W. Va., 1/1993.

104 *"We've been classified":* Author interview with Fess Halcomb, Slemp, Ky., 7/1/01.

104 *"I don't know who made it":* Ibid.

104 *"Roscoe was with":* Author interview with Kermit Asher, Slemp, Ky., 7/1/01.

106 *"He never got nothing":* Ibid.

107 *Hunter was a traveling salesman:* Obituary of Max Hunter, *St. Louis Post Dispatch*, 11/10/1999, A9.

107 *sold refrigeration products:* Kathy Barton, "Max Hunter, Ozark Song Collector," apparently unpublished biography, Max Hunter personal papers, box 3, Springfield-Greene County Library.

107 *His route:* "Keeping Ozarks Culture Alive," *Springfield (Mo.) News-Leader*, 3/7/1998, B1, B10.

107 *His stops included:* Max Hunter personal papers and song transcriptions, Springfield-Greene County Library.

107 *Like many Ozarkers:* Max Hunter, speech prepared for delivery on 2/12/1974, Max Hunter personal papers, Springfield-Greene County Library, box 1.

107 *In 1956:* Kathy Barton, "Max Hunter, Ozark Song Collector," 20.

107 *He had been collecting:* W. K. McNeil, introduction to Vance Randolph's *Ozark Folksongs* (Columbia: University of Missouri Press, 1980), vol. 1, 10–11.

107 *He called 'em:* Article from *Arkansas Gazette*, 11/11/1948, no page number available, from Vance Randolph papers in University of Arkansas Special Collections, box 1, folder 1–9.

108 *His personal papers include:* Recipe, "To Cook Eels," from Vance Randolph papers, box 1, series 3, folder 1.

108 *Even as he was compiling:* G. Legman, introduction to Vance Randolph and G. Legman, *Roll Me in Your Arms: "Unprintable" Ozark Folksongs and Folklore, Vol. 1* (Fayetteville: University of Arkansas Press, 1992), 6–7.

108 *The folks who sang:* Vance Randolph and G. Legman, *Roll Me in Your Arms*, 250–53.

108 *One version:* Ibid.

109 *Beware the red light:* Ibid.

110 *Barely four months later:* Ibid.

110 *"She would not sing it":* Ibid.

111 *Baxter Springs:* Mellinger, Edward Henry, *Folk-Songs from the Southern Highlands*, song no. 125.

111 *One, a lament:* "I'll Never Get Drunk Any More," song sheet from Vance Randolph papers, box 3, folder 1–1, song MC952.

111 *Another the same year:* "If I Was on Some Foggy Mountain Top," song sheet from Vance Randolph papers, box 3, folder 1–6, song 78A1.

111 *And Hunter:* Kay Ohrlin, "Saw Mill Boy," song recording and transcription by Max Hunter, Springfield-Greene County Library, song 1016.

112 *Randolph's future wife:* L. Hardy Wright, manuscript of undated profile of Mary Celestia Parler, in Parler vertical file, University of Arkansas Special Collections.

112 *Soon Parler:* Ibid.

112 *Parler herself:* L. D. "Jack" Franklin, "House in New Orleans," audio recording and corresponding song sheet, University of Arkansas Special Collections, Parler recordings, reel 27, track 1, and Parler papers, box 4, folder 44.

113 *He married a woman:* Max Hunter speech, 2/12/74.

113 *During the early part:* Kathy Barton, "Max Hunter, Ozark Song Collector," 22.

114 *Hunter began:* Max Hunter personal papers and song transcriptions, Springfield-Greene County Library.

114 *"No one":* Ibid.

114 *"Don't try to imitate":* Ibid.

114 *By the time he was done:* Max Hunter personal papers and song transcriptions, Springfield-Greene County Library.

115 *He had "songs written":* Max Hunter speech, 2/12/74.

115 *There were renditions:* Max Hunter personal papers and song transcriptions, Springfield-Greene County Library.

115 *I'll sing you a song:* Fred High, "John Thompson's Dog," Max Hunter personal papers and song transcriptions, Springfield-Greene County Library, song 322.

115 *Hunter collected sixteen:* Max Hunter personal papers and song transcriptions, Springfield-Greene County Library.

115 *Burnett had already:* "The Arkansas Song," song sheet, Mary Celestia Parler papers, University of Arkansas Special Collections, box 3, folder 5.

115 *In a 1958:* Doyle Fulmer, *Folklore Project of Summer 1958* (Fayetteville: University of Arkansas, 1958), 3.

115 *On August 18:* Max Hunter song transcriptions, Springfield-Greene County Library.

115 *"I believe Harrison":* Max Hunter tapes, Springfield-Greene County Library, audio notes before song 539, 8/18/60.

116 *Among them:* Harrison Burnett, "Rising Sun," Max Hunter tapes, Springfield-Greene County Library, song 543, 8/18/60.

116 *Let's jump:* Harrison Burnett, "Rising Sun," recorded by Sandy Paton, 1963. Recording courtesy of Sandy Paton.

116 *Burnett's version:* Ibid.

117 *"It was back here on the hill":* Ibid.

117 *On February 9, 1960:* Max Hunter tapes, Springfield-Greene County Library, audio notes for Joe Walker songs 500–506, 2/9/60.

118 *Walker was a farmer:* Author interview with Lucy Kell, Berryville, Ark., 4/3/05.

118 *lived with his wife:* Unpublished local genealogical records and Shady Grove Cemetery records, Heritage Center Museum, Berryville, Ark.

118 *Though Hunter:* Max Hunter tapes, audio notes for Joe Walker songs, 2/9/60.

118 *People in the tavern:* Ibid.

118 *Then he begins:* Joe Walker, "The Rising Sun," Max Hunter tapes, Springfield-Greene County Library, song 504.

119 *At that:* Ibid.

119 *Here it is:* Vance Randolph and G. Legman, *Blow the Candle Out: "Unprintable" Ozark Folksongs and Folklore, Vol. 2* (Fayetteville: University of Arkansas Press, 1992), 601.

120 *The second related song:* Vance Randolph and G. Legman, *Roll Me in Your Arms: "Unprintable" Ozark Folksongs and Folklore, Vol. 1* (Fayetteville: University of Arkansas Press, 1992), 237–39.

120 *Randolph notes that:* Ibid.

120 *Historian Ed Cray:* Ed Cray, *The Erotic Muse: American Bawdy Songs* (Urbana: University of Illinois Press, 1992/1999), 68–71.

121 *"Well, I got Joe to sing":* Max Hunter tapes, audio notes for Joe Walker songs, 2/9/60.

121 *Joe Walker died:* Unpublished local genealogical records and Shady Grove Cemetery records, Heritage Center Museum, Berryville, Ark.

121 *She grew up:* Lucy Kell, 4/3/05.

122 *I decide:* Author visit to Silver Dollar City, Branson, Mo., 4/3/05.

123 *I ask the clerk:* Author interview with store clerk, Silver Dollar City, Branson, Mo., 4/3/05.

124 *Max Hunter was aware:* Max Hunter, "Evaluation: Mountain Folks Music Festival," letter to Jean Nichols, 6/24/76.

124 *"With a very few exceptions":* Ibid.

124 *"The influence":* Max Hunter speech, 2/12/74.

125 *William Harrison Burnett's daughter:* Funeral notice for William Harrison Burnett, *Northwest Arkansas Times*, 1/12/74, 2.

125 *She invites me over:* Author interview with Dortha Bradley, Fayetteville, Ark., 4/6/05.

126 *"Making music":* Ibid.

126 *Harrison Burnett's mother:* Ibid.

127 *He became a rambler:* Ibid.

127 *All the while:* Ibid.

127 *"He sang it":* Ibid.

128 *After nearly two hours:* Ibid.

129 *Though I find:* Author visit to Branson, Mo., 4/3/05.

129 *After driving the strip:* Author visit to Grand Country Music Hall, Branson, Mo., 4/3/05.

130 *The Bacons:* Ibid.

130 *The show ends:* Ibid.

131 *Blues singer Nina Simone:* Nina Simone, "House of the Rising Sun," *Nina Simone at the Village Gate* (Colpix CP-421, 1962/Roulette Jazz CDP 7950582, 1991), track 3.

131 *A Texas singer named Hally Wood:* Hally Wood, *The Folk Box* (Elektra EKL-9001, 1964), side 6, track 5.

131 *a haunting, ethereal version:* Oscar Brand, *The Ballad Mongers: Rise of the Modern Folk Song* (New York: Funk & Wagnalls, 1962), 146; Dave Van Ronk with Elijah Wald, *The Mayor of MacDougal Street: A Memoir* (New York: Da Capo, 2005), 176.

CHAPTER 5: BLAST OFF

Tracing the journey of "House of the Rising Sun" into the 1960s to Bob Dylan and the Animals, the following sources were used for citation or background: Thurston Clarke, *Ask Not: The Inauguration of John F. Kennedy and the Speech That Changed America*; Bob Dylan, *Chronicles: Volume One*; Clinton Heylin, *Bob Dylan: Behind the Shades Revisited*; Dave Van Ronk with Elijah Wald, *The Mayor of MacDougal Street: A Memoir*; Robert Shelton, *No Direction Home: The Life and Music of Bob Dylan*; Ambrose N. Manning and Minnie M. Miller, "Tom Ashley," from *Tom Ashley, Sam McGee, Bukka White: Tennessee Traditional Singers*; "Clarence Ashley," *Sing Out! The Folk Song Magazine*, August/September 1967; Eric Burdon and J. Marshall Craig, *Don't Let Me Be Misunderstood*; Sean Egan, *Animal Tracks: The Story of the Animals, Newcastle's Rising Sons*; Michael Heatley and Spencer Leigh, *Behind the Song: The Stories of 100 Great Pop & Rock Classics*; Fred Bronson, *The Billboard Book of Number One Hits*, 5th ed.; Greil Marcus, *Like a Rolling Stone: Bob Dylan at the Crossroads*; Mike Marqusee, *Chimes of Freedom: The Politics of Bob Dylan's Art*; Greil Marcus, *Invisible Republic*; David Hajdu, *Positively 4th Street*; Clinton Heylin, *Bob Dylan: The Recording Sessions, 1960–1994*; Howard Sounes, *Down the Highway: The Life of Bob Dylan*; A. J. Weberman, *Dylan to English Dictionary*; Robert Cantwell, *When We Were Good: The Folk Revival*; the websites of Alan Price, Eric Burdon, the Newcastle upon Tyne City Council, and the Rock and Roll Hall of Fame and Museum; interviews with Dylan biographer Clinton Heylin; Clarence Ashley's daughter and grandson, Eva Ashley Moore and Tom Moore; Arthel "Doc" Watson (through proxy); and Animals frontman Eric Burdon.

Audio and video works consulted include: Martin Scorsese, director, *No Direction Home: Bob Dylan; Bob Dylan*; Harry Smith, *The Anthology of American Folk Music*, liner notes; tapes of Clarence Ashley in concert in the 1960s, part of the Thomas G. Burton–Ambrose N. Manning Collection at the Archives of Appalachia, East Tennessee State University; *Golden Throats: The Great Celebrity Sing Off; The Essential Ramblin' Jack Elliott; Best of the 60's: The Animals;* D. A. Pennebaker, director, *Bob Dylan: Don't Look Back;* Alan Price, *Archive.*

132 *The cultural critic Lewis Mumford:* Thurston Clarke, *Ask Not: The Inauguration of John F. Kennedy and the Speech That Changed America* (New York: Henry Holt, 2004), 207.

133 *"You could feel":* Bob Dylan, *Chronicles: Volume One,* 28.

133 *He found a dying:* Clinton Heylin, *Bob Dylan: Behind the Shades Revisited* (New York: William Morrow, 1991/2001), 59–60.

133 *"A song is like a dream":* Bob Dylan, *Chronicles: Volume One,* 165.

133 *"Van Ronk seemed ancient":* Ibid., 261.

133 *Van Ronk sang:* Dave Van Ronk with Elijah Wald, *The Mayor of MacDougal Street: A Memoir,* 176.

133 *"I put a different spin":* Ibid.

134 *"I'd never done that":* No Direction Home: Bob Dylan, Martin Scorsese, director, (Paramount, 2005).

134 *"Bobby picked up":* Ibid.

134 *"He asked me":* Ibid.

134 *Turns out Dylan:* Ibid.

134 *Van Ronk called:* Ibid.

135 *one of his Minneapolis friends:* Robert Shelton, *No Direction Home: The Life and Music of Bob Dylan* (New York: Beech Tree Books, 1986), 68.

136 *"Dylan clearly knew":* Author interview with Clinton Heylin, telephone, 6/19/00.

136 *The kicker: No Direction Home: Bob Dylan,* Martin Scorsese, director.

136 *"A folk song":* Bob Dylan, *Chronicles: Volume One,* 71.

136 *In Dylan's "Risin' Sun":* Bob Dylan, *Bob Dylan* (Columbia 08579, 1962), track 10.

137 *His extensive traveling:* Ambrose N. Manning and Minnie M. Miller, "Tom Ashley," from *Tom Ashley, Sam McGee, Bukka White: Tennessee Traditional Singers,* 35.

137 *The ensuing years:* Ibid., 36–38.

138 *Smith's liner notes:* Harry Smith, *The Anthology of American Folk Music,* liner notes.

138 *In 1966:* Ambrose N. Manning and Minnie M. Miller, "Tom Ashley," from *Tom Ashley, Sam McGee, Bukka White: Tennessee Traditional Singers,* 11–12.

138 *In his case:* Ibid., 37–39.

139 *Ashley, whether genuinely:* Ibid.

139 *On the Saturday:* Author interview with Eva Ashley Moore and Tom Moore, Saltville, Va., 2/25/01.

140 *He learned it from Ashley:* Author interview with Arthel "Doc" Watson, through proxy Kim Fowler of Sugar Hill Records, telephone, 8/28/00.

140 *"There was only one":* Arthel "Doc" Watson at live performance at Merlefest, Wilkesboro, N.C., 4/29/05.

141 *John Cohen:* John Cohen, "Clarence Ashley," *Sing Out! The Folk Song Magazine,* August/September 1967, 30.

141 *"She did take this song":* Tape of Clarence Ashley concert in 1960s, exact date unknown (Thomas G. Burton–Ambrose N. Manning Collection, Archives of Appalachia, East Tennessee State University).

142 *he went to art school:* Eric Burdon and J. Marshall Craig, *Don't Let Me Be Misunderstood* (New York, Thunder's Mouth Press, 2001), 4.

142 *an electrical worker's son:* Author interviews with Eric Burdon, New Orleans, La., 5/00.

142 *"a spotty-faced teenage animal":* Eric Burdon and J. Marshall Craig, *Don't Let Me Be Misunderstood,* 4.

142 *Burdon especially liked:* Eric Burdon, New Orleans, La., 5/00.

143 *Burdon remembers thinking:* Ibid.

143 *When his father:* Ibid.

143 *Burdon realized Griffith:* Ibid.

143 *Griffith's drawl-drenched:* Andy Griffith, "House of the Rising Sun," *Golden Throats: The Great Celebrity Sing Off* (Rhino R270187), track 9.

144 *About a year:* Eric Burdon, New Orleans, La., 5/00.

144 *"I realized":* Ibid.

144 *He played with:* Sean Egan, *Animal Tracks: The Story of the Animals, Newcastle's Rising Sons* (London: Helter Skelter Publishing, 2001), 20–22.

144 *This was a time:* Ibid., 14.

144 *As the members:* Ibid., 14; Eric Burton and J. Marshall Craig, *Don't Let Me Be Misunderstood,* 3.

145 *"I was amazed":* Eric Burdon, New Orleans, La., 5/00.

145 *They were traveling:* Eric Burdon and J. Marshall Craig, *Don't Let Me Be Misunderstood,* 14.

145 *The Dylan and White:* Eric Burdon, New Orleans, La., 5/00.

145 *Elliott's twangy version:* Ramblin' Jack Elliott, "House of the Rising Sun," *The Essential Ramblin' Jack Elliott* (Vanguard VCD-89/90, 1974), track 8.

145 *In spring 1964:* Eric Burdon, New Orleans, La., 5/00.

145 *Burdon remembers:* Ibid.

145 *John Steel told:* Sean Egan, *Animal Tracks: The Story of the Animals, Newcastle's Rising Sons,* 42.

145 *And Alan Price said:* Michael Heatley and Spencer Leigh, *Behind the Song: The Stories of 100 Great Pop & Rock Classics* (London: Blandford, 1998), 90.

146 *Valentine says:* Sean Egan, *Animal Tracks: The Story of the Animals, Newcastle's Rising Sons,* 42.

146 *In rehearsals:* Ibid., 43.

146 *Producer Mickie Most:* Eric Burdon and J. Marshall Craig, *Don't Let Me Be Misunderstood,* 21.

146 *EMI, whose Columbia label:* Sean Egan, *Animal Tracks: The Story of the Animals, Newcastle's Rising Sons,* 45.

146 *They were scheduled:* Eric Burdon, New Orleans, La., 5/00.

146 *On May 18:* Ibid.

146 *There, in ten minutes:* Eric Burdon and J. Marshall Craig, *Don't Let Me Be Misunderstood,* 23.

146 *Valentine's seven-note:* The Animals, "The House of the Rising Sun," *Best of the 60's: The Animals* (Disky Records, SI250722, 2000), track 5.

148 Rolling Stone, *in 1988:* "*Rolling Stone*'s Top 100," Associated Press, 8/19/88.

148 *Animals manager Mike Jeffery:* Eric Burdon and J. Marshall Craig, *Don't Let Me Be Misunderstood,* 23.

149 *The other band members:* Sean Egan, *Animal Tracks: The Story of the Animals, Newcastle's Rising Sons,* 46.

149 *Burdon feels betrayed:* Eric Burdon and J. Marshall Craig, *Don't Let Me Be Misunderstood,* 23.

149 *It would have fit:* Ibid., 67.

149 *The BBC wasn't:* Sean Egan, *Animal Tracks: The Story of the Animals, Newcastle's Rising Sons,* 47.

149 *On September 5, 1964:* Fred Bronson, *The Billboard Book of Number One Hits,* 5th ed. (New York: Billboard Books, 2003), 156.

149 *The Animals found themselves:* Eric Burdon and J. Marshall Craig, *Don't Let Me Be Misunderstood,* 23.

149 *the notoriously prickly host:* Ibid., 28.

149 *Then, only months later:* Sean Egan, *Animal Tracks: The Story of the Animals, Newcastle's Rising Sons,* 62.

150 *Subsequent reports:* "Alan Price Biography," from website *Alan Price Online,* http://alanprice.absoluteelsewhere.net/index.html, accessed 09/06.

150 *Price hung around: Bob Dylan: Don't Look Back,* D. A. Pennebaker, director (Docurama NVG-9447, 1967/1999).

150 *In the 1998 book:* Michael Heatley and Spencer Leigh, *Behind the Song: The Stories of 100 Great Pop & Rock Classics,* 91.

150 *Price's hypnotic arrangement:* "Alan Price Biography," from website *Alan*

Price Online http://alanprice.absoluteelsewhere.net/index.html, accessed 09/06.

150 *The newer arrangement:* Alan Price, "The House of the Rising Sun," *Archive* (Rialto Records RMCD209, 1996), track 4.

150 *The section about the Animals:* "Alan Price Biography," from website *Alan Price Online*, 1.

151 *In 1994:* Website, Rock and Roll Hall of Fame and Museum, www.rock hall.com/hof/inductee.asp?id=58, accessed 09/06.

151 *Burdon is still on the road:* Website, Eric Burdon, www.ericburdon.com, accessed 09/06.

151 *Chas Chandler died:* "Bassist of the Animals, Chas Chandler, dead at 57," Associated Press, 7/17/96.

151 *Steel, in the band biography:* Sean Egan, *Animal Tracks: The Story of the Animals, Newcastle's Rising Sons,* 51.

152 *The fence door:* Eric Burdon, New Orleans, La., 5/00.

152 *I am meeting the performer:* Paul Zach, "The beast in Burdon," *The Straits Times,* Singapore, 11/19/99, L1–L3.

152 *He does wonder:* Eric Burdon, New Orleans, La., 5/00.

153 *Burdon is full of stories:* Ibid.

153 *His autobiography:* Eric Burdon and J. Marshall Craig, *Don't Let Me Be Misunderstood,* 22.

153 *Burdon also says:* Ibid.

153 *Burdon is something:* Eric Burdon, New Orleans, La., 5/00.

154 *I have no choice:* Author visit to Graceland, Memphis, Tenn., 4/29/01.

154 *The conversation:* Eric Burdon, New Orleans, La., 5/00.

155 *"I change it":* Ibid.

155 *A few years back:* Eric Burdon and J. Marshall Craig, *Don't Let Me Be Misunderstood,* 259.

155 *Perusing the list:* Ibid.

CHAPTER 6: EVERYWHERE

To illustrate the song's spread around the world and into different genres, sources that informed and documented this chapter included: Joe Klein, *Woody Guthrie: A Life;* Bernard Violet, *Johnny, Le Rebelle Amoureaux;* Greil Marcus, *Mystery Train: Images of America in Rock 'n' Roll Music;* magazine articles about Adam Sandler, Tony Blair, Johnny Hallyday, and Billy Joel; interviews with Georgia Turner's nephew Gillis Turner; Melissa Swingle and Laura King of the Moaners; Hank Williams Jr. (through proxy); pianist Lorie Line; Dolly Parton (via fax); Jason Coomes of Blinddog Smokin'; Bill Ware of Vibes; Steve Power; Justin Guardipee of Non Prophet Organization; "House of the Rising Sun" collector Paul Meskil; Snakefarm's Anna Domino;

William Schurk of Bowling Green State University; Peggy Bulger of the Library of Congress American Folklife Center; Eric Burdon of the Animals; Nora Guthrie, Woody Guthrie's daughter; and Colleen Long.

Audio works consulted included Miriam Makeba, *The Click Song;* Jerry Garcia, David Grisman, and Tony Rice, *The Pizza Tapes;* Gregory Isaacs, *House of the Rising Sun;* Wyclef Jean and Refugee Allstars, *The Carnival;* The Moaners, *Dark Snack;* Dolly Parton and Mike Post, *9 to 5 and Odd Jobs; Stars 1994;* Lorie Line, *Walking with You: Piano Orchestrations;* Kinnunen, "House of the Rising Sun"; Demis Roussos, *Attitudes + Bonustracks from "Reflection";* Mark O'Connor, *Heroes;* Steve Power, "House of the Rising Sun"; David H. Yakobian, *Alpha States: Exotic Recorders;* John Otway, *Greatest Hits; Seeds Turn to Flowers Turn to Dust: A Collection of Totally Unrelated Garage/Psych Records from the Late 60s;* The Adolescents, *Brats in Battalions;* Sedale, *Pre-Millennial Tension v.2.0; Kenny Rogers: 20 of the Best* (African bootleg); Nate Leath, *Extra Medium;* Maxim, *Hell's Kitchen;* Xavier Cugat, *Invitacion al Mambo y Cha-Cha-Cha;* Johnny Hallyday, *Master Series, Vol. 1;* The Be Good Tanyas, *Chinatown;* Snakefarm, *Songs from My Funeral; Astrological Series, Vol. 1: The Astronomical House of Scorpio;* the Supremes, *A Bit of Liverpool;* Peter, Paul and Mary, *1994 Lifelines;* Lana Cantrell, *Another Shade of Lana;* June Bugg, *Hootenanny Folk Festival: The Incredible Voice of June Bugg;* Billy Strange, *Lloyd Thaxton Presents;* Dave Ray, *Snaker's Here! Blues and Hollers;* the Beatles, *Sweet Apple Trax;* Udo Jurgens, *Udo Live.*

156 *In South Africa:* Miriam Makeba, "House of the Rising Sun," *The Click Song* (Sonod 534, 1999), track 11.

156 *The hard-rock band Frijid Pink:* Author interview with Gillis Turner, telephone, 7/19/00.

157 *Billy Joel has sung it:* Keith Spera, "Joel show slightly clumsy, uniquely brilliant," *The New Orleans Times-Picayune,* 12/4/99, 25A.

157 *Jerry Garcia:* Jerry Garcia, David Grisman, and Tony Rice, "House of the Rising Sun," *The Pizza Tapes* (Acoustic Disc ACD-41), track 20.

157 *Reggae artist Gregory Isaacs:* Gregory Isaacs, "House of the Rising Sun (Vocal Mix)" / "House of the Rising Sun (Wicked Dub Mix)" / "House of the Rising Sun (Slightly Dubful Vocal Mix)," *House of the Rising Sun* (RAS Records CD7040, 1993), tracks 1–3.

157 *When Wyclef Jean:* Wyclef Jean and Refugee Allstars, "Sang Fezi," *The Carnival* (Columbia/Ruff House Records CK67974, 1997), track 13.

158 *"I wonder why":* Skip Wollenberg, "Mercedes-Benz dusts off Janis Joplin song for commercial," Associated Press, 3/9/95.

158 *Even Woody Guthrie's:* Joe Klein, *Woody Guthrie: A Life* (New York: Delta/Dell, 1999), 454.

160 *There is a joint:* The Moaners, "Paradise Club," *Dark Snack* (Yep Roc YEP-2088, 2005), track 9.

160 *"It's just like"*: Author interview with Melissa Swingle and Laura King, Carrboro, N.C., 4/27/05.

161 *"I realized"*: Ibid.

161 *As we've seen*: Ibid.

162 *"I didn't want to"*: Ibid.

163 *I play them*: Ibid.

163 *"If you take something"*: Ibid.

164 *Hank Williams Jr.*: Author interview with Hank Williams Jr., through proxy Kathy Gangwisch, PR representative, 06/00.

164 *Country music icon Dolly Parton*: Dolly Parton and Mike Post, "House of the Rising Sun," *9 to 5 and Odd Jobs* (RCA RCA-3852, 1980), track 3.

165 *Parton learned the song*: Fax from Dolly Parton to author, 6/19/00.

165 *David Allan Coe*: David Allan Coe, "House of the Rising Sun," *Stars 1994* (Power Pak PKCD-10501, 1994), track 6.

165 *Lorie Line*: Author interview with Lorie Line, telephone, 6/8/00.

166 *Her ambient 1994 version*: Lorie Line, "House of the Rising Sun," *Walking with You: Piano Orchestrations* (Time Line, 1994), track 12.

166 *"When we play that song"*: Author interview with Jason Coomes, telephone, 06/00.

166 *The Timo Kinnunen One-Man Band*: Timo Kinnunen, "House of the Rising Sun," no label, downloaded from MP3.com, 2001.

167 *This category has*: Demis Roussos, "House of the Rising Sun," *Attitudes + Bonustracks from "Reflection"* (BR Music, 2002), track 7.

167 *Mark O'Connor*: Mark O'Connor with Vassar Clements, "House of the Rising Sun," *Heroes* (Warner Bros. 45257-2, 1993), track 5.

167 *A fast-paced, honky-tonk*: Steve Power, "House of the Rising Sun," track emailed to author, 2001.

167 *Power, who counts*: Author interview with Steve Power, email, 6/13/01.

167 *The New Age stylings*: David H. Yakobian, "House of the Rising Sun," *Alpha States: Exotic Recorders* (Worldwide Success Records WWS-727272, 1999) track 12.

168 *Does Yakobian's desire*: Ibid., liner notes.

168 *In 2002*: Mary Novakovich, "You're 50 and you want a chart hit. How do you do it?" *Independent on Sunday* (London), 9/29/02, 7.

168 *Here's a bit*: John Otway, "House of the Rising Sun (Live at Abbey Road)," *Greatest Hits* (Cherry Red Records, 2005).

168 *"We sound like"*: Non Prophet Organization artist page on MP3.com, 2001.

168 *With a Yamaha keyboard*: Author interview, Justin Guardipee, telephone, 5/14/01.

169 *They posted it*: Ibid.

169 *But they didn't come close: Seeds Turn to Flowers Turn to Dust: A Collection*

of Totally Unrelated Garage/Psych Records from the Late 60s (Bacchus Archives BA1133, 1999), liner notes.

169 *Their Eminence took:* Their Eminence, "Mary," *Seeds Turn to Flowers Turn to Dust,* track 1.

169 *"Were they serious?":* *Seeds Turn to Flowers Turn to Dust,* liner notes.

170 *The Adolescents:* The Adolescents, "House of the Rising Sun," *Brats in Battalions* (Triple X Records 51061-2, 1991), track 7.

170 *Sedale, an electronic group:* Sedale, "House of the Rising Sun," *Pre-Millennial Tension v.2.0* (1999), track 1.

170 *I was in West Africa:* Unknown performer, "House of the Rising Sun," *Kenny Rogers: 20 of the Best* (bootleg, no information available), track 16.

170 *Nate Leath:* Nate Leath, "House of the Rising Sun," *Extra Medium* (Patuxtent CD-057, 2000), track 10.

170 *A techno-laced song:* Maxim, "Carmen Queasy," *Hell's Kitchen* (XL Recordings, XLCD134, 2000), track 3.

171 *Cuban bandleader:* Xavier Cugat, "Casa del Sol Naciente," *Invitacion al Mambo y Cha-Cha-Cha* (Mediterraneo, 2003), track 2.

171 *In 1964:* Bernard Violet, *Johnny, Le Rebelle Amoureaux* (Paris: Editions Fayard, 2003), 177.

171 *The doors of the penitentiary:* Johnny Hallyday, "Le Penitencier," *Johnny Hallyday, Master Serie, Vol. 1* (Universal, 832-049-2, 1987), track 11. Translated from the French by Lynn A. Higgins.

172 *After three dozen albums:* Robin Eggar, "Vive Johnny," *The Times of London,* 3/8/03.

172 *a Canadian female trio:* The Be Good Tanyas, "House of the Rising Sun," *Chinatown* (Nettwerk 6700-30304-2-7, 2003), track 8.

172 *"We almost didn't":* Dan MacIntosh, "The Be Good Tanyas show their roots," *Country Standard Time* (online magazine), 3/03.

172 *The late Paul Meskil:* Author interview with Paul Meskil, telephone, 11/29/00.

172 *Meskil found:* Ibid.

173 *Their 1999 CD:* Snakefarm, *Songs from My Funeral* (RCA 07863-67687-2, 1999).

173 *"We wanted to give":* Author interview with Anna Domino, telephone, 8/9/00.

173 *To listen to:* Snakefarm, *Songs from My Funeral.*

173 *Snakefarm's take on "Rising Sun":* Ibid., track 2.

174 *Like many musicians:* Anna Domino, 8/9/00.

174 *Domino is entranced:* Ibid.

174 *Critics have tried:* Ibid.

175 *"I can't drive":* Author interview with William Schurk, Bowling Green, Oh., 6/26/01.

175 *In the 1980s:* Ibid.
176 *At Bowling Green:* Ibid.
177 "Astrological Series": *Astrological Series, Vol. 1: The Astronomical House of Scorpio* (GWP-Astro 1008), liner notes.
177 *I learn later:* "Syndicated astrologer Carroll Righter dead at 88," Associated Press, 5/3/1988.
177 *Here is Righter's take: Astrological Series, Vol. 1,* liner notes.
178 *The Supremes:* The Supremes, "House of the Rising Sun," *A Bit of Liverpool* (Motown MT-623, 1964).
178 *Peter, Paul and Mary:* Peter, Paul and Mary, *Lifelines.*
178 *It offers:* Mary Travers and B.B. King, "House of the Rising Sun," *Lifelines.*
179 *A doe-eyed:* Lana Cantrell, "House of the Rising Sun," *Another Shade of Lana* (RCA Victor LSP3862).
179 *Another woman:* June Bugg, "House of the Rising Sun Blues," *Hootenanny Folk Festival: The Incredible Voice of June Bugg* (Palace PST757).
179 *Billy Strange:* Billy Strange, "House of the Rising Sun Ska," *Lloyd Thaxton Presents* (Decca DL-4594).
179 *Dave Ray:* Dave Ray, "Rising Sun Blues," *Snaker's Here! Blues and Hollers* (Elektra EKS7284).
179 *I had heard rumors:* The Beatles, "House of the Rising Sun," *Sweet Apple Trax,* side 4, track 2.
179 *The bass:* Ibid.
179 *Then Udo Jurgens's:* Udo Jurgens, "House of the Rising Sun," *Udo Live* (Ariola 79133-XV, 1968).
181 *"When you delve":* Author interview with Peggy Bulger, Washington, D.C., 7/20/00.
181 *"Once a guitar player":* Eric Burdon, New Orleans, La., 05/00.
182 *And Nora Guthrie:* Author interview with Nora Guthrie, New York, NY, 7/00.
182 *Colleen, a singer:* Author interview with Colleen Long, New York, NY, 5/9/06.
182 *Bon Jovi was fourteen:* Timothy White, "Bon Jovi: Can slippery rock give love a bad name?" *Playboy,* September 1987, 78–84.
182 *Even Tony Blair:* Jason Lewis, "Poptastic PM . . . or just a shameless vote grabber?" *The Mail on Sunday,* 1/23/05, 17.
182 *But it's doubtful:* "Q&A with Adam Sandler, *E Online,* www.eOnline.com/Celebs/Qa/Sandler/interview4.html, undated, accessed 09/06.
183 *"Anybody can learn this song":* From website www.youtube.com/watch?v=2smyS60VSm8, accessed 11/06.
183 *France's Shion2A, meanwhile, offers:* From website www.youtube.com/watch?v=5BnxZWHhLfk, accessed 11/06.

183 *Another user, ggin, films an infant:* From website http://youtube.com/
watch?v=SacjGLQ6sm4, accessed 11/06.

183 *The most entertaining take:* From website http://youtube.com/watch?v
=TqJ1prUhtWA, accessed 11/06.

183 *"The only difference":* Peggy Bulger, 7/20/00.

CHAPTER 7: DIASPORA

Sources for documentation and background in this chapter included: Eric
Burdon and J. Marshall Craig, *Don't Let Me Be Misunderstood;* Gene O'Neill,
House of the Rising Sun; Chuck Hustmyre, *House of the Rising Sun;* "Between
Soup and Soap: Iconic Nationality, Mass Media and Pop Culture," *Lituanus:
Lithuanian Quarterly Journal of Arts and Sciences; An Anthology of English
Songs;* "History of Karaoke," *Karaoke Scene;* news articles about Alvin Ailey,
Christian music, song parodies, and competitive ice skating; the websites of
Adult DVD Empire, Excalibur Films, and Farragut High School in Knoxville,
Tenn.; interviews with Bob and Dale Charnes of the Arizona Gunfighters
and players Jarae Taylor; musician Jimmy Thibodeaux; John Pallini of
Casio; Dustin Cohn of Gatorade and Danny Schuman of Element 79 Part-
ners; Attila Weinberger (email); visits by author to the Festival of the West
in Arizona, to Harbin and Beijing, China, and to Bangkok, Thailand.

Audio and video works consulted included: "Origins 3," nationally aired
commercial by Gatorade, coproduced by Element 79 Partners; the pilot
episode of the NBC television show *Knight Rider;* episodes of the ABC televi-
sion show *Lost;* two adult films entitled *House of the Rising Sun* by
VideoTeam and Legend, respectively; the film *Casino,* directed by Martin
Scorsese; David Harp, *How to Whistle Like a Pro; The United States Navy Band
Presents the Commodores;* Apocalypse Hoboken, *House of the Rising Son of a
Bitch; Charlie Daniels: Super Hits;*

184 *The man named Mad Dog:* Author visit to the Festival of the West,
Scottsdale, Ariz., 3/19/05.

184 *"What have you done":* Ibid.

185 *The place is Scottsdale:* Ibid.

186 *"We are a little careful":* Author interview, Bob and Dale Charnes,
Scottsdale, Ariz., 3/19/05.

186 *Jarae Taylor:* Author interview with Jarae Taylor, Scottsdale, Ariz.,
3/19/05.

186 *Dale Charnes is the den mother:* Bob and Dale Charnes, 3/19/05.

187 *Doing a "Rising Sun":* Ibid.

188 *Even Eric Burdon:* Eric Burdon and J. Marshall Craig, *Don't Let Me Be
Misunderstood,* 204.

188 *Jimmy Thibodeaux:* Author interview with Jimmy Thibodeaux, telephone, 7/18/00.

188 *The late black:* Mary Campbell, "Alvin Ailey American Dance Theater has 30th birthday," Associated Press, 12/8/1988.

188 *In it, female dancers in nightgowns:* Jack Anderson, "Demonstrating Ailey's choreographic versatility," *New York Times,* 12/11/88; Deborah A. Levinson, "Ailey performances blur line between theater and dance," *The Tech,* Massachusetts Institute of Technology, 3/30/93, 7–8.

189 *Casio calibrates:* Author interview with John Pallini, telephone, 6/21/00.

189 *In 2005:* "Origins 3," nationally aired commercial by Gatorade, coproduced by Element 79 Partners, 2005.

189 *Gatorade learned:* Author interview with Dustin Cohn and Danny Schuman, telephone, 6/16/05.

190 *"There were two":* Ibid.

190 *Consider the short story:* Gene O'Neill, *House of the Rising Sun* (Fountain Hills, Ariz.: Eraserhead Press, 2001).

191 *Adrian had never:* Ibid., 6–7.

191 *Chuck Hustmyre:* Chuck Hustmyre, *House of the Rising Sun* (Bend, Ore.: Salvo Press, 2004).

191 *The Rising Sun:* Ibid., 17.

192 *As Jenny finished:* Ibid., 22.

192 *The director, Ron Judkins:* "A feature film project of Mustang Films to be directed by Ron Judkins," announcement by director on website http://houseoftherisingsun.tv/pages/1/page1.html, accessed 06/06.

192 *In recent years: Knight Rider,* pilot episode, "Knight of the Phoenix," parts one and two, NBC, 9/26/82.

192 *And in the popular: Lost,* season one, episode 6, "House of the Rising Sun," ABC, 10/27/04.

193 *A little-known 1987 film: House of the Rising Sun,* Greg Gold, director (Mediacom Productions, 1987).

193 *In 2004: Slaughterhouse of the Rising Sun,* Vin Crease, director (Perceramborol Productions, 2005).

193 *The first, made in 1993: House of the Rising Sun,* Wesley Emerson, director (VideoTeam, 1993).

194 *The second, a 1999 production: House of the Rising Sun,* Jerome Tanner, director (Legend, 1999).

194 *At least three:* Film synopses from AdultDVDEmpire.com website, http://adult.dvdempire.com, accessed 09/06.

194 *In this scintillating sexvid:* Film synopsis from Excalibur Films website, http://excaliburfilms.com/AdultDVD/112753D1 Bordello House of the Rising sun dvd.htm, accessed 09/06.

194 *This harks back:* Vance Randolph and G. Legman, *Roll Me in Your Arms: "Unprintable" Ozark Folksongs and Folklore, Vol. 1,* 250–53.

195 *The most effective transference: Casino,* Martin Scorsese, director (MCA/ Universal Pictures, 1995).

195 *The opening credits:* Ibid.

195 *The use of popular music:* Ibid.

196 *If "House of the Rising Sun":* Ibid.

197 *David Harp's 1989 album:* David Harp, *How to Whistle Like a Pro* (Eva-Tone 105876, 1989).

197 *the fall 2002 repertoire:* "Fall 2002 Marching Season," Farragut High School Marching Band website, www.farragutband.org, accessed 09/06.

197 *In 1969, the Commodores:* Larry Kreitner, band director, "House of the Rising Sun," *The United States Navy Band Presents the Commodores* (USNB 37192, 1980).

197 *In 1996, it provided:* Anne M. Peterson, "Michelle Kwan leads after short program," Associated Press, 1/20/96.

197 *In 1998, a group:* Apocalypse Hoboken, *House of the Rising Son of a Bitch* (Kung Fu Records 78766, 1998).

197 *In 2001, a fourteen-year-old:* Jodi Fuson, "Lincoln teen travels coast to coast to dance," *Lincoln Journal Star,* 9/26/01.

197 *Attila Weinberger:* Email to author from Attila Weinberger, 5/30/01.

197 *It's even been quoted:* Charlie Daniels, "The Devil Went Down to Georgia," *Charlie Daniels: Super Hits* (Sony EK 64182, 1994).

198 *Religion, too:* Susie P. Gonzalez, "Christian music: Growing variety of forms attracts modern worshippers," *San Antonio Express-News,* 11/15/97, 7B.

198 *And a few years ago:* "Notebook: Just give me that Biblical rock 'n' roll," *Time,* 2/19/01, 19.

198 *There in the House in Washington:* W. Tong, "House of the White-Haired One," from website bootnewt.tripod.com/housewht.htm, accessed 09/06.

198 *For political fairness:* Bubba, "House of the Rising Son," from website www.amiright.com/parody/60s/theanimals0.shtml, accessed 09/06.

199 *Tom Smith:* Tom Smith, "The Dread Ensign Wesley," from website of Tom Smith, www.tomsmithonline.com/lyrics/dreadwesley.htm, accessed 06/06.

199 *Virgis Stakenas:* Arturas Tereskinas, "Between Soup and Soap: Iconic Nationality, Mass Media and Pop Culture," *Lituanus: Lithuanian Quarterly Journal of Arts and Sciences,* vol. 46, no. 2, summer 2000.

201 *The streets and shops of Harbin:* Author visit to Harbin, China, 1/28/03.

202 *The Chinese music cognoscenti:* Margaret McGreevey, Richard Lawrence

and Grant Tyreman, *An Anthology of English Songs* (Beijing: Huaxia Publishing, 1994).

202 *And on page 63:* Ibid., 63.

202 *On the fourth floor:* Author visit to Harbin, China, 1/28/03.

203 *The following day:* Author visit to Harbin, China, 1/29/03.

203 *Meanwhile, Dawei:* Ibid.

204 *Room 329:* Author visit to PartyWorld Cash Box karaoke, Beijing, China, 5/12/04.

205 *We are here:* Ibid.

205 *In the three-ring binder:* Ibid.

206 *I have done the Asian karaoke:* Author visit to BMG Karaoke Box, Bangkok, Thailand, 6/29/00.

207 *"It is said":* "History of Karaoke," *Karaoke Scene,* online magazine at website www.karaokescene.com/history/, accessed 09/06.

CHAPTER 8: FAMILY

To tell the story of finding Georgia Turner, the author consulted works that included: Bill C. Malone, *Singing Cowboys and Musical Mountaineers: Southern Culture and the Roots of Country Music;* letters from Alan Lomax and Georgia Turner, Alan Lomax Archives; a contract between Ludlow Music Inc. and John A. Lomax, Alan Lomax, and Georgia Turner, 9/1/59, courtesy of Reno Taylor; Peter Goldsmith, *Making People's Music: Moe Asch and Folkways Records;* a check stub from TRO Songways Services, Inc., courtesy of Faye Stromberger; interviews with Edward Hunter of Middlesboro, Ky.; author David Morton; Georgia Turner's children, sister-in-law, nephew, and great-niece.

Audio works consulted included Alan Lomax field recordings of Georgia Turner from his 1937 Kentucky trip held by the Library of Congress American Folklife Center.

208 *Music historian Bill C. Malone:* Bill C. Malone, *Singing Cowboys and Musical Mountaineers: Southern Culture and the Roots of Country Music* (Athens: University of Georgia Press, 1993), 25.

209 *The one that prompted it:* Letter from Georgia Turner Connolly to Alan Lomax, 1963, on file at Alan Lomax Archives.

210 *Hunter seemed to recognize:* Edward Hunter, 7/17/00 and 7/23/00.

210 *The voice sounded excited:* Author interview with Jana Bruce, telephone, 7/18/00.

211 *"Instead, it brought":* Author interview with David Morton, telephone, 7/17/00.

212 *"It was like being on the moon":* Author interview with Reno Taylor, June Turner and Jana Bruce, Monroe, Mich., 8/19/00.

213 *Reno never knew:* Ibid.

214 *"So," I say:* Ibid.

214 *I pull out:* Audiotape, Library of Congress American Folklife Center, batch 4872, track AFS-1404-A1.214

214 *I watch him intently:* Reno Taylor, June Turner, and Jana Bruce, 8/19/00.

215 *The song ends:* Ibid.

216 *Five months later:* Author interview with Georgia Turner's children, 2/17/01.

216 *Barbara Wilson:* Ibid.

217 *Because Reno Taylor was away:* Ibid.

217 *Royalties began reaching:* Letter from Georgia Connolly to Alan Lomax, 1963.

217 *Sometime later:* Pauline Inman, 7/00.

218 *A September 1, 1959, contract:* Contract between Ludlow Music Inc. and John A. Lomax, Alan Lomax, and Georgia Turner, 9/1/59, courtesy of Reno Taylor.

218 *The contract was apparently:* Ibid.

218 *by the 1960s:* Letter from Alan Lomax to Georgia Turner Connolly, 1963, on file at Alan Lomax Archives.

218 *Peter Goldsmith:* Peter Goldsmith, *Making People's Music: Moe Asch and Folkways Records* (Washington, D.C.: Smithsonian Institution Press, 1998), 288.

218 *Checks did trickle:* Georgia Turner's children, 2/17/01.

219 *Today, Faye has:* Check stub, TRO Songways Services, Inc., New York, N.Y., 10/30/68, courtesy of Faye Stromberger.

219 *Each has stacks:* Georgia Turner's children, 2/17/01.

219 *"Why is music important?":* Ibid.

CHAPTER 9: GOING BACK TO NEW ORLEANS

Documenting the legend of a "House of the Rising Sun" in New Orleans and finishing up his search, the author consulted background and documentary sources that included: editions of the *Louisiana Gazette* from 1821 and 1822, courtesy of the Historic New Orleans Collection (HNOC); French Quarter tract maps, also on file at the HNOC; Herbert Asbury, *The French Quarter;* Al Rose, *Storyville, New Orleans;* Bob Dylan, *Chronicles: Volume One;* visits by the author to New Orleans in 2000, 2001, and 2005; Vance Randolph and G. Legman, *Roll Me in Your Arms: "Unprintable" Ozark Folksongs and Folklore, Vol. 1;* Dave Van Ronk with Elijah Wald, *The Mayor of MacDougal Street: A Memoir;*

New Orleans city directories from 1850 to 1920 at the New Orleans Public Library; a 2003 letter to the editor by New Orleans historian Pamela D. Arceneaux in *The Times-Picayune;* Eric Burdon and J. Marshall Craig, *Don't Let Me Be Misunderstood;* a March 2005 *Times-Picayune* article by Bruce Eggler, "A French Quarter excavation may yield some tantalizing clues: evidence of the infamous Rising Sun brothel as well as a pre-New Orleans settlement"; John Schwartz, "Archaeologist in New Orleans finds a way to help the living," *New York Times;* Robert Andrews, Mary Biggs, and Michael Seidel et al., *The Columbia World of Quotations;* Dr. Seuss, *McElligot's Pool;* Harold Sinclair, *Music Out of Dixie;* Grace Lichtenstein and Laura Dankner, *Musical Gumbo: The Music of New Orleans;* Rick Koster, *Louisiana Music;* interviews with Bruce Raeburn of the Tulane Jazz Archives; Eric Burdon of the Animals; archaeologist Shannon Dawdy; bed-and-breakfast owner and music historian Kevin Herridge and his wife, Wendy; Priscilla Lawrence, executive director of the Historic New Orleans Commission; Virginia Lee and David Blood of the band Mixt Company; Reno Taylor, Georgia Turner's eldest son; June Turner and Jana Bruce, Georgia Turner's sister-in-law and great-niece.

Audio and video works consulted included: director Louis Malle's 1978 film *Pretty Baby;* Woody Guthrie, "Tom Joad."

221 *Rising Sun Hotel:* "Rising Sun Hotel, Conti Street, Nearly opposite the State Bank," *Louisiana Gazette,* 1/27/1821, 2.
222 *About two o'clock:* No headline, *Louisiana Gazette,* 2/28/1822, 2.
223 *Asbury spends:* Herbert Asbury, *The French Quarter* (New York: Alfred A. Knopf, 1936).
223 *"Every flatboat man":* Ibid, 59.
223 *"The visitor to New Orleans":* Al Rose, *Storyville, New Orleans* (Tuscaloosa: University of Alabama Press, 1974), 73.
224 *They seem like ghosts themselves:* Ibid., 2–100.
224 *In Louis Malle's: Pretty Baby,* Louis Malle, director (Paramount, 1978).
224 *"New Orleans, unlike a lot":* Bob Dylan, *Chronicles: Volume One,* 180.
224 *On one occasion:* Author visit to New Orleans, 3/22/05–3/24/05.
225 *Vance Randolph:* Vance Randolph and G. Legman, *Roll Me in Your Arms: "Unprintable" Ozark Folksongs and Folklore, Vol. 1,* 250–53.
226 *Dave Van Ronk:* Dave Van Ronk with Elijah Wald, *The Mayor of MacDougal Street: A Memoir,* 178.
226 *"I've never seen it":* Author interview with Bruce Raeburn, New Orleans, La., 5/9/00.
226 *One bed and breakfast:* New Orleans, La., 3/22/05–3/24/05.
226 *New Orleans city directories:* City directories, 1850–1900, New Orleans Public Library.

227 *New Orleans reference librarian:* Pamela D. Arceneaux, "Fact: It's been the ruin of many a poor myth," letter to the editor, *The Times-Picayune,* 2/3/03, 4.

227 *Eric Burdon thinks:* Eric Burdon, 05/00.

227 *A few years back:* Eric Burdon and J. Marshall Craig, *Don't Let Me Be Misunderstood,* 277–84.

227 *The Herridges:* Author interview with Kevin and Wendy Herridge, New Orleans, La. 5/10/00.

228 *In early 2005:* Author interview with Priscilla Lawrence, executive director of the Historic New Orleans Commission, New Orleans, La., 3/23/05.

228 *The tract was:* New Orleans, 3/22/05–3/24/05.

228 *Five months before:* Author interview with Shannon Dawdy, New Orleans, La., 3/23/05.

229 *Here was a hotel:* "Rising Sun Hotel, Conti Street, Nearly opposite the State Bank," *Louisiana Gazette,* 2.

229 *Dawdy found:* Shannon Dawdy, 3/23/05.

229 *"It is true":* Ibid.

229 *That may be why:* Bruce Eggler, "A French Quarter excavation may yield some tantalizing clues: evidence of the infamous Rising Sun brothel as well as a pre-New Orleans settlement," *The Times-Picayune,* 3/6/05, 1.

229 *When I visited:* Shannon Dawdy, 3/23/05.

230 *Dawdy ended up embedded:* John Schwartz, "Archaeologist in New Orleans finds a way to help the living," *New York Times,* 1/3/06, F1.

230 *Four years after:* Author interview with Virginia Lee and David Blood, Nashville, Tenn., 5/24/05.

231 *It's past 10 p.m.:* Virginia Lee and David Blood, 5/24/05.

233 *"Civilization," the historian Will Durant wrote:* Robert Andrews, Mary Biggs and Michael Seidel et al., *The Columbia World of Quotations* (New York: Columbia University Press, 1996).

234 *"Everybody might be":* Woody Guthrie, "Tom Joad" (TRO-Ludlow Music Inc., 1963).

235 *An underground river:* Dr. Seuss, *McElligot's Pool* (New York: Random House, 1947), 7.

235 *I follow Reno Taylor:* Author interview with Reno Taylor, Monroe, Mich., 8/19/00.

235 *I think of what:* Reno Taylor, June Turner, and Jana Bruce, 8/19/00.

AFTERWORD: MY RACE IS ALMOST RUN

Sources consulted for the afterword included an interview with musician and radio host Oscar Brand; and the CD *Alan Lomax: Popular Songbook*.

237 *A few years ago:* Oscar Brand, 8/16/00.
238 *"Write a book":* Ibid.
238 *The title was: Alan Lomax: Popular Songbook* (Rounder 82161-1863-2, 2003), liner notes.

Further Reading

I have selected the books below to offer a cross-section of resources for readers who wish to dig deeper into some of the themes explored in this book. The list is heavy on several topics: further reading on the musicians who sang "House of the Rising Sun"; biographies of individual songs; regional and cultural histories, particularly those of the Southern Appalachians and New Orleans; folklore, the folk revival, and the history of musical genres; and the marketing of music in the twentieth century. There are also a few works of fiction tossed into the mix that deal with similar themes.

Anderson, Ann. *Snake Oil, Hustlers and Hambones: The American Medicine Show*. Jefferson, N.C.: McFarland & Company, 2000.

Asbury, Herbert. *The French Quarter: An Informal History of the New Orleans Underworld*. New York, London: A. A. Knopf, 1936.

Ayers, Edward L. *Southern Crossing: A History of the American South, 1877–1906*. Oxford, New York: Oxford University Press, 1995.

Bindas, Kenneth J. *All of This Music Belongs to the Nation: The WPA's Federal Music Project and American Society*. Knoxville: University of Tennessee Press, 1995.

Bishop, Stephen. *Songs in the Rough: From Heartbreak Hotel to Higher Love*. New York: St. Martin's Press, 1996.

Blecha, Peter. *Taboo Tunes: A History of Banned Bands & Censored Songs*. San Francisco: Backbeat Books, 2004.

Blevins, Brooks. *Hill Folks: A History of Arkansas Ozarkers and Their Image*. Chapel Hill: University of North Carolina Press, 2002.

Botkin, Benjamin Albert. *A Treasury of American Folklore: Stories, Ballads, and Traditions of the People*. New York: Crown Publishers, 1944.

Brand, Oscar. *The Ballad Mongers: Rise of the Modern Folk Song*. New York: Funk & Wagnalls, 1962.

Bronson, Fred. *The Billboard Book of Number One Hits*, 5th ed. New York: Billboard Books, 2003.

Brown, Cecil. *Stagolee Shot Billy*. Cambridge, Mass.: Harvard University Press, 2003.

Brown, Rodger Lyle. *Ghost Dancing on the Cracker Circuit: The Culture of Festivals in the American South.* Jackson: University Press of Mississippi, 1997.

Brunvand, Jan Harold. *American Folklore: An Encyclopedia.* New York: Garland, 1996.

Brunvand, Jan Harold. *The Study of American Folklore: An Introduction.* New York: Norton, 1998.

Burdon, Eric, and J. Marshall Craig. *Don't Let Me Be Misunderstood.* New York: Thunder's Mouth Press, 2001.

Cantwell, Robert. *Bluegrass Breakdown: The Making of the Old Southern Sound.* New York: Da Capo, 1984.

———. *When We Were Good: The Folk Revival.* Cambridge: Harvard University Press, 1996.

Caudill, Harry M. *Night Comes to the Cumberlands: A Biography of a Depressed Area.* Boston: Little, Brown, 1963.

Charters, Samuel B. *The Country Blues.* New York: Da Capo, 1975.

———. *The Roots of the Blues: An African Search.* New York: Da Capo, 1981.

Cohen, Norm. *Folk Music: A Regional Exlporation.* Westport, Conn.: Greenwood Press, 2005.

Collins, Shirley. *America over the Water: An Emotional Journey into the Cultural Roots of Traditional American Music with Legendary Archivist Alan Lomax.* London: SAF Publishing, 2004.

Collins, Terry. *The Andy Griffith Story: An Illustrated Biography,* 1st ed. Mount Airy, NC: Explorer Press, 1995.

Conway, Cecelia. *African Banjo Echoes in Appalachia: A Study of Folk Traditions.* Knoxville: University of Tennessee Press, 1995.

Crawford, Martin. *Ashe County's Civil War: Community and Society in the Appalachian South.* Charlottesville: University Press of Virginia, 2001.

Cray, Ed. *The Erotic Muse: American Bawdy Songs.* Urbana: University of Illinois Press, 1992/1999.

———. *Ramblin' Man: The Life and Times of Woody Guthrie.* New York: Norton, 2004.

Dawidoff, Nicholas. *In the Country of Country: A Journey to the Roots of American Music.* New York: Pantheon, 1997.

DeSalvo, Debra. *The Language of the Blues: From Alcorub to Zuzu.* New York: Billboard Books, 2006.

Douglas, Susan J. *Listening In: Radio and the American Imagination.* New York: Times Books, 1999.

Dylan, Bob. *Chronicles, Volume One.* New York: Simon & Schuster, 2004.

Egan, Sean. *Animal Tracks: The Story of the Animals.* London: Helter Skelter Publishing, 2001.

Emerson, Ken. *Doo-Dah!: Stephen Foster and the Rise of American Popular Culture*. New York: Simon & Schuster, 1997.

Erbsen, Wayne. *Rural Roots of Bluegrass: Songs, Stories & History*. Pacific, Mo.: Mel Bay Publications, 2004.

Escott, Colin. *Roadkill on the Three-Chord Highway: Art and Trash in American Popular Music*. New York: Routledge, 2002.

Mari-Lynn Evans, Robert Santelli and Holly George-Warren, editors. *The Appalachians: America's First and Last Frontier*. New York: Random House, 2004.

Ewen, David. *Panorama of American Popular Music: The Story of Our National Ballads and Folk Songs, the Songs of Tin Pan Alley, Broadway and Hollywood, New Orleans Jazz, Swing, and Symphonic Jazz*. Englewood Cliffs, N.J.: Prentice-Hall, 1957.

Ferris, William R. *Blues from the Delta*. New York: Da Capo, 1984.

Filene, Benjamin. *Romancing the Folk: Public Memory & American Roots Music*. Chapel Hill: University of North Carolina Press, 2000.

Gill, Andy. *Don't Think Twice, It's All Right: Bob Dylan, the Early Years*. New York: Thunder's Mouth Press, 1998.

Glassie, Henry H., Edward D. Ives, and John F. Szwed. *Folksongs and Their Makers*. Bowling Green, Oh.: Bowling Green State University Popular Press, 1970.

Goldsmith, Peter. *Making People's Music: Moe Asch and Folkways Records*. Washington, D.C.: Smithsonian Institution Press, 1998.

Goodman, Fred. *The Mansion on the Hill: Dylan, Young, Geffen, Springsteen, and the Head-on Collision of Rock and Commerce*. New York: Vintage, 1997.

Guthrie, Woody. *Woody Guthrie Songbook*. New York: Ludlow Music, 1994/1999.

Hajdu, David. *Positively 4th Street: The Lives and Times of Joan Baez, Bob Dylan, Mimi Baez Fariña, and Richard Fariña*. New York: Farrar, Straus and Giroux, 2001.

Handy, W. C. *Father of the Blues: An Autobiography*. New York: Da Capo, 1941/1969.

Hamby, Zetta Barker. *Memoirs of Grassy Creek: Growing Up in the Mountains on the Virginia–North Carolina Line*. Jefferson, N.C.: McFarland & Co., 1998.

Heatley, Michael with Spencer Leigh. *Behind the Song: The Stories of 100 Great Pop & Rock Classics*. London: Blandford, 1998.

Hemphill, Paul. *The Nashville Sound: Bright Lights and Country Music*. New York: Simon & Schuster, 1970.

Heylin, Clinton. *Bob Dylan: Behind the Shades Revisited*. New York: William Morrow, 1991/2001.

———. *Bob Dylan: The Recording Sessions, 1960–1994,* 1st ed. New York: St. Martin's Press, 1995.

Heyrman, Christine Leigh. *Southern Cross: The Beginnings of the Bible Belt.* New York: A. A. Knopf, 1997.

Hill, Fred. *Grass Roots: An Illustrated History of Bluegrass and Mountain Music.* Rutland, Vt.: Academy Books, 1980.

Ives, Burl. *The Burl Ives Song Book.* New York: Ballantine Books, 1953.

Jones, LeRoi. *Blues People: Negro Music in White America.* New York: William Morrow, 1963/1999.

Kemp, Mark. *Dixie Lullaby: A Story of Music, Race, and New Beginnings in a New South.* New York: Free Press, 2004.

Klein, Joe. *Woody Guthrie: A Life.* New York: Delta/Dell, 1999.

Koster, Rich. *Louisiana Music.* New York: Da Capo, 2002.

Lanza, Joseph. *Elevator Music: A Surreal History of Muzak, Easy-Listening, and Other Moodsong.* New York: Picador, 1994.

Ledbetter, Huddie (Lead Belly). *Lead Belly: No Stranger to the Blues: The Songs of Huddie Ledbetter.* New York: Folkways Music Publishers, 1998.

Lichtenstein, Grace and Laura Dankner. *Musical Gumbo: The Music of New Orleans.* New York: Norton, 1993.

Logsdon, Guy. *The Whorehouse Bells Were Ringing, and Other Songs Cowboys Sing.* Urbana: University of Illinois Press, 1989.

Lomax, Alan. *The Folk Songs of North America, in the English Language.* Garden City: Doubleday, 1960.

———. *The Land Where the Blues Began.* New York: New Press, 2002.

———. *The Penguin Book of American Folk Songs.* Baltimore: Penguin Books, 1966.

Lomax, Alan and Ronald D. Cohen. *Alan Lomax: Selected Writings, 1934–1997.* New York: Routledge, 2003.

Lomax, Alan, Woody Guthrie, and Pete Seeger. *Hard Hitting Songs for Hard-Hit People.* Lincoln: University of Nebraska Press, 1999.

Lomax, John Avery and Alan Lomax. *American Ballads and Folk Songs.* New York: MacMillan/Dover, 1934/1994.

———. *Our Singing Country: Folk Songs and Ballads.* Mineola, N.Y.: Dover, 1941.

Magoffin, Richard. *Waltzing Matilda: The Story Behind the Legend.* Sydney: ABC Television, 1983.

Malone, Bill C. *Country Music U.S.A.: A Fifty-Year History.* Austin: University of Texas Press/American Folklore Society, 1968.

———. *Don't Get Above Your Raisin': Country Music and the Southern Working Class.* Urbana: University of Illinois Press, 2002.

———. *Singing Cowboys and Musical Mountaineers: Southern Culture and the Roots of Country Music.* Athens: University of Georgia Press, 1993.

Marcic, Dorothy. *Respect: Women and Popular Music.* New York: Texere, 2002.

Marcus, Greil. *Invisible Republic: Bob Dylan's Basement Tapes.* New York: Henry Holt, 1997.

———. *Like a Rolling Stone: Bob Dylan at the Crossroads.* New York: PublicAffairs, 2005.

———. *Mystery Train: Images of America in Rock 'n' roll Music.* New York: Dutton, 1982.

Margolick, David. *Strange Fruit: The Biography of a Song.* New York: Ecco Press, 2001.

Marqusee, Mike. *Chimes of Freedom: The Politics of Bob Dylan's Art.* New York: New Press, 2003.

Marsh, Dave. *Louie Louie: The History and Mythology of the World's Most Famous Rock 'n' Roll Song.* New York: Hyperion, 1993.

McCrumb, Sharyn. *The Songcatcher.* New York: Signet Fiction, 2001.

McGee, Marty. *Traditional Musicians of the Central Blue Ridge.* Jefferson, N.C.: McFarland & Co., 2000.

McGreevey, Margaret, Richard Lawrence, and Grant Tyreman. *An Anthology of English Songs.* Beijing: Huaxia Publishing, 1994.

McLagan, Ian. *All the Rage: A Riotous Romp Through Rock & Roll History.* New York: Billboard Books, 2000.

Miller, Calvin. *Jesus Loves Me: Celebrating the Profound Truths of a Simple Hymn.* New York: Warner Books, 2002.

Moore, Warren. *Mountain Voices: A Legacy of the Blue Ridge and Great Smokies.* Winston-Salem, N.C.: John F. Blair, 1988.

Morton, David. *Off the Record: The Technology and Culture of Sound Recording in America.* New Brunswick, N.J.: Rutgers University Press, 2000.

Ownby, Ted. *Subduing Satan: Religion, Recreation, and Manhood in the Rural South, 1865–1920.* Chapel Hill: University of North Carolina Press, 1990.

Palmer, Robert. *Deep Blues.* New York: Penguin Books, 1982.

Parris, John. *Roaming the Mountains with John A. Parris.* Asheville, N.C.: Citizen-Times Pub. Co., 1955.

Partridge, Elizabeth. *This Land Was Made for You and Me: The Life and Songs of Woody Guthrie.* New York: Viking Juvenile, 2002.

Peattie, Roderick, editor. *The Great Smokies and the Blue Ridge: The Story of the Southern Appalachians.* New York: Vanguard Press, 1943.

Poole, Cary Franklin. *A History of Railroading in North Carolina.* Johnson City, Tenn.: The Overmountain Press, 1995.

Porterfield, Nolan. *Last Cavalier: The Life and Times of John A. Lomax, 1867–1948.* Urbana: University of Illinois Press, 1996.

Remini, Robert V. *The Battle of New Orleans: Andrew Jackson and America's First Military Victory.* New York: Penguin Books, 2001.

Ritchie, Jean. *Folk Songs of the Southern Appalachians*. Lexington: University Press of Kentucky, 1965/1997.

———. *Singing Family of the Cumberlands*. Oxford/Lexington, Ky.: Oxford University Press/University Press of Kentucky, 1955/1988.

Robb, Ian G. *A Century of Lowestoft: Events, People and Places over the Last 100 Years*. Phoenix Mill, England: Sutton Publishing Ltd., 1999.

Rose, Al. *Storyville, New Orleans: Being an Authentic, Illustrated Account of the Notorious Red-Light District*. Tuscaloosa: University of Alabama Press, 1974.

Rosen, Jody. *White Christmas: The Story of an American Song*. New York: Scribner, 2002.

Rosenberg, Neil V. *Bluegrass: A History*. Urbana: University of Illinois Press, 1985.

Sackheim, Eric. *The Blues Line: A Collection of Blues Lyrics*. New York: Schirmer Books, 1975.

Sandburg, Carl. *The American Songbag*. New York: Harcourt Brace, 1927/1990.

Santelli, Robert, Holly George-Warren, and Jim Brown. *American Roots Music*. New York: Harry N. Abrams, 2002.

Schlappi, Elizabeth. *Roy Acuff, the Smoky Mountain Boy*. Gretna, La.: Pelican, 1978/1993.

Schneider, Richard H. *Taps: Notes from a Nation's Heart*. New York: William Morrow, 2002.

Sherr, Lynn. *America the Beautiful: The Stirring True Story Behind Our Nation's Favorite Song*. New York: PublicAffairs, 2001.

Seeger, Pete and Jo Metcalf Schwartz. *The Incompleat Folksinger*. New York: Simon & Schuster, 1972.

Shelton, Robert. *No Direction Home: The Life and Music of Bob Dylan*. New York: Beech Tree Books, 1986.

Shelton, Robert and Burt Goldblatt. *The Country Music Story: A Picture History of Country and Western Music*. Secaucus, N.J.: Castle Books, 1966.

Sounes, Howard. *Down the Highway: The Life of Bob Dylan*, 1st ed. New York: Grove Press, 2001.

Stambler, Irwin and Grelun Landon. *The Encyclopedia of Folk, Country and Western Music*, 2d ed. New York: St. Martin's Press, 1983.

Tichi, Cecelia. *High Lonesome: The American Culture of Country Music*. Chapel Hill: University of North Carolina Press, 1994.

Tosches, Nick. *Country: The Twisted Roots of Rock 'n' Roll*. New York: Da Capo, 1977/1985.

———. *Where Dead Voices Gather*. Boston: Little, Brown, 2001.

Turner, Steve. *Amazing Grace: The Story of America's Most Beloved Song*. New York: Ecco, 2002.

Van Ronk, Dave with Elijah Wald. *The Mayor of MacDougal Street: A Memoir.* New York: Da Capo, 2005.

Von Schmidt, Eric and Jim Rooney. *Baby, Let Me Follow You Down: The Illustrated Story of the Cambridge Folk Years.* New York: Anchor, 1979.

Wald, Elijah. *Josh White: Society Blues.* Amherst: University of Massachusetts Press, 2000.

Weberman, A. J. *Dylan to English Dictionary.* New York: Yippie Museum Press, 2005.

Weidensaul, Scott. *Mountains of the Heart: A Natural History of the Appalachians.* Golden, Colo.: Fulcrum Pub., 1994.

Weisbard, Eric and Experience Music Project. *This Is Pop: In Search of the Elusive at Experience Music Project.* Cambridge: Harvard University Press, 2004.

Weller, Jack E. *Yesterday's People: Life in Contemporary Appalachia.* Lexington: University of Kentucky Press, 1965.

West, John Foster. *Lift Up Your Head, Tom Dooley: The True Story of the Appalachian Murder That Inspired One of America's Most Popular Ballads.* Asheboro, N.C.: Down Home Press, 1993.

White, Mark. *You Must Remember This . . . : Popular Songwriters 1900–1980.* New York: Charles Scribner's Sons, 1985.

Whitehead, Colson. *John Henry Days.* New York: Doubleday, 2001.

Williamson, J. W. *Hillbillyland: What the Movies Did to the Mountains and What the Mountains Did to the Movies.* Chapel Hill: University of North Carolina Press, 1995.

Wilson, Charles Reagan, William R. Ferris, and University of Mississippi Center for the Study of Southern Culture. *Encyclopedia of Southern Culture.* 4 vols. New York: Anchor Books, 1991.

Zwonitzer, Mark and Charles Hirshberg. *Will You Miss Me When I'm Gone?: The Carter Family and Their Legacy in American Music.* New York: Simon & Schuster, 2002.

Selected Discography

The instances of "House of the Rising Sun" listed here by no means represent a complete collection; new versions are being recorded by fresh artists every month. This discography offers a cross section that includes most of the recordings significant to the song's evolution and dozens of others from various genres. Catalog numbers are listed where available. The earliest versions, from the 1930s, are marked with the year they were recorded.

50 Mission Blues Band, album version.
Roy Acuff, *Greatest Hits, Vol. 2* (Elektra/Asylum Records, 9E-303).
Roy Acuff, "The Rising Sun" (Vocalion 4909B, 1938).
Adolescents, *Brats in Battalions* (Triple X Records 510610-2).
Almanac Singers, *The Almanac Singers: Their Complete General Recordings* (MCA MCAD-11499).
Animals, *Best of the 60's* (SI 250722).
Clarence Ashley and Doc Watson, "Rising sun Blues," *The Original Folkways Recordings 1960–62* (disc one) (Folkways).
Tom Ashley and Gwen Foster, as "Rising Sun Blues," *The Rising Sun Blues:* (Vocalion 02576, 1933).
Hoyt Axton, *House of the Rising Sun.*
Bachman-Turner Overdrive, *Trial by Fire—Greatest & Latest* (CMC Records 5216112).
Joan Baez, *Joan Baez* (Vanguard Records VMD-2077).
Be Good Tanyas, *Chinatown* (Nettwerk Productions 0 6700 30304 2 7).
Mac Benford and the Woodshed All-Stars, *Willow* (Rounder CD 0371).
Bruno Bertone Orchestra, *Strangers in the Night* (LaserLight Digital/Delta 21 705).
Blind Boys of Alabama, as "Amazing Grace," *Spirit of the Century* (Real World Records 7243 8 50918 2 7)
Blinddog Smokin, *Ain't from Mississippi* (Crying Tone Records).
Bohemian Vendetta, *Bohemian Vendetta.*
Bone Brothers, *Less = More.*
Bremson and Owen, *One Day in September.*
Sarah Brooks, *What Is My Heart For?* (Whaling City Sound WCS 015).

Bobby Broom, *Stand!* (Premonition Records: 66917 90754 2 6).

Eric Burdon, *Roxy Live* (One Way Records 35131).

Eric Burdon and the New Animals, *The Official Live Bootleg 2000* (Flying Eye Records).

Harrison Burnett, as "Rising Sun," *Rising Sun* (Max Hunter Collection, Springfield-Greene County Library, Springfield, Mo., catalog no. 0543).

Charlie Byrd, *The Guitar Artistry of Charlie Byrd* (Riverside Records RLP-9451).

Donald Byrd, *Up with Donald Byrd* (Verve Records V6-8609).

Callahan Brothers, as "Rounder's Luck," *The Callahan Brothers* (Old Homestead Records OHCD-4031, 1934).

Ace Cannon, *Ace Cannon Plays Gold Favorites* (Power Pak PKCD-10520).

Fred Carter Concepts, *Songs of the British Isles* (Music Mill Entertainment MME-70012-2).

Dillard Chandler, as "Sport in New Orleans," *The End of an Old Song* (Smithsonian/Folkways FA 2418).

Tracy Chapman, *Rubaiyat—Elektra's 40th Anniversary, Disc One* (Elektra).

John Cheshire, *Singalong with JC*.

David Allan Coe, *Stars 1994* (Power Pak PKCD 10501).

Country Gentlemen, *The Country Gentlemen, featuring Ricky Skaggs* (Vanguard 73123-2).

Xavier Cugat, Invitación al Mambo y Cha-Cha-Cha.

Dame Darcy, *Greatest Hits*.

David, *David* (Gear Fab Records GF163).

Kelsy Davis and the Radical Soul, *Break the Mold* (Azure Blue Entertainment 857 068 001-00).

Difanga, "Les Portes Du Penitencier," on L'Hip-Hopee, *La Grande Epopee du Reggae et du R&B francais* (various artists) (Blackdoor Music 5 25662 2).

DocWood, *The GoldenVanity* (Neoga Records NM0005).

Bob Dylan, as "House of the Risin' Sun," *Bob Dylan* (Columbia Records/CBS Records 08579).

Ramblin' Jack Elliott, *The Essential Ramblin' Jack Elliott* (Vanguard VCD-89/90).

Empire State Radio with Rhe De Ville, *Damsel in This Dress*.

Santa Esmeralda, *Santa Esmeralda 2—The House of the Rising Sun* (Atoll Records/Hot Productions HTCD 6635-2).

EverEve, *Regret* (Nuclear Blast NB 402-2).

Everly Brothers, *The Hit Sound of the Everly Brothers* (Collectors' Choice Music CCM-559).

Donna Fargo, *Made in America—Folk Favorites* (Delta Entertainment 46 075).

Lester Flatt and the Nashville Grass, *Mountain Music Collection, Vol. One— Wild & Reckless Men* (CMH Records CD-8002).

Forever Love Song, Vol. 3, as "The House of the Kising Sun," (Chinese pirated release of various artists).

The Noel Freidline Quintet, *Four Nights at the Slammer* (Free Lion Records FLCD 6911-2).

Frijid Pink, "House of the Rising Sun" *Hard Rock Essentials—1970s* (various artists) (Polygram 314 520 278-2).

Jerry Garcia, David Grisman, and Tony Rice, *The Pizza Tapes* (Acoustic Disc/ Handmade Music ACD-41).

Geordie, *Can You Do It?* (Delta Music Ltd. CD 6190).

Gerry and the Pacemakers, *Ferry Cross the Mersey* (Pulse PLS CD 129).

Andy Griffith, *Golden Throats: The Great Celebrity Sing Off* (Rhino Records R2 70187).

Golden Trumpet Favorites, Vol. 3 (C-5623-3).

Smoky Greenwell, *Smoke Alarm* (Greenwell Records).

Guster, *House of the Rising Sun.*

Woody Guthrie, *The Original Folkways Recordings (Pete Seeger, Woody Guthrie and Leadbelly)* (Legacy International CD 463).

Johnny Hallyday, as "Le Penitencier," *Johnny Hallyday, Vol. 1* (Universal 832 049-2).

Daw Henson, as "The Rising Sun Blues" (Library of Congress AFS1508-B2, 1937).

Roscoe Holcomb, as "House in New Orleans," *The High Lonesome Sound* (Smithsonian Folkways FW 2363).

Misako Honjoh, *Twin Very Best Collection 1984–1990* (Imperial Records/ Teichiku Entertainment TECN-32909).

Il Mondo Di Papetti, *No. 2* (Kubaney Publishing Corp. CD 9504).

Gregory Isaacs, *House of the Rising Sun* (several mixes) (RAS Records RASCD 7040).

Wyclef Jean, chords used in song "Sang Fezi," *The Carnival Featuring Refugee Allstars* (Sony Music Entertainment CK 67974).

Waylon Jennings, *Phase One—The Early Years 1958–1964* (Universal Music Enterprises 314 584 096-2).

Waylon Jennings, *Waylon Live* (Buddha Records 7446599640-2).

Joe and Eddie, *Gene Norman Presents the Best of Joe & Eddie* (GNP Crescendo Records GNPD 2032).

Joseph, *Stoned Age Man* (Radioactive Records RRCD 134).

Udo Jurgens, *Was ich Dir sagen will.*

Susannah Keith, *Torchlight.*

James Last, *Meine schonsten Erfolge* (Spectrum 552 841-2).

Phil Leadbetter, *Philibuster!* (Rounder Select 0459).

Lead Belly, *Lead Belly's Last Sessions* (Smithsonian/Folkways SF CD 40068/71).

Lead Belly, as "In New Orleans," *Tradition Runs Deep* (Tradition 1006).

Lead Belly, as "New Orleans (The Rising Sun Blues)," *Where Did You Sleep Last Night—Lead Belly Legacy, Vol. 1:* Smithsonian/Folkways SF 40044

Nate Leath, *Extra Medium* (Patuxent CD-057).

Lorie Line, *Walking with You* (Time Line Productions TLP 07).

Lari Lucien, *House of the Rising Sun.*

Miriam Makeba, *Miriam Makeba* (Esperance CD 5564).

Bert Martin, as "The Rising Sun Blues" (Library of Congress AFS1496, 1937).

Maxim, chord used in song "Carmen Queasy," *Hell's Kitchen* (XL Recordings XLCD134).

Micaroni and Vulcano, *House of the Rising Sun.*

Ronnie Milsap, *The Country Soul of Ronnie Milsap* (Trip Records TLX-8508).

Jon Morris with Assid, *House of the Rising Sun.*

Muddyharp, *From the Delta to the Piedmont* (Hippjoint Productions).

New Toys, *House of the Rising Sun (Live).*

The Nixon Grin, *BiPolar* (The Nixon Grin LLC).

Non Prophet Organization, *House of the Rising Sun* (Mellow Edit).

Northstar Orchestra, *Morning Mood Easy Listening* (Direct Source Special Products DT62172).

Mark O'Connor, with Vassar Clements, *Heroes* (Warner Bros. Records 9 45257-2).

Odetta, as "House of the Rising Son," *Best of the Vanguard Years* (Vanguard Records 79522-2).

Odetta, *Livin' with the Blues* (Vanguard 79557-2).

Valdeci Oliveira y Banda Tropical, as "Latin Medley III," *Macarena—Latin Summer Hits* (LaserLight Digital 12 861).

101 Strings Orchestra, *The Best of 101 Strings* (Madacy Entertainment Group AL-2-2409).

Opportunity Knocks, as "Amazing Grace," *Unhinged Live!* (Open Door Ministries).

John Otway, as "House of the Rising Sun—Live at Abbey Road, *Greatest Hits.*

Oysterhead, *House of the Rising Sun.*

The Larry Page Orchestra: *Lounge with Larry—Mood Mosaic, Vol. 4* (RPM/Cherry Red Records RPM 214).

Miltiades Papastamou and Marcos Alexiou, *Dialogue Blue* (CC N'C Records - 1102).

Dolly Parton, *9 to 5 and Odd Jobs* (Buddha Records 7446599641-2).

Peter, Paul and Mary, *PP&M: Lifelines* (Warner Bros. Records 9 45851-2).

Pivo, as "Rising Sun," *Rising Sun.*

Buster Poindexter, *Buster Poindexter* (BMG Music 6633-2-R).

Steve Power, *House of the Rising Sun.*

Alan Price, *Alan Price Archive* (Rialto Records RMCD 209).

Dinu Radu, *Die Faszination Der Panflote* (LaserLight Digital 12 359).

Rage, *Rage* (Rialto RMCD 235 [Z]).

Mary Ranieri, *ARIEL*.

Ian Raven, *Bloody Merry*.

Redeye Carl and the Pirates, *Home from Shipwreck Island*.

Rhodeside, *Production Demo*.

The Tony Rice Unit, *Unit of Measure* (Rounder 11661-0405-2).

Robot Surfer, *Road to the Moon*.

Sex Mob, *Din of Inequity* (Columbia/Knitting Factory Records CTDP 095683).

Joey Scarbury, *House of the Rising Sun*.

Nina Simone, *At the Village Gate* (EMI Records CDP 7950582).

Edward Simoni, *Pan-Phantasien* (Sony Music Entertainment 12-474881-10).

Scum, *Mother Nature* (Black Mark BMCD 46).

Liz Skillman and Joaquim, *In the Middle* (Hermione Records 80766-88001-2).

Snakefarm, as "Rising Sun," *Songs from My Funeral* (BMG Music 67687-2).

Speculations, *Walking the Dog in the Midnight Hour with the Speculations* (Collectables Records COL-0621).

The Supersonics, *The Supersonics* (BIS/EMI 529157 2).

Hiroko Sutra, *House of the Rising Sun*.

Swinging Crossovers, *House of the Rising Sun*.

Synthesonic Sounds, "House of the Rising Sun," on the Easy Project, *20 Loungecore Favourites* (various artists) (Sequel Records/Castle Music CMAR 671).

Jimmy Thibodeaux, *Jimmy Thibodeaux with Gumbo Cajun Band* (Swallow Records SW 6096-2).

Their Eminence, as "Mary," *Seeds Turn to Flowers Turn to Dust* (Bacchus Archives BA1133).

Don Thompson, *Hot Dog: Don Thompson Plays Ragtime and Blues* (Arkay Records AR 6168).

Timo Kinnunen One-Man Band, *House of the Rising Sun*.

Georgia Turner, as "The Rising Sun Blues" (Library of Congress AFS1404-A1, 1937).

Conway Twitty, *To See My Angel Cry / That's When She Stopped Loving You* (Decca Records DL 75172).

unlisted artist, "House of the Rising Sun," *Party Dancing Around the World, Vol. 1* (various artists) (Madacy Inc. S-4571).

Orchester Anthony Ventura, *Je T'aime Traum-Melodien 3* (WEA Music/ Warner Music Germany LC-4281).

Ventures, *The Ventures: Stars on Guitars* (disc two) (Celebrity Licensing Inc./ Snapper Music LC 1770).

Vibes, *Withdrawn* (Knitting Factory Records KFR-242).

Doc Watson (with Merle Watson), as "Rising Sun Blues," *The Best of Doc Watson 1964–1968* (Vanguard Records 79535-2).

Doc and Richard Watson, *Third Generation Blues* (Sugar Hill SHCD-3893).

Weavers, *The Weavers Greatest Hits* (Vanguard Records VCD-15/16).

A. G. Weinberger, *Standard Weinberger.*

Josh White, *Josh White in Chronological Order, Vol. 6, 1944–45* (Document Records DOCD-5572).

Josh White Jr., *In Tribute to Josh White—House of the Rising Son* (Silverwolf SWCD 1015).

Hank Williams Jr., *Hank Live* (Curb Records D2 77917).

John Williams, as "New Sun Rising," *The Collection* (Castle Communications CCSCD 190).

Warren Williams, "The House of the Rising Sun," *A Night Out with Australian Rock'N'Roll* (various artists) (Canetoad Records CTCD-037).

Mac Wiseman, *50 Years of Bluegrass Hits—4* (CMH Records CD-9036).

Hally Wood, *The Folk Box* (Elektra EKL-9001).

David H. Yakobian, *Alpha States* (Worldwide Success Records 727272).

Jubal Lee Young, *House of the Rising Sun.*

Acknowledgments

My first acknowledgment must be to the children of Georgia Turner who were so good to me—Reno, Roy ("Whitey"), and Ron ("Tootie") Taylor, Faye Stromberger, Joyce Proskie, Barbara Wilson, and Brenda Stowell, and Robert Taylor, whom I didn't have the fortune of meeting. In their friendliness, their generosity of spirit and their dedication to their mother, they demonstrated that the cliché is true—no one is dead as long as someone remembers. Without their cooperation and their trust in me to tell their mother's story, this book would not exist.

My editor at Simon & Schuster, Alice Mayhew, deserves my gratitude for believing in this project and trusting an unknown writer. Serena Jones at S&S also has my thanks. Patty Romanowski's and Lisa Healy's careful copyediting saved me from myself. And my agent, Paul Bresnick, who kept me motivated and excited throughout the process, is owed several drinks.

Special gratitude goes to the three Associated Press editors who believed in this story when most laughed at it: Bruce DeSilva, who spent five years generously giving me the space to pursue this and so many other windmill-tiltings; Chris Sullivan, who did an expert job of shaping the original AP piece; and Jerry Schwartz—colleague, friend, hero—who saw this idea through as a critic, guerrilla editor, and father confessor, across the years and the continents. My current bosses at the AP—Sally Jacobsen, Mike Silverman, and Kathleen Carroll—offered support, inspiration, and flexibility through the entire writing process, even when they didn't know it.

I must thank my editors through the years who have helped me understand storytelling better. Each taught me something that echoes in this book: Carolyn Sorisio, Lauren Young, Diane Davis, David S. Martin, Roger Quigley, Bob Heisse, John Troutman, Kelly Kissel, Bob Vucic, Cate

Barron, John Kirkpatrick, Nancy Eshelman, Tony Perry, Jim Agnello, Pete Mattiace, John Raby, John Curran, Jana Moore, Ted Duncombe, Dick Lawyer, Nate Polowetzky, Darrell Christian, Bill Ahearn, Tom Kent, Frank Crepeau, Kevin Noblet, Kristin Gazlay, Alice Klement, Jon Wolman, Patricia Bibby, Ann Levin, Paula Froke, Barbara King, Marcus Eliason, Kit Frieden, Ellen Nimmons, Mary Sedor, Joe McDonald, John Leicester, Meg Richards, Michelle Boorstein, Nick Tatro, Larry Heinzerling, Paul Alexander, Paul Haven, Robin McDowell, Ian Mader, Laura Myers, Debbie Seward, Lisa Tolin, Eric Carvin, and Caryn Brooks. And finally Bob Reid, an irascible Blue Ridger and extraordinary journalistic field marshal who warrants his own sentence fragment. "This isn't a stupid idea," he once told me.

Thanks also go to Alisa Blackwood, Christy Lemire, Elizabeth Kennedy, Eliza Cooke Browning, Megan Stack, and Jamie Tarabay; each insisted I could do this when I doubted it the most. To Frazier Moore and Dave Bauder, whose takes on American culture and music were invaluable, and to Dolores Barclay, whose passion for arts journalism inspired me. To Munir Ahmad, journalist, author, and poet, who makes me want to be a better person. And to Matt Crenson, Niko Price, and Tim Sullivan, colleagues and irreplaceable friends, for their welcoming ears and editing help over six years.

The good people at the Library of Congress's American Folklife Center helped me start my search—Jennifer Cutting, Judith Gray, Peggy Bulger, and Joe Hickerson. Various folks at assorted libraries also deserve recognition (I wish I could name them all): the University of Arkansas Library Special Collections (particularly Anne Prichard); the Louis Round Wilson Library at the University of North Carolina–Chapel Hill; the Springfield-Greene County Library in Springfield, Mo.; the Middlesboro (Kentucky) Historical Society; the public libraries in West Jefferson, North Carolina, and Asheville, North Carolina, and Fayetteville, Arkansas; the historical society in Carroll County, Arkansas; the Woody Guthrie Archives in New York; the Historic New Orleans Collection; Matt Barton at the Alan Lomax Archives; the W. L. Eury Appalachian Collection at Appalachian State University; and the Archives of Appalachia at East Tennessee State University. Thanks to the Experience Music Project, where my presentation of the "Rising Sun" story led to this project, and to Greil Marcus, whose early encouragement motivated me. Years later, I continue to appreciate Janet Caporizzo, who taught me how to write, and Susan Lockette, who taught me how to care.

And, of course, there are the people who populate this book and who have taught me so much about my country. But a few: Virginia, Letitia, and David, now family friends; Tom Moore; Joe Bussard; Ed Hunter; Dortha Bradley; and the late—and missed—Homer Callahan and Eva Ashley Moore.

I owe the energy for this journey to Pat Maloney, who taught me long ago that death does not necessarily silence precious voices.

I owe much to Edward Mason Anthony Jr. and Ann Terbrueggen Anthony, who instilled in me an unlikely combination of intellectual curiosity and sentimentality that has served me well. My sisters Lynn Higgins and Jan Anthony first introduced me to cultural studies and 1960s music respectively (Jan: I'm *really* sorry about the Beatles records). My three-year-old son, Mason, reminds me daily about the stake I have in the future (and does a mean version of "Go Tell Aunt Rhody"). And Wyatt, who I can't wait to start learning about.

My wife and the love of my life, Melissa Rayworth, should have her name on this book as well. She has listened to countless versions of The Song and has been dragged hither and yon across the landscape, fed cheap beers, lodged in sketchy motels, and forced to listen to her husband sing karaoke over and over and charge thousands of dollars on Amazon—and has insisted she loved every minute of it. She has read every version of this story since its inception, made suggestions and revisions, issued heartfelt compliments and much-needed criticism. I can imagine no one better to share my world with. Melissa: You know where I keep all the CDs. If you want to set them afire, I'll understand completely.

Index

About the Author

Ted Anthony joined The Associated Press in 1992 in Charleston, West Virginia. He was nominated for the Pulitzer Prize for beat reporting by the AP in 1998 and for feature writing in 2001. In 2001, he won the National Headliner Award for feature writing, and in 2006 he was named one of the Newspaper Association of America's "20 under 40" in *Presstime* magazine. He has worked for the AP as a national correspondent and a foreign correspondent in China, Afghanistan, and Iraq, and has reported from more than twenty countries. Anthony is currently the editor of asap, a multimedia news service produced by the AP. He lives in Montclair, New Jersey, with his wife and two sons.

Printed in the United States
By Bookmasters